8/04

AMERICAN
TRANSPORTATION POLICY

AMERICAN TRANSPORTATION POLICY

Robert Jay Dilger

Westport, Connecticut
London

Library of Congress Cataloguing-in-Publication Data

Dilger, Robert Jay, 1954–
    American transportation policy / Robert Jay Dilger.
        p.   cm.
    Includes bibliographical references and index.
    ISBN 0–275–97853–2 (alk. paper)
    1. Transportation and state—United States—History.   I. Title.
HE206.2.D55   2003
388′.0973—dc21   2002026962

British Library Cataloguing in Publication Data is available.

Library of Congress Catalog Card Number: 2002026962
ISBN: 0–275–97853–2

First published in 2003

Praeger Publishers, 88 Post Road West, Westport, CT 06881
An imprint of Greenwood Publishing Group, Inc.
www.praeger.com

Printed in the United States of America

The paper used in this book complies with the
Permanent Paper Standard issued by the National
Information Standards Organization (Z39.48–1984).

10 9 8 7 6 5 4 3 2 1

CONTENTS

1

AN OVERVIEW OF AMERICAN TRANSPORTATION POLICY, 1789 TO 1956

The American transportation system plays a central role in the American economy. It connects the country spatially, allowing people and commerce to move from place to place, through a network of over 5.5 million miles of public roads, railroads, waterways, and oil and gas pipelines and 18,770 public and private airports. More than 240 million vehicles, railcars, aircraft, ships, and recreational boats use the network. It supports over 4.5 trillion miles of passenger travel, and 4 trillion ton-miles of goods movement annually. In addition, consumer and government transportation-related expenditures ($1 trillion annually) account for over 11 percent of the nation's gross domestic product, ranking it the fourth highest activity in the economy, behind housing, health care, and food. The typical American family spends nearly $7,000 annually on transportation-related expenses, about one-fifth of total household spending. Moreover, almost 4.5 million people are employed by transportation industries, including 1.8 million by trucking and warehousing companies, 1.2 million by air transportation companies, 485,000 by public transit operators, 435,00 by transportation service companies, 223,000 by rail transportation companies, 205,000 by water transportation companies, and 14,000 by pipeline companies. Several million more are employed in industries that supply transportation-related goods and services. Overall, transportation accounts for approximately 13 percent of all jobs in the United States.[1]

The American transportation system has an enormous effect on both the national economy and American society. The sociological effects resulting from increased mobility are immense. Age-old customs and family traditions have been shattered by improvements in the nation's transportation system. Individual family members are more likely than ever before to be separated geographically and are less likely to be rooted in any one community or way of life. The interstate highway system's completion during the early 1990s, coupled with the airline industry's dramatic growth since World War II, has enabled millions of Americans to visit the far corners of the United States and the world. Combined with satellite broadcasts, the development of the nation's transportation system has changed the way that Americans perceive themselves and their place in the world. As one author put it: "In this day and age, all ends of the earth are in immediate touch with one another. . . . The fact that we can and do come face to face with other members of society in other parts of the world certainly modifies our values and our actions much more than if we had merely read or heard about a way of life or a problem in a distant land."[2]

Transportation policy's importance to the nation's economic future and American society is indisputable, but there has been considerable debate concerning the public and private sector's role in determining the scope and nature of the national transportation system and whether current policies and institutional arrangements are appropriate. For example, some have argued that most transportation decisions should be left to the private sector and that government intervention has created an inefficient transportation system that is both costly and not very good at moving either people or goods. Others argue that government intervention is a good idea but that government transportation policies should take into account their effect on society as well as traffic. They contend that government policies have historically favored highways over mass transit and intercity passenger rail service and that this has caused irreparable harm to the nation's cities. They argue that highways have encouraged the suburbanization of American society and contributed to the spread of unsightly suburban sprawl. They advocate smart growth strategies that integrate the various transportation modes into a single, comprehensive transportation system; make greater use of metropolitan planning organizations and regional planning councils to create a more seamless, less fragmented transportation system for the nation's metropolitan regions; increase funding for mass transit and intercity passenger rail; impose higher fuel taxes and other pricing strategies to encourage people to travel less, carpool more, and use mass transit and other alternatives to the automobile when traveling; and enact zoning ordinances and other laws to preserve open space, combat sprawl, and encourage people to live closer to their places of employment.

Others want transportation policies to focus solely on the efficient movement of people and goods. They note that government spends approximately $180 billion annually on transportation projects, and the private sector spends at least $20 billion annually, yet traffic congestion, both on land and in the air, especially in and over the nation's largest cities, is at record levels. Moreover, automobile congestion is worsening, especially in the wake of the September 11, 2001, terrorist attacks on the World Trade Center and Pentagon. In their view, worrying about nontraffic-related issues diverts scarce resources, making it more difficult to deal with traffic congestion. They note that the average American spends 36 hours each year stuck in traffic, up from 11 hours in 1982; highway traffic congestion in the nation's 68 largest cities alone results in over $78 billion annually in wasted fuel and lost wages; and rush "hour" is now a misnomer in most of America's larger cities, where city streets and highways are congested for up to seven hours each weekday.[3]

Others agree with David Schultz, county executive in Milwaukee, Wisconsin, who noted that debates over public policies and institutional arrangements are important but, that, as a practical matter, the influence of public preferences and behavior on the success or failure of public policies and institutional arrangements should never be underestimated:

[T]hose of us concerned with transportation in urban America can no longer wait for people to start to behave as we would like them to: living in compact, high density residential development patterns; traveling short distances to work along well-defined corridors to destinations in orderly, compact business districts; using public transit in large numbers because they want to and not because they have to; and being very socially conscious in their selection and very limited personal use of an automobile. We have to recognize the reality that people are very unlikely to accept, and are in fact likely to strongly resist, significant changes of this sort, especially if they perceive that such changes are limiting their personal freedom of choice.[4]

This book examines these and other debates affecting the formation and implementation of transportation policy in the United States and concludes with several recommendations for improving the American transportation system and the policy-making process. It begins by describing the evolution of government's increasingly dominant role in determining the scope and nature of the nation's transportation system from the nation's birth in 1789 to the enactment of the landmark *Federal Aid to Highways Act of 1956*, which authorized the construction of the interstate highway system. Because the national government has focused most of its transportation resources on highways, the next two chapters examine the creation and implementation of the nation's highway and mass transit policies. Chapter 2 examines developments from 1956 to 1990 (the construction of the interstate highway system), and Chapter 3 examines developments since 1990 (the postinterstate era). Chapter 4 describes the formation and implementation of the national government's policy on intercity passenger rail service, focusing on Amtrak's creation in 1970 and its subsequent effort to become operationally self-sufficient. Chapter 5 analyzes the formation and implementation of the national government's policy on civilian air transportation. As will be shown, political expediency, coupled with the decentralization of the congressional policy-making process, led the national government to enhance transportation capacity in all of these transportation modes indiscriminately, rather than develop an integrated, coordinated, intermodal strategy to improve the nation's mobility. While this served Congress's short-term political interests well, it resulted in a fragmented transportation system that by most accounts is not only less than optimal but inferior to those in several European nations that compete with the United States in an increasingly global economic marketplace. Given America's global economic dominance during the late twentieth century, the inefficiencies evident in the American transportation system were not considered a major concern. Now that America's economic dominance is less than it once was, these inefficiencies are being called into question.

TRANSPORTATION POLICY: PRIVATE OR PUBLIC SOLUTIONS

According to economic theory there are four types of goods and services (private, common-pool, toll, and public), and the manner in which they are consumed (either individually or collectively) and the relative ease or difficulty of preventing their free use should determine government's role in supplying and regulating them.[5] Private goods and services, such as clothes and household appliances, are consumed individually, and it is relatively easy to prevent their free use by arresting and prosecuting thieves. Common-pool goods and services, such as drinking water, are also consumed individually (each person breathes air and drinks water, and may hunt a wild animal), but it is relatively difficult to prevent their free use. Toll goods and services, such as education and transportation, are consumed collectively (e.g., hundreds and, in some cases, thousands of people can travel on a highway simultaneously), and their free use can be prevented relatively easily by imposing a fee or toll to allow entrance or exit. Public goods and services, such as the provision of police and fire protection and national defense, are also consumed collectively (all residents of the community benefit from the provision of public safety services), but it is relatively difficult to prevent their free use.

Economic theory suggests that government should intervene in the private marketplace to prevent cheating (by outlawing false advertising, the stealing of trade secrets, etc.) and when the economic law of supply and demand for goods and services fails. One of the most common causes of market failure is the presence of free riders (people who consume goods and services but refuse to pay for them). Individuals and companies are reluctant to supply goods and services subject to free riders because no one is willing to put time and effort into economic endeavors that do not have a reasonable expectation of turning a profit. Because public goods and services are subject to free riders, individuals and companies are, understandably, reluctant to provide them. This creates a market imperfection, where the supply of public goods and services is expected to fall short of demand. Economic theory suggests that government should perfect the marketplace by assuring that public goods and services are supplied in appropriate amounts (either by supplying them directly or, preferably, indirectly by contracting out their provision to the private sector).[6] The opposite problem exists for common-pool goods and services. They are prone to overconsumption (air and water supplies will be polluted, and animals will be hunted to extinction) because the private marketplace cannot prevent their free consumption easily. In this instance, government should perfect the private marketplace by regulating (restricting) the consumption of common-pool goods.

These market imperfections do not exist for private goods and services and for toll goods and services. Individuals and companies supply them because, in the absence of free riders, they have a reasonable expectation of making a profit. Moreover, the economic law of supply and demand ensures that there are enough of these goods and services to meet demand and that they are supplied at a reasonable (competitive) price. In a truly competitive market, suppliers also have an incentive to continually improve their product or service to remain competitive. As a result, government's role in private goods and services and toll goods and services should be restricted to preventing cheating (punishing suppliers who make false claims or use misleading advertising, etc.).

Nevertheless, as the remainder of this chapter demonstrates, the public sector's role in determining the scope and nature of the American transportation system has increased over time to the point where it now plays the leading role in those decisions. Governments at all levels currently finance transportation projects; establish safety standards; plan and promote "better" transportation systems; regulate many aspects of transportation operations; research and develop new transportation technologies; subsidize various transportation modes, either directly with cash assistance or indirectly with in-kind services; and operate public transportation systems. Moreover, governmental policies—such as environmental regulations, energy conservation measures, labor laws, nondiscrimination statutes, relocation assistance provisions, the imposition of user fees and various transportation trust funds, and even the compilation of transportation statistics—all affect the structure and operation of America's transportation system.[7]

PRIVATE OR PUBLIC SOLUTIONS: 1789–1850

From the nation's formation in 1789 through the early 1800s, the national government's role in transportation policy was minimal. State and local governments, on the other hand, were very active, providing financial subsidies to private companies that built and maintained a somewhat haphazard system of wagon roads, canals, and ferries to move people and goods from place to place. The settlement of the western frontier states received a large boost in 1807 from Robert Fulton's introduction of the first steam-powered boat, the *Claremont*. The steamboat ushered in a new era in American transportation. Its ability to overcome constraints of prevailing winds and currents opened up trading routes throughout the United States and expedited the nation's expansion into the interior. Over the next 50 years, over 4,000 miles of canals were built, providing the nation with its first extensive transportation network. By 1860, steamboats were carrying over $300 million in cargo annually along the Mississippi River alone, and New Orleans had grown into the fourth largest port in the world, processing less cargo than only London, Liverpool, and New York.[8]

Local governments often subsidized canal construction because water transportation was vital to a community's economic survival, especially for those located along the western frontier. State governments were also active. They often subsidized canal construction by selling bonds and using the proceeds to purchase stock in companies building and operating canals and, occasionally, provided canal companies low interest loans and, less frequently, cash. State governments provided about 70 percent of the $125 million invested in canal construction during the 1800s.[9]

At first, the national government did not offer financial assistance for transportation projects because transportation, other than postal roads, was considered either a private endeavor outside the scope of governmental authority or a state and local government responsibility. However, postal roads were specifically mentioned in the U.S. Constitution as a national government responsibility. As a result, there was little opposition to Colonel Ebenezer Zane's offer in 1796 to build a postal road from Wheeling, Virginia (now West Virginia), to the river port at Limestone (now Maysville), Kentucky, in exchange for a national government land warrant totaling three square miles where the road crossed the Muskingum, Hackhocking, and Scioto Rivers. The road was 100 miles shorter and less expensive to operate than the postal route over the winding Ohio River. The road, known as Zane's Trace, became an important route for settlers headed into southeastern Ohio. It was the national government's first road subsidy. In 1802, the *Ohio Statehood Enabling Act* set aside 5 percent of the proceeds from the sale of nationally owned land in that state for road construction. Similar laws were subsequently adopted for Louisiana, Indiana, Mississippi, Illinois, Alabama, and Missouri, except that the proceeds could also be used for canals, levees, river improvements, and schools.[10] In 1803, President Thomas Jefferson (D/R, 1801–1809) ordered improvements to the Natchez Trace, an Indian trail through the Allegheny Mountains, to promote interstate commerce. In 1806, national government funds were appropriated to construct the Cumberland Road from Cumberland, Maryland, to Wheeling and the Ohio River. The road was completed in 1817 and became known as the National Road. In 1808, President Jefferson's secretary of the treasury, Albert Gallatin, proposed the construction of a publicly owned turnpike extending from Maine to Georgia, with four major east–west roads through the Allegheny Mountains. Congress rejected the plan, claiming that its $20 million cost over 10 years was excessive.[11]

There were numerous congressional efforts throughout the early 1800s, especially from representatives from western states, to provide direct cash assistance for transportation projects. Representative, and later Senator, Henry Clay's famous program of internal improvements, for example, provided subsidies for canal construction and port improvements, but the expenditures were relatively modest, and very little was provided for governmentally owed projects. In 1823, the national government spent funds to remove navigational obstructions from the Mississippi River and, following the British practice, also purchased, from time to time, corporate stock in private companies building canals and roads. These companies, in turn, charged customers a toll to use the canal or road. However, most bills authorizing the expenditure of national government funds for transportation projects were vetoed by presidents convinced that the bills were unconstitutional infringements on states' rights. For example, just before leaving office, President James Madison (R, 1809–1817) vetoed a bill that would have funded road construction from dividends earned on the national government's stock in the National Bank. He argued that the bill's sponsors were incorrect in their assertion that the bill was allowable under the national government's constitutional powers to regulate commerce and provide for the national defense. Later that year, his successor, President James Monroe (R, 1817–1825), announced in his first inaugural address that he personally advocated direct expenditures for roads and canals as a means to assist economic development but would support legislation to that effect only if the national government was provided that power by constitutional amendment.[12] In 1822, he vetoed legislation authorizing tolls on the National Road because he believed that a national toll unconstitutionally violated state sovereignty over the use of state-owned land. The following year, he signed legislation appropriating $498,000 for improvements to the National Road and its extension to Zanesville, Ohio, declaring that road improvements were welcomed by states and did not infringe on their sovereign rights.[13]

President Andrew Jackson's (D, 1829–1837) election and the ascendancy of the Democratic Party and its advocacy of states' rights slowed the national government's increased involvement in transportation policy for nearly a generation. President Jackson's veto of the Maysville Road project on May 27, 1830, is considered by some as a turning point in the history of American internal improvements during the nineteenth century. The 64-mile road project from Maysville to Lexington was located entirely within Kentucky. The bill would have provided $150,000 to purchase 1,500 shares of stock in the Maysville Turnpike Road Company. The road would have extended the existing overland postal road that followed the National Road at Zanesville, Ohio, and Zane's Trace to the Ohio River. Its sponsors argued that funding postal roads was constitutional. President Jackson vetoed the bill anyway, declaring that it was wholly local in nature and, therefore, unconstitutional. He also argued that internal improvement projects were less important than reducing taxes and paying off the national debt. The veto forestalled pending legislation providing funds for other internal improvement projects, including the Baltimore and Ohio Railroad, the nation's first commercial railroad company chartered in 1827.[14] Still, congressional members, intent on securing politically popular internal improvement projects for their home districts, secured over $10 million for internal improvements during President Jackson's eight years in office by attaching specific improvement projects into general appropriation bills. This forced President Jackson to choose between his constitutional scruples and signing appropriation bills needed to keep the government operating. The practice of attaching internal improvement projects to appropriation bills continued throughout the pre–Civil War era. As a result, the national government funded internal improvement projects throughout this period but left most of the responsibility for funding internal improvement projects to state and local governments and the private sector.[15] The national government's acquiescence to states in transportation policy was, perhaps, best symbolized by its turning over the National Road to them in 1834.

Although political factors prevented the national government from spending large sums of money on transportation projects, it did donate to states over 3 million acres of nationally owned land that was subsequently auctioned to raise revenue for wagon road construction. It also gave states another 4.5 million acres for canal construction, 2.25 million acres for river navigation, and 64 million acres for flood control.[16] Despite this, prior to 1850, the national government's involvement in transportation policy is best characterized as indirect and limited.

State governments, on the other hand, were much more active. In addition to financing canals, they routinely purchased stock in private companies or provided companies tax exemptions to build turnpikes. Originally, a "turnpike" was a long pole or pike that barred the traveler's way at each toll gate. After paying the required fee, the pike was turned or swung out, allowing the traveler to pass. The term turnpike became synonymous with any stone-surfaced road. Pennsylvania, for example, chartered over 80 turnpike companies that constructed over 3,110 miles of roads by the mid-1830s, and New York chartered 278 companies that built over 4,000 miles of roads by 1830.[17]

Local government officials, especially city government officials, constructed publicly owned and maintained roads and bridges, but there was little or no coordinated road building by government entities over long distances. As a result, there were few publicly owned thoroughfares in the United States during this period. Nearly all long-distance land travel was done on privately held turnpikes. For example, the private Philadelphia–Lancaster Turnpike, chartered in 1792, was considered the finest long-distance road in the United States for many years.

PRIVATE OR PUBLIC SOLUTIONS: 1850–1900

From just before the middle of the nineteenth century until its end, railroads surpassed highway and water transportation as the primary means to move goods and people over long distances. Except for relatively short runs, horse-drawn carriages and wagons could not compete with the steam-driven railroads' speed and passengers' comfort.[18]

At first, railroads were not developed to compete with steamboats as the primary means of moving people and goods over long distances. They were built, often with state government assistance, to serve as an all-weather route to adjacent towns and nearby canals. Prior to 1850, most railroads used different track gauges, making it impossible to develop through traffic over long distances. But, as steam engines became more reliable, the number of railroad companies and the miles of trackage increased. In 1838, the national government gave the fledgling railroad industry a financial boost by designating them all postal routes, a pattern of government subsidy that would later repeat itself as technological breakthroughs created new transportation modes. At that time, there were about 3,000 miles of railroad track in the United States. By 1850, that figure had tripled to 9,000 miles, thanks, at least in part, to the revenue provided by the national government's postal contracts.

The national government subsidized railroad expansion across the continent, primarily because railroads were seen as a means to promote interstate commerce.

However, given constitutional constraints, the national government did not fund railroads directly. Instead, it donated nationally owned land to the states. They, in turn, sold that land at auction and gave the proceeds to railroads. In 1850, the first land grant for railroad construction sent 3.7 million acres of nationally owned land to Illinois, Mississippi, and Alabama. The proceeds from the land sales were given to the Illinois Central Railroad and Mobile and Ohio Railroad companies to subsidize their expansion in those states. By 1860, there was more than 30,000 miles of railroad track in the United States. Most of the shorter rail lines at that time had linked up into larger systems, made possible by the industry's adoption of the 56.5-inch standard gauge for tracks. The agreement on a standard track gauge, coupled with the financial assistance provided by the national government's land grants and postal contracts, helped the railroads become the dominant means of long-distance transportation in the United States during the latter half of the nineteenth century.[19]

The number of railroad companies and the miles of railroad track continued to expand, largely because of government subsidies. By 1871, the national government had given away 36 million acres of land to assist over 50 railroads expand their operations across the continent. By the end of the century, the national government had provided 130.3 million acres for railroad improvements, and states had contributed another 48.9 million acres of state-owned land.[20]

Despite numerous attempts to attach steam engines to wagons, early efforts to build an overland steam-powered vehicle failed miserably. These early "automobiles" were not reliable, their axles could not handle the rough cobblestone streets in most American cities, and they could not escape the mud on the unimproved roads outside the nation's cities. The bulk and weight of the early steam engines made it easier to apply them to railroad locomotives than to highway vehicles. The absence of motor-driven automobiles meant that the steamboat remained the railroad industry's primary competition for long-distance travel.

The competition for rail lines among local communities, especially those located in the western frontier states, was intense. Wherever the railroads went, towns followed. For topographical reasons, rail lines often ran parallel or close to established turnpikes and canals. Unable to compete with the railroad's speed and freight-hauling capabilities, the freight wagon and stagecoach companies that operated on the nation's turnpikes disappeared. Without their revenue, the turnpike companies also disappeared, leaving their roadways to the elements or donating them to the nearest local government. One of the last holdouts was the famous Lancaster Turnpike Road Company. It lasted until February 1902.[21]

By the late 1800s, Chicago had became the rail center of the United States, serving as the go-between for the West's natural resources and East Coast consumers. By 1890, there were 163,597 miles of rail track in the United States, including several transcontinental lines connecting California, Oregon, and Washington to the rest of the nation.[22]

Because railroads provided a convenient and relatively cost-effective means of traveling long distances, there was relatively little pressure on public officials during the 1800s to improve roads outside the nation's cities. In 1903, the United States had more than 2 million miles of roads, but more than 90 percent of them were almost impassable during inclement weather.[23] At that time, the main sources of revenue for local road construction in rural areas were the property tax and poll (head) tax. In 1904, these taxes raised $53.8 million nationally, barely enough to keep existing roads from being overgrown by brush and other plant life. Many southern states did not set aside any tax revenue for road construction. They relied on statute labor (convicts) to build and maintain roads. The situation was better in the nation's cities. They also relied on property taxes, often supplemented by special assessments, to fund road construction, but their larger tax bases provided sufficient revenue to construct most of their main streets out of granite block or hard paving bricks. These all-weather roads were strong enough to handle horse-drawn trucks and drays hauling up to 18 tons of cargo. Most city side streets were built with macadam or gravel. By the 1890s, many of these side streets were made mud-free by asphalt surfacing. Also, by that time, electric streetcars were operating in over 100 American cities, ending the reliance on horse-drawn carriages for most city travel.[24]

When one spoke of transportation policy in the United States during the late-1800s, the conversation would have included steamboats and wagons, but it would have centered on railroads. This was especially true in the West, where the absence of a natural river waterway system made water travel relatively difficult. As the rail lines continued to expand, offering shippers and passengers ready access to multiple service areas and destinations, water transportation's role in the American transportation system began to diminish. New canal construction was almost nonexistent by the late 1800s as the industry's focus shifted to serving the Great Lakes region and, later, international cargo.[25] Also, pipelines transporting crude oil to refiners appeared during the late 1800s but were mostly confined to western Pennsylvania and surrounding states.

The private sector was particularly important in the development of the water and railroad industries. For example, in 1890, there were more than 1,000 private railroad companies operating in the nation. Largely unregulated by local, state, or national government officials, most of the important decisions concerning the nation's transportation system (routing, pricing, etc.) were made by these companies.

The private sector's dominant role in determining the scope and nature of the American transportation system began to change following the establishment of the five-member Interstate Commerce Commission in 1887. It was created in the wake of allegations, most of them true, that railroads behaved in a monopolistic manner by setting prices artificially high and used bribes and other means (including free and reduced price tickets) to ensure that state and local government officials did nothing to interfere with their activities. They also routinely provided large suppliers with secret rebates, undercutting the ability of smaller suppliers to compete.

The Interstate Commerce Commission's establishment marked the beginning of a new era. The national government was now an active participant in determining both the physical development and use of the American transportation system.

It was authorized to prescribe just, reasonable, and nondiscriminatory rates; grant or deny operating authority to common carriers; approve or deny proposed consolidations and mergers of carriers and forwarders; and investigate alleged violations of antitrust laws and transmit its findings to the U.S. attorney general.

In 1890, the national government attempted to prevent monopolies and encourage price competition in the railroad industry by passing the *Sherman Anti-Trust Act*. It made it nearly impossible for railroads to merge. In 1906, the national government attempted to prevent John D. Rockefeller's Standard Oil Company, which owned nearly 90 percent of the nation's 7,000 miles of pipeline, from creating a monopoly in the emerging crude oil pipeline business by passing the *Hepburn Act*. It gave the Interstate Commerce Commission jurisdiction over the pipeline industry. In 1911, the U.S. Supreme Court ruled unanimously that the Standard Oil Company was a monopoly and broke it into 10 common carriers and three holding companies. Soon afterward, additional pipeline companies appeared in Illinois, Kansas, Oklahoma, and Texas to transport crude oil to Gulf of Mexico tankers serving the Eastern seaboard.[26]

PRIVATE OR PUBLIC SOLUTIONS: 1900–1956

At the turn of the century, automobile ownership was still largely limited to the wealthy and upper middle class. There were only 8,000 motor vehicles registered in the entire country in 1900.[27] There was, however, a growing awareness that better roads might benefit farmers who, for the most part, relied on horse-drawn wagons to transport their goods to market. There was a large disparity in quality between city roads and country roads, but city residents taxed themselves to build roads and objected to any proposal that required them to contribute to the construction and maintenance of roads used primarily by farmers. Residents of rural areas, on the other hand, lacked the population density and commercial and industrial development necessary to create a tax base large enough to finance roads without government subsidies. Farm-to-market roads also lacked the volume of traffic necessary to pay for themselves through tolls. This led the National Grange and other farm organizations to lobby during the early 1900s for publicly financed farm-to-market roads. They were joined by numerous bicycle clubs across America that had earlier started what had become known as the Good Roads Movement. Initially, their lobbying efforts were not very successful, but, in 1902, two events took place that would have a significant affect on the policy-making process. First, the American Automobile Association was founded. It provided a strong voice for those desiring public investment in roads and bridges. Second, Henry Ford's Model T appeared. The Model T was initially designed as a large, heavy touring car capable of handling the hard pounding of country roads. Then, in 1906, Ford used vanadium alloy steel, developed in Europe, to redesign the Model T into a much lighter and smaller vehicle. At the same time, Ford adopted the moving assembly line process, used in the munitions industry, to standardize and shorten the automotive production process. The introduction of the assembly line enabled Ford to increase production from 1,599 units in 1905 to 8,729 units in 1906 and 14,887 units in 1907. It also reduced expenses, enabling Ford to lower the Model T's price. As sales increased, further economies of scale were realized, and Ford was able to continually lower the Model T's price until, by 1917, it sold for less than $300.[28] Thanks to the Model T and competitor companies, including General Motors and Chrysler, that copied Ford's assembly line production process, automobile prices decreased, and automobile sales increased dramatically. By 1915, over 2 million motor vehicles were on America's roads. Importantly, trucks replaced horse-drawn wagons as the primary means of transporting goods over short distances. As automobile and truck ownership increased, the public began to drive out into the countryside. Often finding themselves stuck in mud or with a flat or broken tire from the rough ride, the public's demand for improved roads, in both cities and rural areas, intensified.[29]

Despite the growing demand for publicly financed roads and bridges, the national government continued to appropriate token amounts for internal improvements during the early 1900s. As mentioned previously, due to constitutional considerations, the national government relied primarily on land grants to states to subsidize railroad expansion and canal and road construction. However, by the early 1900s much of the national government's land had been given away and auctioned off. The new emphasis was on land preservation. For example, President Benjamin Harrison (R, 1889–1893) set aside millions of acres of national land in 1891 by declaring them forest preserves. In 1906, President Theodore Roosevelt (R, 1901–1908) started the National Park System. It looked as if the national government's role in providing subsidies for transportation projects was about to wane just as the public's demand for subsidies was on the rise. Then, in 1913, the 16th Amendment, establishing the national income tax, was ratified.

The national income tax was not broadly applied and did not, at least initially, generate significant amounts of additional revenue. In 1915, the income tax generated only $125 million, or 24 percent of the $513 million generated by national taxes. However, the income tax's legalization provided the national government with an elastic revenue generator that gave it an unprecedented opportunity to expand its role in domestic policy. One of the first things that national government officials did with the added revenue was to fund highway construction projects.

The *Federal Road Act of 1916* created, by far, the national government's most significant intergovernmental grant program prior to the New Deal era. It authorized the expenditure of $75 million over five years to improve rural postal roads. The funds were provided to states on a 50-50 matching basis.[30] States did not object to this intrusion into one of their domestic policy areas because funds were directed to rural areas. At that time, state apportionment rules allocated most of the seats in state Houses and Senates to representatives and senators from rural districts. In addition, rural roads were the primary means for farmers to get their produce to market. It would have been politically foolish for state politicians to turn down a national subsidy for agriculture when most constituents at the time were farmers.[31]

The *Federal Road Act of 1916* had administrative requirements that foreshadowed conditions routinely attached to many contemporary grants-in-aid programs. For example, expenditures were prohibited in communities with populations exceeding 2,500, and states had to establish a highway department or commission to oversee program operations and set priorities and detailed plans. At that time, only 39 of the 48 states had a state road department. Advanced examination of projects, detailed progress reports, audits of expenditures, and examination of finished work were also required.[32]

By 1917, all 48 states had a state road agency. This marked the beginning of the centralization and professionalization of highway policy in the United States. Prior to this time most road construction planning was left to local government officials, many of whom had relatively little professional training and often let political and economic considerations influence where roads and bridges were located and how they were designed. By the mid-1920s, national and state road engineers communicated with each other regularly and devised strategies to centralize their authority over the construction of highways and bridges. In 1925, the national government's Bureau of Public Roads had worked out arrangements with all of the state road agencies for uniform route markings with roads running east–west having even numbers and roads running north–south having odd numbers. Although the collaboration between national and state road engineers was not viewed as a power grab by local government officials, it was systematic of a fundamental shift in power from local government officials to state and national government officials. By the mid-1930s, national and state engineers increasingly wrote project specifications, supervised the work of local transportation officials, and limited their transportation initiatives. State road engineers, for example, developed sophisticated rationales for maintaining or extending highway systems and routinely imposed those standards on local government officials. These standards were typically based on the premise that highways were financed by users and, consequently, should serve traffic, not bolster local property values.[33]

The United States' entry into World War I temporarily interrupted the expansion of national government funding for road construction and improvement. At that time, railroads dominated the transportation of goods and people over long distances, carrying 84 percent of intercity freight and 85 percent of all passenger miles traveled by public carriers. Intercity automobile and air travel was negligible.[34] World War I, however, made it abundantly clear that the country needed an integrated network of roads, not just a piecemeal improvement in local roads. The railroads, especially in the Northeast, were overwhelmed as freight cars shipping war goods became mired in monumental traffic jams. The railroad's difficulties in accommodating a wartime economy highlighted the need to create an alternative system of transportation for national defense purposes. The situation became so severe that the national government temporarily took over the railroad system on December 26, 1917, in an attempt to unsnarl the threatened paralysis of the national economy.[35]

By 1920, World War I was over, but memories of the railroads' troubles were still vivid in the minds of the nation's political leaders. The congressional re-authorization of the *Federal Highway Act* focused on the need to create a more integrated, national system of roads and bridges capable of moving both troops and goods over long distances during a national emergency. The *Federal Highway Act of 1921* did precisely that by mandating that the program's funds be concentrated on roads that were interstate in character and expedited the completion of "an adequate and connected system of highways."[36] In addition, each state was required to designate 7 percent of its road mileage as primary, and only that mileage (about 200,000 miles) was eligible for funding, still on a 50-50 cost share basis. National funding was increased to $75 million annually, and the U.S. Bureau of Public Roads, under the leadership of Thomas H. MacDonald, used the funds to begin the nation's first genuine national highway system.

By the end of the decade, funding for the *Federal Highway Act* was increased to nearly $200 million annually, accounting for more than three-quarters of national intergovernmental expenditures. Farmers and agricultural distributors interested in promoting the nascent trucking industry lobbied hard for additional highway funding. Although railroads were the primary means to transport agricultural products to market, trucks provided a competitive alternative, especially for perishable items, that helped keep railroad freight rates in check.[37]

The 1920s were called the "golden age" for road building, with most of the projects providing gravel surfaces. By the end of the 1920s, there were 23 million cars and 3.5 million trucks on the roads (about 60 percent of American families owned a car), and their owners were increasingly anxious about road conditions. Also at this time the American love affair with cars became apparent.[38] As one author put it, automobile ownership became a powerful social symbol, a cultural icon, and an emotional outlet for millions of Americans. Part of automobile ownership's appeal, he argued, was that it empowers people, allowing them to make

a vastly wider range of choices relating to personal mobility than he or she would have without a car. Auto drivers are freed from the constraints of the fixed routes and rigid schedules of train or bus riders. They can choose many more destinations; select the companions, if any, traveling in their vehicle; carry much more luggage than they could on a bus; never have to stand because all the seats are taken; stop for refreshment when they want to; listen to their favorite music or news; and not worry (too much) about being mugged while waiting at the bus stop or subway station.[39]

By the 1930s, getting "your" driver's license had become a major life event, signifying for the nation's population of 16-year-olds the beginning of their transition from youth to adulthood and, for others, the means to participate more fully in American society. Not having a driver's license was tantamount to being un-American. However, despite the automobile's emergence as a central part of American society, national government funding for highways and bridges remained at the $150–$180 million level throughout the 1930s, primarily because the Great Depression reduced business activity, which, in turn, caused the national government's revenue to decline. In 1932, the national government imposed a one cent per gallon tax on gasoline to address an escalating annual budget deficit approaching $1 billion. The gasoline tax generated $125 million in 1933 and averaged about $200 million annually through the rest of the decade. The funds were deposited into the national government's general revenue account and were not set aside for transportation projects.

The nation's massive unemployment, peaking at over one-third of the workforce, altered the way that elected officials viewed highway construction. They continued to view it as a means to address constituents' demand for relief from traffic congestion, foster long-term economic development opportunities, and appease the politically active highway lobby (oil and gasoline companies, automobile manufacturers, concrete and asphalt suppliers, etc.). However, they now also saw highway construction as a vital component of an overall effort to combat short-term unemployment. As always, elected officials could point to highway construction projects in their districts as a visible signal to their constituents that they were doing something about the nation's unemployment problem.

Congress purposively targeted most of its transportation assistance during this era to smaller, district-level projects. By "spreading the wealth," Congress enabled its members to claim credit for doing something about unemployment. As part of the movement to spread funding to as many districts as possible, urban segments of the primary road system were made eligible for national funding in 1934. Two years later, secondary "feeder" roads were also made eligible. Unlike Germany, which built the autobahn, the world's first freeway system, the United States focused its highway construction resources on local and state road systems, where traffic congestion was an increasing problem.[40]

Although the nation's road system was still fragmented and in relatively poor condition, by the 1930s automobiles were displacing streetcars as the primary means of travel within cities, and trucks were challenging railroads for moving goods, especially perishable produce, over short and medium distances. However, many national government officials were worried that the trucking industry might collapse from cutthroat price competition as truckers competed for dwindling business during the Great Depression. They also worried that price competition between the trucking industry and the regulated railroad industry would lead to bankruptcies in both industries. In an effort to promote the trucking industry's growth and protect railroads, the national government regulated the trucking industry in 1935.

The *Motor Carrier Act of 1935* empowered the Interstate Commerce Commission to establish regulations governing which trucking routes were available for service, the discontinuation of services, mergers within the industry, and shipping rates. Trucking companies that operated entirely within one state, carried only unprocessed agricultural products, operated within designated concentrated commercial areas, or were owned by a company and used to ship only its own goods were exempt from the regulations (about 60 percent of all trucking companies were exempt). The 18,000 trucking firms in business in 1935 that were now under the Interstate Commerce Commission's jurisdiction were granted grandfather rights to maintain their routes and services. The Interstate Commerce Commission subsequently restricted the entry of new trucking firms to reduce price competition in the industry. New applicants, for example, had to prove that existing firms were not already providing the service and that they would not cause economic damage to an existing firm. The Interstate Commerce Commission also tended to approve rates based on what the market could bear rather than on the actual cost of transporting goods. Because entry was tightly restricted, the only way that most new trucking companies got started was by buying hauling rights from an existing carrier. The Interstate Commerce Commission's operating certificates became many trucking companies most valuable asset, and banks routinely accepted them as loan collateral.[41]

The Interstate Commerce Commission typically refused to allow trucking firms to eliminate nonprofitable routes if it had lucrative ones to offset the losses. This practice protected smaller communities from becoming isolated from the economic mainstream. Consumer advocates and the trucking industry complained that cross-subsidization of nonprofitable routes with profitable ones often resulted in empty or nearly empty backhauls and the retention of unnecessary trucking capacity. This, in turn, resulted in artificially high costs for haulers and higher prices for consumers.[42] A similar circumstance existed for both the railroad industry and, starting in 1938, airlines. For example, the Interstate Commerce Commission routinely required railroads to provide intercity passenger rail service, regardless of its profitability, to protect smaller communities from becoming economically isolated from the rest of the nation. In exchange, the entry of new railroads was restricted, and freight rates were set at levels based on what the market could bear rather than on the actual cost of transporting goods. The national government, through the Civil Aeronautics Board, regulated the airline industry in a similar fashion.

In anticipation of its entry into World War II, the national government increased its gasoline tax to one and a half cents per gallon in 1940. The funds, averaging about $300 million annually during the early 1940s, went into the general revenue account and were not set aside for highway projects. Although defense expenditures became the national government's top priority during World War II, the national government continued to spend $180 million to $200 million annually on highways and bridges until the war's conclusion in 1945.

After the war, national funding for highway and bridge construction increased incrementally, reaching $498 million in 1950. This was approximately the same amount generated by the gasoline tax. Although no state refused funding, the National Governors' Conference (now called the National Governors' Association) repeatedly asked the national government to give states the national tax dollars used to fund the program and allow them to build highways and bridges without national interference. Also, although the national government was not legally required to spend the funds on highways, the highway lobby strongly opposed the diversion of those funds to other uses and routinely publicized comparisons between the amount raised by the national government's gasoline tax and the amount appropriated for highways.[43]

State and local governments continued to outspend the national government on highway projects during the 1930s, 1940s, and early 1950s. For example, in 1940 the national government spent $392 million on highways and bridges, and the states and localities spent $854 million. In 1950, the national government spent $967 million on highways and bridges, and the states and localities spent $2.4 billion. Instead of using general revenue to fund road construction and repair, by 1929 every state had imposed a tax on gasoline sales, ranging from two to six cents per gallon. The revenue financed road and bridge construction, primarily main trunk roads and, to a lesser extent, secondary roads. Between 1930 and 1940, state gasoline tax revenue soared from $494 million to $870 million annually. Motorist and trucking organizations disagreed over specific gasoline and diesel fuel tax rates, with motorist organizations, like the American Automobile Association, advocating higher fees on truckers to compensate for their heavy rigs' extra wear and tear on roadways. However, they both supported the imposition of state gasoline taxes as the primary means of generating highway revenue so long as the funds were spent on highways. At that time, many states diverted motor fuel tax revenue to other uses. For example, 19 percent of state gasoline tax revenue in 1936 was diverted to schools. Motorist and trucking organizations also strongly objected to using tolls to finance highway projects. In their view, not only did tolls restrict traffic flow, but the combination of imposing a toll as well as motor fuel taxes on motorists and truckers was a form of double taxation. At that time, tolls were used by some states, primarily in the Northeast, to fund unusually costly highway projects, typically bridges and tunnels. Tolls, at that time, were prohibited on nearly all nationally financed road projects (exceptions were granted for several high-cost bridges and tunnels) in large part due to opposition from the trucking industry and the American Automobile Association.[44]

Between 1921 and 1940, the number of paved miles in the United States increased to 3 million, and limited-access highways were opened in Chicago, Los Angeles, New York City, and Pittsburgh. In 1939, Thomas H. MacDonald, chief of the U.S. Agriculture Department's Bureau of Public Roads, promoted the idea of constructing a 30,000 mile-national expressway system to improve rural and urban traffic flow, eliminate urban and rural decay, and create thousands of jobs.[45] Two years later, President Franklin D. Roosevelt (D, 1933–1945) appointed a National Interregional Highway Committee, headed by MacDonald, to further evaluate the need for a national expressway system. The committee's January 1944 report, *Interregional Highways*, recommended the construction of a 33,900-mile national highway system, plus an additional 5,000 miles of auxiliary urban routes. Congress later authorized $20 billion for a 40,000-mile National System of Interstate Highways in the *Federal-Aid Highway Act of 1944*. However, World War II precluded spending billions on highways, and only token amounts were appropriated for their construction.

Although there was little opposition to the construction of publicly owned and maintained highways and bridges, there was little consensus about how to go about it. City planners and local government officials saw highway and road construction as a means to address and revitalize decaying urban centers. State highway engineers, whose views were articulated by the American Association of State Highway Officials and defended by the National Highway Users Conference (composed of trucking, manufacturing, and oil companies), viewed highways as a means to move traffic. These differences created much debate over highway design standards, the location of highways, and the diversion of gasoline tax revenue.[46]

State highway engineers favored limited-access highways and expressways because they were the most efficient means to move traffic over fairly long distances. City planners and local government officials favored roads with multiple access points because they encouraged construction of homes and businesses along the highway's rights-of-way, which, in turn, generated additional tax revenue for localities.

State highway engineers also clashed with city planners and local government officials over the location of highways. City planners and local government officials often recommended using highway construction projects to eliminate residential slums and decaying industrial areas. State highway engineers were less interested in slum clearance and urban renewal than in locating highways in places that moved the most traffic at the least cost, regardless of the economic, social, and/or political status of affected neighborhoods.

State highway engineers also objected to the tendency of both state and local government officials to divert gasoline tax revenue to other uses. In their view, using gasoline tax revenue for urban renewal, schools, and other social causes was tantamount to theft from the pockets of highway users. Many government officials saw nothing wrong with diverting state gasoline tax dollars to nontransportation uses. They considered transportation users' fees as one of several revenue sources available to assist them in their effort to improve their community.

PRIVATE OR PUBLIC SOLUTIONS: *THE FEDERAL HIGHWAY ACT OF 1956*

The nation's economic expansion following World War II led to a virtual explosion in both car and truck ownership. Motor vehicle registration jumped from 31 million vehicles in 1945 to 49 million in 1950. The phenomenal growth in automobile and truck ownership led to increased traffic congestion throughout the nation. State and local governments reacted to angry motorists' demands for traffic relief (and opposition to increases in user fees) by issuing hundreds of millions of dollars in bonds for road and bridge construction (over $650 million in bonds were issued in 1950 alone). Most states also stopped, or dramatically curtailed, the diversion of highway user fees to nonhighway uses. By 1950, 21 states had adopted legislation outlawing the diversion of highway user fees for nonhighway purposes. Yet, despite the increased expenditures, it was becoming increasingly clear that state and local government officials lacked the fiscal resources necessary to meet the growing demand for highways and other surface transportation projects. As traffic congestion became a salient political issue for local, state, and national government officials alike, it became increasingly clear that the national government was going to have to play an increasingly important role in what had traditionally been primarily a state and local government responsibility.

As mentioned earlier, Congress authorized the construction of a $20 billion, 40,000-mile interstate highway system in 1944 but subsequently appropriated relatively token amounts for the system. When President Dwight Eisenhower (R, 1953–1961) was first elected to the White House, the national government was spending around $100 million annually on interstate highways. At that time, there was consensus within Congress that an interstate highway system would boost the national economy and was needed to move military equipment and personnel during a national emergency. It also had President Eisenhower's strong support. As a result, several members of Congress expressed interest in reexamining the question of how to find the resources to fund a complete, national interstate highway system.

President Eisenhower was a fiscal conservative who, as a general rule, did not support national intrusion into areas typically viewed as state and local government responsibilities. However, as the commander in chief of the Allied forces, he experienced first hand the advantages that Germany enjoyed during World War II because of their autobahn network of highways. Also, as a young man, he participated in the U.S. Army's first transcontinental motor convoy in 1919. During the 62-day trip from Washington, D.C., to San Francisco, California, then-Lieutenant Colonel Eisenhower experienced all of the woes known to motorists at the time: a seemingly endless series of mechanical breakdowns, vehicles stuck in mud and sand, and trucks crashing through wooden bridges. Given his experiences, President Eisenhower was a strong advocate for road-building projects. However, the nation's involvement in the Korean conflict from June 25, 1950, to July 27, 1953, precluded major increases in funding for domestic projects. Once the cease-fire was in place, President Eisenhower focused, once again, on the interstate highway system by naming General Lucius D. Clay chair of the President's Committee on a National Highway Program.[47]

To no one's surprise, the Clay Committee recommended that the national government go forward with plans to construct an interstate highway system. General Clay summed up the arguments of those favoring the creation of an interstate highway system in his testimony before the House Committee on Public Works on April 20, 1955:

[T]he automobile has become a very vital part of our economy.... It has become more than a means of transportation. It has become a very vital part of our family life, both for recreation and for the movement of children to schools, for the movement of the housewife to shopping, and for the movement of the worker to work. Loss of lives in accidents due to inadequate highways is very real. Moreover, ... the ... interstate system is a system designated by the

Defense Department as essential to national defense for the movement of troops in the event of war, more important for the movement of industrial products and, with civil defense now a more important factor, for the dispersal of population in the event of atomic attack.[48]

The military's support for the interstate highway system, coupled with support from the National Governors' Conference, National Association of Counties, American Municipal League, U.S. Conference of Mayors, and other state and local government organizations, was critical in garnering support of conservative congressional Democrats who normally opposed national expenditures in areas traditionally seen as a state and/or local government responsibility. However, there was little consensus on how to raise the necessary funds. The U.S. Bureau of Public Roads had reported in 1939 that most roads outside of the Northeast, southern California, and Florida did not have traffic volumes necessary to cover costs through tolls.[49] Moreover, the American Automobile Association, other organizations representing motorists, and the trucking industry vehemently opposed the use of tolls to finance the system. All interested parties were also reluctant to raise motor fuel taxes to pay for it. Clay's committee recommended the creation of a Federal Highway Corporation that would float 30-year bonds to finance the system. The bonds would be paid by the national government's two cents a gallon tax on gasoline, which, at that time, generated over $800 million annually. However, state highway officials viewed the Federal Highway Corporation as a threat to their autonomy, and Senator Harry Byrd (D-VA), chair of the Senate Finance Committee, opposed borrowing money to finance the system. He wanted a pay-as-you-go plan that avoided interest charges. The disagreement over financing prevented any final action during the 1955 legislative session. The following year, the logjam was broken when it was decided to follow the National Governors' Conference's suggestion to create a Highway Trust Fund, similar to state highway trust funds. The Highway Trust Fund's revenue would be generated from national fuel taxes and taxes on tires and motor oil. The elimination of the Federal Highway Corporation and the offer to pay for 90 percent of the interstate highway system's cost appeased state highway officials. Prohibiting tolls on nationally financed interstate highways, with an exception granted for the 2,447 miles of toll expressways already in operation, and a relatively small increase in motor fuel taxes from two to three cents per gallon appeased motorist and trucking organizations. The funding compromise solved the problem of how to fund what President Eisenhower later called the "greatest public works program in history."[50] Specifically, the *Federal Aid to Highway Act of 1956* created a 41,000-mile national system of interstate and defense highways with a target completion date of 1972. To help finance the national government's share of the cost ($23.6 billion of an anticipated $27 billion), the Highway Trust Fund was expected to collect an estimated $14.8 billion over the program's 16-year construction period from a three cents per gallon excise tax on gasoline, diesel, and special motor fuels; a nine cents per pound excise tax on inner tubes; an eight cents per pound excise tax on automobile tubes; a three cents per pound excise tax on tire retreads; half of the 10 percent manufacturer's tax on trucks, buses, and truck trailers; and a $1.50 per pound weight fee on trucks and buses, excluding local transit vehicles weighing over 26,000 pounds. The weight fee was imposed to account for the extra wear and tear that heavy trucks caused to the nation's roadways. The intent was to target the interstate highway system's cost onto those who used it without resorting to tolls that would impede traffic. Congress planned to appropriate money from the general treasury to make up the difference between the program's anticipated cost and the revenue generated in the Highway Trust Fund.[51]

The *Federal Aid to Highway Act of 1956* was a defining moment in the development of the nation's transportation policy. In theoretical terms introduced by James Wilson, it transformed highway policy from a primary focus on client politics to a blend of both client and majoritarian politics.[52] This blend was an important factor in helping to explain why the nation's highway policy remained relatively the same for a generation. Unlike client politics, where benefits are targeted to specific groups, and costs are spread relatively widely, majoritarian politics have benefits and costs that are widely dispersed. The *Federal Aid to Highway Act of 1956* continued the client politics focus by providing subsidies to the highway lobby. At the same time, the public perceived the program in majoritarian terms because it promised to make the entire nation accessible by automobile and truck through the construction of toll-free roads; ensure economic growth throughout the nation, without adversely affecting one region at the expense of the other; and disperse costs relatively widely through the program's user fees.[53] As one author explained: "As long as the trust fund principle was broadly accepted, its client politics operated smoothly and unobtrusively behind the majoritarian elements, like a road project being built behind a large 'Your Highway Tax Dollars at Work' sign."[54]

For the next 35 years, the national government focused most of its surface transportation resources on the construction of interstate highways. Moreover, the *Federal Aid to Highway Act of 1956* centralized highway policy-making authority in the United States by elevating the role of national and state highway department officials in determining the scope and nature of the nation's highway system. Local government officials and urban planners still played a role, but the overall design and location of the interstate system and, increasingly, primary and secondary highways as well were decided by national and state government officials whose goals often conflicted with those held by local government officials. As mentioned previously, local government officials were interested in fostering local economic growth as well as improving traffic flow. They were also more interested than state or national government officials in using interstate highway construction to clear slums and other blighted areas, a difference in outlook that led to many conflicts with state and national government officials over route locations. In addition, national and state highway engineers imposed professional, uniform road construction and design standards throughout the nation. Local government officials resented the imposition of these standards because they increased construction costs and impinged on their autonomy.[55]

CONCLUSION: FOLLOWING THE PATH OF LEAST POLITICAL RESISTANCE

From 1956 to 1991, five issues dominated American surface transportation policy: the escalating cost of completing the interstate highway system, using Highway Trust Fund revenue for nonhighway uses, crossover sanctions, suburban sprawl, and the use of highways to clear slums and blighted areas and that practice's effect on minority neighborhoods and the urban poor. There was also considerable debate over the national government's regulation of the trucking industry. These debates and their resolution are examined in the next chapter. It is important to note that each of these issues was debated and decided by Congress, signifying the public sector's growing hegemony in surface transportation decision making, and the national government's increasingly dominant role in that decision-making process. It is also important to note that up until this point the national government acted on each transportation mode separately, reacted to issues as they arose, rarely anticipating issues or taking a long-term, proactive approach. It also did not attempt to develop an integrated, intermodal strategy to address traffic congestion. Instead, it expanded transportation capacity in all available transportation modes, with an added emphasis on expanding highway capacity. There was little interest in coordinating transportation modes to maximize transportation efficiencies or to address transportation inadequacies.[56] This was the path of least political resistance. By focusing on enhanced capacity, national, state, and local government officials garnered political support from all affected industries. Coordination and integration of the various transportation modes would have required them to make choices according to hard-to-agree-upon principles and then prioritize and allocate resources accordingly. These decisions were certain to upset one organization or another and turn highway policy into a zero-sum game, with winners and losers. When presented with a choice, elected officials avoid making enemies. The developmental system in place appeased many politically active organizations whose support on Election Day was greatly appreciated.

As mentioned earlier, the participants in surface transportation policy making during the 1940s and early 1950s were engaging in what James Q. Wilson described as client politics. This occurs when the program's benefits (in this case, government subsidies) are targeted to specific groups (construction companies, engineering firms, automotive manufacturers and dealers, oil refiners, gasoline retailers, etc.), and the program's costs are dispersed widely to all taxpayers. Because costs are dispersed, taxpayers do not organize in opposition, and conflict in the policy-making process is relatively low.[57] However, the economic regulation of the trucking industry was a different matter. It had elements of what Wilson called interest group politics. It occurs when specific groups try to grab all of a program's benefits and shift all of the costs onto other groups. Interest group politics often pits one interest group against the other and is marked by relatively high levels of conflict.[58] In this case, the railroad industry wanted to use the national government's regulatory powers to prevent cutthroat price competition from the trucking industry, its main competitor for long-distance freight hauling. However, the trucking industry welcomed economic regulation because it guaranteed profits in an era of very great economic uncertainty. From their perspective, the imposition of economic regulations was an extension of the Federal Aid to Highways program's client politics because the program's benefits (restricted entry of new trucking companies and price regulations based on what the market will bear) were targeted to their industry, and costs (higher prices) were dispersed relatively widely to consumers.

Although national policymakers did not attempt to create a comprehensive, systemwide solution to the nation's traffic congestion problems during their deliberations on the Federal Aid to Highways program, the regulation of the railroad, trucking, and aviation industries had systemwide effects. For example, the cross-subsidization of nonprofitable routes, typically in rural areas, with profitable ones, typically in urban areas, in all transportation modes had a systemwide effect. Instead of pitting one type of transportation industry against the other, cross-subsidization pitted one type of area (rural) against another (urban). Without these regulations, transportation costs in the nation's rural areas would have been higher, and service would have been lower. Conversely, without these regulations, transportation costs in the nation's urban areas would have been lower, and service would have been higher. Cross-subsidization was popular in the U.S. Senate, where each state, regardless of its population, has two senators. The two senators per state rule augmented the rural states' political clout in the U.S. Senate, enabling this policy to survive the congressional policy-making process for many years.

NOTES

1. U.S. Department of Transportation, *Transportation Statistics Annual Report 1998* (Washington, DC: U.S. Government Printing Office, 1998), pp. 56–72; and U.S. Department of Transportation, *Transportation Indicators: January 2002* (Washington, DC: U.S. Government Printing Office, 2002), p. 63.

2. Richard E. Ward, "Transportation and Society," in *Introduction to Transportation*, ed. Paul W. DeVore (Worcester, MA: Davis Publications, 1983), p. 21.

3. Jonathan D. Salant, "U.S. Traffic Congestion Has Increased Greatly, Study Finds," *The Charleston Gazette*, May 8, 2001, p. 2A.

4. David F. Schultz, "Keynote Address: Decision Makers Need Help," in *Transportation, Urban Form, and the Environment* (Washington, DC: Transportation Research Board, 1990), p. 12.

5. Milton Friedman and Rose Friedman, *Free to Choose* (NY: Avon Books, 1979), pp. 183–192; and E. S. Savas, *Privatization and Public-Private Partnerships* (NY: Chatham House, 2000), pp. 44–49.

6. E. S. Savas, *Privatization: The Key to Better Government* (Chatham, NJ: Chatham House, 1987), pp. 33–51, 137–148; and E. S. Savas, *Privatization and Public-Private Partnerships*, pp. 92–107, 237–258.

7. Bruce D. McDowell, "Transportation and Governmental Organizations," in *Introduction to Transportation*, ed. Paul W. DeVore (Worcester, MA: Davis Publications, 1983), p. 326.

8. Rodney Leis and Thomas F. Murphy, "Marine Systems," in *Introduction to Transportation*, ed. Paul W. DeVore (Worcester, MA: Davis Publications, 1983), p. 52; Herman Mertins, Jr., *National Transportation Policy in Transition* (Lexington, MA: Lexington Books, 1972), p. 5; and John L. Hazard, *Transportation: Management Economics Policy* (Cambridge, MD: Cornell Maritime Press, Inc., 1977), pp. 333, 334.

9. Bruce D. McDowell, "Transportation and Governmental Organizations," p. 327; and John L. Hazard, *Transportation*, p. 5.

10. U.S. Department of Transportation, Federal Highway Administration, *America's Highways, 1776/1976* (Washington, DC: U.S. Government Printing Office, 1976), p. 16.

11. Ibid.; and Mark S. Foster, "Roads," in *Encyclopedia of Urban America: The Cities and Suburbs*, vol. 2, ed. Neil Larry Shumsky (Santa Barbara, CA: ABC-CLIO, 1998), pp. 671–675.

12. Douglas E. Clanin, "Internal Improvements in National Politics, 1816–1830," in *Transportation and the Early Nation*, papers presented at an Indiana American Revolution Bicentennial Symposium (Indianapolis: Indiana Historical Society, 1982), pp. 34, 35; and Herman Mertins, Jr., *National Transportation Policy in Transition*, p. 5.

13. U.S. Department of Transportation, Federal Highway Administration, *America's Highways, 1776/1976*, pp. 20–22.

14. Ibid., pp. 14, 22, 23.

15. Douglas E. Clanin, "Internal Improvements in National Politics, 1816–1830," pp. 47–53.

16. Morton Grodzins, *The American System* (Chicago: Rand McNally, 1966), pp. 33–37.

17. John B. Rae, *The Road and Car in American Life* (Cambridge, MA: MIT Press, 1971), pp. 16, 17; and U.S. Department of Transportation, Federal Highway Administration, *America's Highways, 1776/1976*, p. 8.

18. John B. Rae, *The Road and Car in American Life*, p. 23.

19. Stanford Erickson, "Rail Systems," in *Introduction to Transportation*, ed. Paul W. DeVore (Worcester, MA: Davis Publications, 1983), p. 83; and Herman Mertins, Jr., *National Transportation Policy in Transition*, pp. 6, 7.

20. U.S. Department of Transportation, Federal Highway Administration, *America's Highways, 1776/1976*, pp. 32–34.

21. Ibid., p. 15.

22. Ibid., p. 29; and Stanford Erickson, "Rail Systems," p. 85.

23. John B. Rae, *The Road and Car in American Life*, pp. 23–27; and Mark S. Foster, "Roads," pp. 672, 673.

24. U.S. Department of Transportation, Federal Highway Administration, *America's Highways, 1776/1976*, p. 39.

25. Rodney Leis and Thomas F. Murphy, "Marine Systems," pp. 53, 54; and Herman Mertins, Jr., *National Transportation Policy in Transition*, p. 8.

26. Herman Mertins, Jr., *National Transportation Policy in Transition*, pp. 10, 11; and John L. Hazard, *Transportation*, p. 12.

27. John B. Rae, *The Road and Car in American Life*, p. 49.

28. U.S. Department of Transportation, Federal Highway Administration, *America's Highways, 1776/1976*, p. 55.

29. John B. Rae, *The Road and Car in American Life*, pp. 33–39.

30. U.S. Advisory Commission on Intergovernmental Relations (ACIR), *Categorical Grants: Their Role and Design* (Washington, DC: ACIR, 1978), pp. 16, 17.

31. "Postwar Highway Program," in *Congress and the Nation, 1945–1964* (Washington, DC: Congressional Quarterly Service, 1965), pp. 525–527.

32. ACIR, *Categorical Grants*, p. 17.

33. Mark H. Rose, *Interstate: Express Highway Politics, 1939–1989*, rev. ed. (Knoxville, TN: The University of Tennessee Press, 1990) pp. 8, 9.

34. Herman Mertins, Jr., *National Transportation Policy in Transition*, p. 13.

35. John B. Rae, *The Road and Car in American Life*, pp. 36–39.

36. Ibid., p. 38.

37. Herman Mertins, Jr., *National Transportation Policy in Transition*, p. 14.

38. Ibid., pp. 14, 15.

39. James A. Dunn, Jr., *Driving Forces: The Automobile, Its Enemies, and the Politics of Mobility* (Washington, DC: The Brookings Institution Press, 1998), p. 2.

40. John B. Rae, *The Road and Car in American Life*, pp. 74–76; and Richard F. Weingroff, "From 1916 to 1939: The Federal-State Partnership at Work," *Public Roads* 60:1 (Summer 1996). Available on-line at: http://www.tfhrc.gov/pubrds/summer96/p96su7.htm.

41. Dorothy Robyn, *Braking the Special Interests: Trucking Deregulation and the Politics of Policy Reform* (Chicago: The University of Chicago Press, 1987), pp. 12–16.

42. Bruce D. McDowell, "Transportation and Governmental Organizations," p. 342.

43. James A. Dunn, Jr., *Driving Forces*, p. 34.

44. Jose A. Gomez-Ibanez and John R. Meyer, *Going Private: The International Experience with Transport Privatization* (Washington, DC: The Brookings Institution, 1993), p. 167.

45. Mark H. Rose, *Interstate*, p. 4.

46. Ibid., pp. 5–10.

47. Richard F. Weingroff, "Federal-Aid Highway Act of 1956: Creating the Interstate System," *Public Roads* 60:1 (Summer 1996). Available on-line at: http://www.tfhrc.gov/pubrds/summer96/p96su10.htm.

48. General Lucius D. Clay, Chairman of President Eisenhower's Committee on a National Highway Program, "Statement before the House Committee on Public Works," in *National Highway Program*. Hearings before the House Committee on Public Works, 84th Congress, First Session (Washington, DC: U.S. Government Printing Office, April 20, 1955), p. 128.

49. Jose A. Gomez-Ibanez and John R. Meyer, *Going Private*, p. 167.

50. "Postwar Highway Program," in *Congress and the Nation, 1945–1964*, p. 524; Walter J. Kohler, Governor of Wisconsin and Chair, National Governors' Conference Committee on Highways, "Statement before the House Committee on Public Works," in *National Highway Program*. Hearings before the House Committee on Public Works, 84th Congress, First Session (Washington, DC: U.S. Government Printing Office, May 4, 1955), p. 366; and James A. Dunn, Jr., *Driving Forces*, pp. 34, 35.

51. "Postwar Highway Program," in *Congress and the Nation, 1945–1964*, pp. 524, 531; and John R. Meyer and Jose A. Gomez-Ibanez, *Autos, Transit and Cities* (Cambridge, MA: Harvard University Press, 1981), p. 7.

52. James Q. Wilson, "The Politics of Regulation," in *The Politics of Regulation*, ed. James Q. Wilson (NY: Basic Books, 1980), pp. 357–394.

53. James A. Dunn, Jr., *Driving Forces*, p. 31.

54. Ibid.

55. Mark H. Rose, *Interstate*, pp. 95–104.

56. Herman Mertins, Jr., *National Transportation Policy in Transition*, p. 37.

57. James Q. Wilson, "The Politics of Regulation," pp. 357–394.

58. Ibid.

2

Highway and Mass Transit Policy, 1956 to 1990

Disagreements over funding, particularly how to deal with the escalating cost of completing the interstate highway system, dominated American highway and mass transit policy throughout the 1956 to 1990 period. Other recurring issues involved efforts to divert revenue from the Highway Trust Fund to mass transit, use crossover sanctions to achieve political goals not necessarily associated with moving people and goods from place to place, alter routing decisions and funding patterns to help cities and prevent suburban sprawl, and alter routing decisions and funding patterns to keep minority neighborhoods intact and promote the interests of the urban poor. During the 1970s, the deregulation of the trucking industry also became a hot political issue.

Congress addressed each of these issues in isolation from the others and from its decisions concerning other transportation modes, including intercity passenger rail service and civilian air service. It did this, even though numerous studies, conducted by academics as well as government-sponsored blue-ribbon panels, criticized the national government for failing to develop a unified and integrated transportation system that reflected the strengths and weaknesses of each transportation mode. For example, in 1942 the National Resources Planning Board criticized the national government for promoting the expansion of each transportation mode indiscriminately instead of coordinating the modes to maximize the nation's mobility. In 1949, the Hoover Commission argued that the fragmentation of authority brought about by a host of promotional, regulatory agencies prevented the national government from effectively developing or coordinating the nation's transportation system.[1] In 1961, the Doyle Report, written for the U.S. Senate Committee on Interstate and Foreign Commerce, cited Congress's decentralized committee system, which provides jurisdiction over the various transportation modes to different committees and subcommittees, as one of the primary reasons that the national government had failed to develop an integrated national transportation policy that took into account the various transportation modes' strengths and weaknesses. It proposed the creation of a U.S. Department of Transportation within the executive branch to serve as a counterweight to Congress's decentralized decision-making process and the consolidation of the Civil Aeronautics Board (which regulated the airline industry), the Interstate Commerce Commission (which regulated the trucking, pipeline, and railroad industries), and the Federal Maritime Board (which regulated the inland water transportation industry) into a single National Transportation Commission to regulate the economic activities of all transportation modes in a single place. It also recommended the creation of a House and Senate Joint Committee on Transportation to serve as a focal point for coordinating transportation legislation in Congress.[2]

The U.S. Department of Transportation was created in 1966. Instead of formulating a grand design to weave the various transportation modes into a single, cohesive system, the national government continued to follow the path of least political resistance, which was to act in a piecemeal fashion; appease the various transportation industries' lobbying organizations by increasing funding for all transportation modes indiscriminately; and, in recognition of the highway lobby's political power, focus most of its transportation resources on the completion of the interstate highway system.

One new development was the intrusion of "outsiders" into the surface transportation policy-making process who were interested in raising gasoline taxes for purposes other than funding transportation projects, such as reducing the national budget deficit and conserving energy. Although the highway lobby (automotive and truck manufacturers and their related unions, oil companies and refineries, tire manufacturers, asphalt and concrete suppliers, trucking companies, etc.) and other transportation interests fought to retain their hegemony over surface transportation policy outcomes, outside interests won several key battles during the 1980s that changed the nature of the national government's transportation policy-making process, making it more partisan, more prone to conflict, and less predictable.

ESCALATING HIGHWAY CONSTRUCTION COSTS

Escalating highway construction costs arose as an issue almost from the very start of the interstate highway project. In 1957, national highway administrators reported that the initial cost estimate of $27 billion to complete the interstate highway system was unrealistic. They estimated that it would cost at least $37 billion, with the national government's share being $33.9 billion. Most of the additional cost was due to legitimate expenses, such as purchasing land for the system and incorporating improved, more expensive highway design and safety features. Congressional conservatives complained that a good portion of the additional cost was due to the *Davis-Bacon Act's* prevailing wage rule. It required construction companies working on interstate highways to pay employees the locally prevailing wage as determined by the U.S. secretary of labor. Labor organizations and many Democrats, primarily because they were politically allied with organized labor, defended the prevailing wage rule. A largely unexpected additional expense was due to corruption among state highway officials. Investigations in 1957 revealed that Indiana state highway officials used their insiders' knowledge of where the interstate highway system was to be constructed to purchase land along the highway's right-of-way. After the route was announced publicly, they sold the land to the state highway department, making a 500 percent profit. Similar practices were discovered in Oklahoma and Florida in 1961 and in Massachusetts in 1962.[3]

By this time, the highway lobby was widely recognized as one of the nation's politically most powerful lobby organizations, spending millions of dollars to help elect or defeat candidates and employing millions of voters. The highway lobby's political strength, coupled with the public's support for the interstate highway system's completion, led Congress in 1959 to increase the national government's gasoline excise tax to four cents a gallon to prevent the interstate highway system from falling hopelessly behind schedule. This increased the Highway Trust Fund's revenue from about $1.5 billion annually to $2.9 billion annually (see Table 2.1).

In a testimonial to the highway lobby's influence, in 1961 Congress appropriated an additional $900 million from general revenue to keep the construction of the interstate highway system on schedule. It also increased excise taxes on inner tubes, tire retreads, and other automobile-related products to further ensure that the 1972 completion date was met. Most policymakers thought that the cost overrun problem was solved. However, in 1965, the U.S. Department of Commerce increased the interstate system's construction cost estimate to $46.8 billion. Three years later, the newly formed U.S. Department of Transportation revised that figure to $56.5 billion. Faced with the escalating cost of financing the Vietnam War and with the prospect of incurring large budget deficits, in 1966 Congress delayed the interstate system's targeted completion date to 1973. Two years later, Congress extended the deadline to 1974.[4]

In 1972, the interstate highway system was still only 70 percent complete, and the estimated cost to complete the system had risen to $76.3 billion. Faced with increased pressure from public interest groups (such as the National League of Cities and U.S. Conference of Mayors) to spend more on mass transit and noninterstate highways and slower than anticipated revenue growth in the Highway Trust Fund due to the introduction of more fuel-efficient automobiles, Congress considered three options: raise fuel and transportation-related taxes, increase highway spending from the general revenue account, and/or extend the interstate system's completion date even further. Groups representing those who would have to pay the higher taxes, such as the American Automobile Association and the Highway Users Federation, did not strongly oppose higher fuel taxes, but they wanted a guarantee that those funds would be used for highways. Moreover, they were not enthusiastic about raising taxes and refused to provide Congress political cover from motorists who, as a group, opposed gasoline tax increases. Fiscal conserva-

Table 2.1
Federal Highway Trust Fund Revenue, 1958–2005 (millions of dollars)

Year	Gasoline Excise Tax	Revenue
2005 est.	18.4¢	$28,093
2000	18.4	27,867
1995	18.4	23,233
1990	14.0	16,233
1985	9.0	13,894
1980	4.0	9,569
1975	4.0	4,947
1970	4.0	4,300
1965	4.0	3,980
1960	4.0	2,913
1958	3.0	1,493

Sources U.S. Office of Management and Budget. 2002. *The Budget of the United States Government for FY 2003: Historical Tables.* Washington, DC: U.S. Government Printing Office, pp. 220–228.

tives opposed using general revenue funds for highway construction because the national government's budget was already in deficit. In the absence of a consensus, Congress delayed action until 1976, when it decided to extend the interstate system's completion date to 1990.

During the mid-1970s, environmentalists, worried about automotive exhaust's adverse effect on the ozone layer, and organizations worried about the nation's increasing dependence on foreign oil, especially in the aftermath of the Arab oil embargo of 1973, demanded an increase in national gasoline taxes. They wanted to discourage automobile use, not raise revenue for additional highway construction. In 1975, they convinced President Jimmy Carter (D, 1977–1981) to recommend the imposition of an oil import fee, to be collected only on gasoline, to promote energy conservation.[5] Congress rejected the proposal, but it was a milestone event in the history of surface transportation policy making in the United States. It was the first of several attempts by "outsiders" to alter the outcome of national transportation policy. As will be shown, most of these attempts involved the diversion of Highway Trust Fund revenue for deficit reduction or mass transit. These attempts pitted interest group against interest group, transforming the normally closed and relatively consensus-based client politics that had dominated surface transportation policy for many years into a much more open, partisan, and conflict-prone political environment.

When President Ronald Reagan (R, 1981–1989) began his first term of office, 95 percent of the interstate highway system (40,438 of the proposed 42,500 miles) was complete. The national government had spent $63 billion and states $7 billion on the system. The U.S. Department of Transportation estimated that it was going to cost another $48 billion to complete the last 2,062 miles in the system and bring the system up to final construction standards (the U.S. Department of Transportation reported that 25 percent of existing interstate highways needed immediate repair or replacement, and nearly half would need repair or rehabilitation by 1995).

Worried about the budget deficit and unwilling to support tax increases, President Reagan recommended that those segments of the interstate system not already under construction be eliminated and existing resources focused on interstate highway maintenance. The Democratic Congress agreed to increase funding for maintenance but rejected the president's proposal to eliminate the last segments of the interstate highway system. Congress's reluctance was rooted in its members' relentless desire to search for opportunities to engage in credit-claiming as a means to enhance their reelection prospects.[6] The construction of bridges and roads and their subsequent ribbon-cutting ceremonies are one of Congress's prime sources of credit-claiming.

In recognition of Congress's desire to complete the interstate highway system, U.S. Secretary of Transportation Andrew Lewis crafted compromise legislation in 1982 that would have increased the excise tax on gasoline from four cents to nine cents and imposed higher fees on heavy trucks. The plan would have generated an additional $5.5 billion annually, enough to increase funding for the "4R" interstate highway maintenance program (the resurface, restore, rehabilitate, and reconstruct program) from $500 million to $2 billion annually and complete the interstate highway system by 1991. Lewis' plan won bipartisan congressional support but was initially rejected by President Reagan. He was more interested in claiming credit for reducing taxes and spending than for securing additional highway and bridge projects. However, the Republican Party subsequently lost an unusually large number of congressional seats in the November 1982 elections. The nation was mired in a recession and, in the wake of the disappointing election returns, President Reagan decided that he needed to demonstrate to the public that he was willing to work with Congress to combat the nation's unemployment problem. Carefully avoiding the word "tax," he endorsed Lewis' plan to increase user fees as a means to create thousands of construction jobs.[7]

When President George Bush (R, 1989–1993) entered the White House, gasoline prices had fallen to levels below those in place prior to the 1982 nickel per gallon gasoline tax increase. Concerned that low gasoline prices were encouraging motorists to burn fuel needlessly, environmentalists lobbied for a significant increase in fuel taxes to encourage motorists to conserve fuel. Others, including Alan Greenspan, chair of the Federal Reserve Board, testified before Congress that increasing the gasoline tax would also be an easy, relatively pain-free way for the national government to increase revenue and reduce its budget deficit, which, in their view, threatened the nation's economic recovery. Congressional leaders not associated with the Transportation Committees floated various "trial balloon" proposals before the press to determine the American public's reaction to a possible increase in gasoline taxes. Seeing no strong, adverse reaction, congressional leaders included the possibility of a 5 or 10 cents per gallon increase in the gasoline tax as part of a larger package of proposals that it was negotiating with the White House to reduce the budget deficit. In a classic, textbook example of "iron triangle" politics in action, members of the House and Senate Transportation Committees, the highway lobby, and U.S. Department of Transportation officials denounced the use of gasoline tax revenue to offset the budget deficit. However, the House and Senate Budget Committees and Finance Committees have jurisdiction over tax legislation. After extended negotiations and over objections from the House and Senate Transportation Committees, the Budget Committees recommended, and the House and Senate later approved, increasing the national government's gasoline tax from 9 cents to 14 cents per gallon starting in 1990. To appease the highway lobby and Transportation Committees, half of the revenue went into the Highway Trust Fund, and half went into the general revenue account to help offset the budget deficit.[8]

For the first time since 1956, national gasoline tax revenue was diverted from the Highway Trust Fund and used for nonhighway purposes. Outsiders had successfully broken the highway lobby's policy monopoly, forcing it to accept policy changes that it opposed.[9] Sensing vulnerability, other groups, including mass transit and intercity passenger railroad lobbies, soon launched their own attacks on the Highway Trust Fund. They were not alone. Shortly after his election in 1992, President Bill Clinton (D, 1993–2000) proposed a broad-based energy tax based on the Btu (British thermal unit) content of different fuels. His twin goals were to generate additional revenue to reduce the national budget deficit and encourage Americans to conserve energy. His proposal taxed petroleum products at a higher level than coal and natural gas. After much bickering marked by sectional and regional rivalries, Congress rejected the broad-based tax concept. Instead, it increased the national government's gasoline excise tax another 4.3 cents per gallon. All of the additional revenue was earmarked for deficit reduction. The gasoline tax vote divided along party lines, with Vice President Al Gore casting the tiebreaking vote in the U.S. Senate. Because all of the tax increase's revenue went to deficit reduction, and none was set aside for highway or mass transit, the vote was perceived in purely partisan terms. The 1990 and 1993 gasoline tax increases demonstrated that the highway lobby's policy monopoly had disappeared, and the client and majoritarian politics that had marked the making of surface transportation policy for nearly a generation was now largely a thing of the past.

MASS TRANSIT

Prior to the 1960s, most forms of mass transit (bus, subway, ferryboat, and commuter rail) were provided by private firms.[10] Competition from government-subsidized highways and the public's preference to drive to work caused many private firms to go out of business or reduce service to selected, profitable routes. As private firms withdrew from the mass transit field, their stranded customers lobbied state and local government officials to subsidize specific routes or offer mass transit as a public service. At the same time, environmentalists lobbied for the expansion of mass transit operations as a means to get people out of their cars. Their goal was to reduce traffic congestion to conserve energy, reduce air and noise pollution, and protect the ozone layer. City planners, especially those in America's larger population cities, and many academics studying urban America also advocated an expansion of public mass transit. Many of them blamed the national government's highway program for the social and economic ills afflicting the nation's larger population cities, primarily because that program contributed to the expansion of the nation's suburbs. In their view, mass transit was necessary to make cities more competitive with suburbs as a place to live and conduct business. Also, civil rights organizations and groups advocating the interests of the poor favored subsidized, public mass transit as a means to enable the nation's most economically vulnerable citizens to participate more fully in American society.

At first, these disparate interests did not behave as a cohesive lobby. One reason for this was that bus operators, represented by the American Transit Association, opposed government assistance because they feared the imposition of unwanted mandates and other regulations. However, facing increased public pressure to provide additional mass transit services, mayors from the nation's largest population cities began to lobby the national government for financial assistance for mass transit. The national government's response to the mayors' lobbying provided the means to bring these disparate groups into a more cohesive and influential lobbying force.

The mayors, primarily through the lobbying efforts of the U.S. Conference of Mayors, convinced the Democratically controlled Congress to provide $25 million in grants and $50 million in low-interest loans for mass transit in the *Housing Act of 1961*. Indicative of the highway lobby's power, the law originated in Congress's banking committees, not its transportation committees.[11] They then convinced President John F. Kennedy (D, 1961–1963), who was very aware of the Democratic Party's need to attract urban voters, to endorse a bill authorizing $500 million for urban transit systems. The highway lobby did not oppose the bill because its funds came from the general revenue account, not from the Highway Trust Fund. President Lyndon Baines Johnson (D, 1963–1968) later included an expanded version of the mass transit bill in his Great Society program.

The *Urban Mass Transportation Act of 1964* provided states $375 million over three years to pay for up to two-thirds of the cost to plan, engineer, and design urban mass transit systems; all of the costs of relocating families displaced by mass transit; and half of the cost of mass transit projects that showed urgent need but lacked required planning reports. Although far below highway funding levels, mass transit advocates hailed the *Urban Mass Transportation Act* as a milestone achievement. Cities used the funds to purchase mass transit companies on the brink of bankruptcy and expand existing public bus services. The *Urban Mass Transportation Act* was subsequently renewed and, by 1970, had an annual appropriation of $175 million.

The *Urban Mass Transportation Act* had a galvanizing effect on the previously disjointed organizations advocating the expansion of public mass transit. The act's regulations protecting wages and working conditions won organized labor's support. The availability of money attracted support from rail equipment and bus manufacturers, engineering and public works construction firms, consultants, urban planners, and the American Transit Association.[12] These groups, led by the U.S. Conference of Mayors, lobbied hard for increased mass transit funding throughout the 1970s. By the decade's end, funding for mass transit capital expenses had grown to $1.5 billion annually. Funding covered two-thirds of the cost to plan, design, and construct mass transit systems. Congress also appropriated $700 million annually for mass transit operating expenses.

Some mass transit lobbyists advocated a "balanced transportation system," a phrase that generally meant less funding for highways and more for mass transit. One of their proposals was to dedicate a portion of Highway Trust Fund revenue to mass transit. That would guarantee funding for mass transit projects and prevent the necessity of having to fight for funding during Congress's annual appropriations process. Lobby organizations representing automotive and trucking industries, road builder associations, oil companies, gasoline retailers, real estate developers, and construction unions opposed efforts to take funds from "their" trust fund.[13] Their economic arguments for retaining the Highway Trust Fund's "purity" were augmented by those who viewed mass transit as a state and local government responsibility. This view, held primarily by Republicans and conservative Democrats, was based on the idea that because mass transit's benefits typically accrue to residents of a single cluster of jurisdictions that rarely involve more than one state, mass transit was primarily a state and local government responsibility. Liberals disagreed. They argued that mass transit was a national government concern because air pollution generated by automotive exhaust is often carried by prevailing winds across state lines. Since mass transit provides people an alternative to driving, it helps reduce air pollution. Because air pollution is a national government concern, mass transit is a national government concern. This fundamental disagreement over which level of government should deal with mass transit policy, coupled with the importance of urban voters to the Democratic Party and the importance of suburban and rural voters (who generally do not view mass transit as a high priority) to the Republican Party, gave mass transportation policy making a distinctive partisan flavor that, at least during the 1960s and 1970s, was typically absent during debates over other transportation modes.

In 1981, President Reagan announced that mass transit operating subsidies should be phased out over four years because they were inefficient and too costly given the size of the national budget deficit. He also opposed increased funding for mass transit capital construction projects because, in his view, mass transit was a state and local government responsibility. Under a threat of a presidential veto, Congress reduced mass transit operating grants to $1.3 billion annually and capital construction-related grants to $1.5 billion annually.

A breakthrough, of sorts, for mass transit occurred in 1982. At that time, President Reagan agreed not to veto a congressional effort to increase Highway Trust Fund revenue by raising the gasoline excise tax from four cents to nine cents a gallon. Revenue from one of the five-cent increases was earmarked for mass transit capital construction projects (approximately $1.1 billion annually). He did not oppose the one cent set-aside for mass transit because the funds were used for capital projects, not operating subsidies, and Congress agreed to convert the mass transit program into a block grant. Under the new format, cities no longer applied to the U.S. Department of Transportation for funding. Instead, funding was allocated according to a formula based on several factors, such as total miles of existing mass transit routes and population. This widened the distribution of funds, decreasing funding in the nation's largest, primarily Democratic cities and increasing funding in suburbs and smaller, primarily Republican cities. Although the block grant was initially funded at $3.5 billion, the Reagan administration urged Congress throughout the remainder of the 1980s to reduce the program's funding to help balance the national budget. By 1990, the program's funding had fallen to approximately $2 billion annually.[14]

CROSSOVER SANCTIONS

The national government has a long history of imposing administrative conditions on its highway assistance programs. Dating as far back as the *Federal Road Act of 1916*, the national government has routinely applied various "good government practices" regulations to highway assistance. Among these regulations are guidelines to assure fair competitive bidding practices for contractors, auditing requirements to prevent embezzlement and fraud, and specific design requirements, such as those concerning noise abatement, traffic interchanges, width of traffic lanes (12 feet), and width of median areas to promote uniform safety and health standards across the nation.[15]

Although state and local government officials have long argued that the administrative red tape tied to highway assistance was burdensome, most of their complaints were not directed at the aforementioned regulations. Instead, they strongly objected to the use of crossover sanctions as a condition of aid. Crossover sanctions impose a penalty on a recipient of a particular program, typically a reduction in assistance, for failing to comply with requirements of another, independent program.[16] In their view, crossover sanctions infringed on states' rights and were an inappropriate use of national government power that bordered on blackmail.

In 1990, there were 14 crossover sanctions attached to national highway assistance, including mandates to remove junkyards and billboards along interstate highways, create a U.S. Department of Transportation-approved highway safety program, limit maximum speeds on nationally financed highways, set blood alcohol concentration levels for determining when motorists are driving under the influence, and establish the drinking age. Many crossover sanctions have goals that are supported by the vast majority of Americans. For example, the first highway crossover sanction was contained in the *Highway Beautification Act of 1965*. President Lyndon Baines Johnson's wife, Lady Bird Johnson, had made highway beautification her top priority. With her support, the *Highway Beautification Act* was approved by Congress with little opposition. Among its many provisions was one that threatened the withdrawal of 10 percent of a state's national highway funds if it did not comply with new, more stringent controls on outdoor advertising billboards located within 660 feet of interstate and primary highways and on junkyards located within 1,000 feet of interstate and primary highways. The national government promised states 75 percent of the cost to comply with the regulations. All 50 states announced shortly after the law's enactment that they would participate in the program. The national government, however, did not appropriate funds to reimburse states' compliance costs. The mandate soon evolved into a voluntary effort to restrict billboards and junkyards along the interstate and primary road systems.[17]

Throughout the 1980s, several public interest groups, especially the National Governors' Conference, lobbied Congress for regulatory relief, especially from crossover sanctions. As part of this effort, 20 U.S. senators, calling themselves the States' Rights Coalition, sponsored legislation in 1986 to raise the speed limit from 55 miles per hour to 65 miles per hour on interstate highways outside urban areas with populations exceeding 50,000. With the Reagan administration's blessing, Congress subsequently amended the *Federal Highway Act of 1987* to provide states additional flexibility concerning the national speed limit. Within 24 hours of the law's enactment, New Mexico and Arizona raised speed limits on their interstate highways, and within a year of the law's enactment another 36 states had raised speed limits on at least a portion of their highway system. In 1995, Congress repealed the national speed limit sanctions altogether but added another: states that do not make it illegal for drivers under the age of 21 to drive with a blood alcohol level of 0.02 percent or higher forfeit 5 percent of their highway trust-fund money starting in 1998 and 20 percent each succeeding year.[18]

HIGHWAYS AND SUBURBAN SPRAWL

Academics and practitioners have debated the cost-benefits of American surface transportation policy for decades. Most studies conclude that highways and other surface transportation-related construction projects have a measurable, positive effect on economic growth. For example, the Federal Highway Administration has estimated that 42,000 new jobs are created for every $1 billion spent on highway construction. Moreover, these new jobs have a positive multiplier effect on economic growth as the newly employed spend their wages in the local economy. Highway construction and improvement projects also increase property values along its right-of-way because highways make it more convenient, or possible, for people to access the property. Highways also attract both residential and nonresidential development, especially commercial development. In addition, transportation expenditures create a more efficient transportation system that, in turn, reduces private firms' transportation expenses, enabling them to be more productive and profitable. Although this latter boost to economic growth is more difficult to quantify than the creation of new jobs and residential and nonresidential development, the Federal Highway Administration conducted several econometric analyses of the national highway program's effect on economic growth from 1950 to 1991. Their analyses suggested that highway construction had a positive effect on economic growth during this period, with the highest rates of return occurring during the early years of the interstate highway system's construction (+.54 during the 1960s) and lower rates in later years (just +.09 in 1991). The declining rate of return was attributed to the large efficiency gains achieved by the construction of the interstate highway system in an era when the nation lacked an interconnected network of modern highways.[19]

Although most scholars and practitioners agree that nationally funded highways have had a positive effect on economic growth, some environmental groups and environmentally conscious "think tanks," such as the Surface Transportation Policy Project (a coalition of environmentalists, urban planners, bicycle enthusiasts, and various transportation consultants), disagree. They argue that adding highway capacity in the postinterstate era may actually inhibit economic development. They point to studies conducted by the U.S. Department of Transportation and U.S. Department of Housing and Urban Development that found that constructing beltways around metropolitan areas did not enhance the region's economic position and to other studies that suggest that highway construction merely shifts economic activity from one area to another, with little overall improvement when examined on a regional basis. They also note that other studies have concluded that the national government's emphasis on highway and bridge construction has had a number of negative, and often unintended consequences, especially for cities. These studies suggest that highways have enabled suburbs to exist as viable options for both residential and nonresidential development, primarily at the expense of the nation's cities. Moreover, they argue that the national government's emphasis on highway and bridge construction and improvement over other modes of transportation, such as commuter trains and mass transit, has contributed to suburban sprawl. Although there is some disagreement over precisely what suburban sprawl is, it is generally defined as the spread-out, skipped-over development that characterizes non-central city metropolitan areas throughout the United States. It typically consists of one- or two-story, single-family residential development located on an acre or less of land and accompanied by strip commercial centers and industrial parks.[20]

Others have suggested that the suburbanization of America was inevitable. They point out that the desire to escape the noise and congestion of American cities by migrating to the suburbs can be traced back to the early and mid-1800s. At that time, the nation's cities were clustered around deepwater sites on long-distance river and oceanic routes, primarily because their chief economic function was funneling raw materials from the nation's interior regions to Europe.[21] The invention and spread of steam-driven passenger and cargo trains substantially broadened urban access to the country's raw materials and encouraged the development of inland towns and small cities. The railroads enabled those with sufficient resources, primarily business owners and professionals, to commute from their single-family, suburban residences to their places of employment in central cities. Acquiring a suburban residence became one of the major goals of the growing middle class. It was a testimonial to their success, marking them as different and above those who could not afford to escape the noise, foul odors, and diseases associated with city life at that time.[22]

Although many of those living in urban areas may have wanted to escape the noise and congestion of the central city, few of them could afford it at the turn of the century. At that time, the concept of suburban sprawl was meaningless because America was still primarily a rural nation. In 1900, nearly three out of every four people (74 percent) resided in rural areas, 20 percent in urban areas, and just 6 percent in suburban areas. Those numbers changed dramatically over the next 30 years as nearly 20 million immigrants from Europe arrived in the United States seeking work and/or improved economic opportunities. Many of them settled in America's cities as the industrialization of the national economy created numerous economic opportunities there, including many relatively high-paying manufacturing jobs. These economic opportunities, coupled with the excitement of "the bright lights" of city life, also attracted many of the nation's rural residents.

What was once a rural nation was, in less than a single lifetime, transformed into an urban nation. As the population of America's cities increased, many urban residents looked to the suburbs as a means to pursue a slower, more peaceful lifestyle while maintaining spatial proximity to their jobs and the city's cultural amenities. The electric streetcar, invented in 1888 and known affectionately as the trolley, enabled the middle class to join the more affluent in the suburbs. By the end of the 1920s, America's cities were crisscrossed with electric trolley lines that stretched out and into the surrounding suburbs. At the same time, automobile ownership skyrocketed. The introduction of the redesigned Ford Model T in 1906 and cost efficiencies brought about by the Ford Motor Company's assembly-line production system made automobile ownership possible for many in the middle class.[23] Initially sold for $850, by 1917 the Model T was priced under $300, bringing the possibility of automobile ownership to millions of Americans.[24] The number of automobiles in the United States increased exponentially, from 500,000 in 1910 to 8 million in 1920 and to 26 million in 1929. As automobile ownership increased, so too did the demand for paved highways. Highway and bridge construction, paid mostly by state and local governments intent on fostering economic growth, made the suburbs increasingly accessible to all economic classes. Although zoning codes were enacted in many suburban communities to keep "riffraff" and certain "nondesirable" businesses (especially heavy manufacturing) out, the advent of the automobile made it possible for all economic classes to dream of the day when they could own a home in the suburbs, complete with a yard surrounded by a "white picket fence" and a short, leisurely, daily commute to their jobs in the city.

To meet the demand for new and improved roads, in 1919 Oregon became the first state to enact gasoline taxes to finance road construction. Within a decade of Oregon's penny per gallon excise tax on gasoline, every state had imposed a similar tax. Thanks in large part to the revenue from these taxes, state expenditures on road and bridge construction more than doubled during the 1920s, jumping from $1.38 billion in 1921 to $2.85 billion in 1930.[25]

The 1920s boom in road construction made it possible for large numbers of people to move to the suburbs and for the suburbs to begin to develop economic independence from the central city. Manufacturers and wholesalers found that older, urban street patterns with their winding, narrow rights-of-way were not conducive to automobile and truck movement. Traffic congestion, lack of employee parking spaces, and problems involving freight transfers increased both direct and indirect costs of conducting business in the city. The development of suburban highway systems and increased dependence by both manufacturers and wholesalers on trucks for moving their goods made the relatively noncongested and low-tax suburbs an increasingly attractive alternative for locating their businesses. In addition, as the suburbs' population increased, large retailers such as Sears Roebuck and J. C. Penny found it increasingly necessary to establish suburban branches to maintain profitability.

Although the Federal Housing Administration's intent in 1934 was to encourage homeownership and reduce unemployment in the various construction industries, its policies had the unintended consequence of contributing to the exodus to the suburbs. Its home mortgage subsidization program encouraged suburban migration because real estate appraisers engaged in a process called redlining, where government subsidized and/or guaranteed loans were not granted in neighborhoods classified as physically or economically deteriorated or populated by African Americans or working-class immigrants. Because most of these "bad risk" neighborhoods were located in cities, most of the subsidized loans were awarded in the suburbs. In addition, the deductibility of home mortgage interest on the national income tax encouraged homeownership everywhere, bringing suburban housing costs within the reach of millions of Americans who otherwise would have purchased homes in the city.[26]

Following World War II, suburbs rapidly became the location of choice for the burgeoning middle class. During the 1950s, millions of mass-produced, affordable, single-family homes were constructed on the metropolitan periphery. The suburbs' continued popularity was so great that many social commentators during the 1960s and 1970s worried about "white flight," a reference to the increasingly widening economic gulf between the predominantly white, middle- and upper-income classes locating in suburbs and the increasingly nonwhite, lower-income classes that remained in cities. Many social commentators complained that suburbs had become the haven for middle- and upper-class white residents

who "deserted" cities, leaving cities in a vicious, no-win situation. As their populations became increasingly poor, cities were faced with increased demands for social
and other services. At the same time, their capacity to raise revenue became increasingly constrained as middle- and upper-income taxpayers exited to the suburbs. This situation worsened as businesses joined the exodus to the suburbs in
search of lower taxes, cheaper land, and, among other factors, proximity to a more
educated workforce. Moreover, many retail businesses either relocated to suburbs
or expanded there in an attempt to maintain their customer base. By 1970, there
were over 14,000 strip-mall shopping centers dotting the suburban landscape,
each a testament to the suburbanization of American society.[27]

Critics of suburban sprawl argue that it is visually displeasing, causes significantly higher infrastructure costs, longer travel distances, more traffic congestion,
more automotive pollution, and a greater loss of agricultural land and open space
than more compact, planned development. Although some of the additional infrastructure costs caused by suburban sprawl are captured by local governments
through impact fees, developer extractions, and proffers, critics claim that sprawl
has an adverse effect on the quality of life, especially in the way that it reduces social
connections among people. They blame suburban sprawl for segregating neighborhoods by economic class and for fostering an "us versus them" mentality when
it comes to relations with its neighboring city. They point to five national public
opinion polls conducted in 2000 that named suburban sprawl, unfettered growth,
and traffic congestion the number one problem facing urban America, edging out
more traditional issues such as crime, the economy, and education. The concern
about sprawl was strongest in America's largest cities. Over 60 percent of the respondents in Denver and 47 percent of the respondents in San Francisco named
sprawl as their number one concern.[28]

Not everyone believes that suburban sprawl is bad. Some argue that it epito-
mizes the public's preference for that lifestyle. As one author put it, suburban
sprawl "produces relatively safe and economically heterogeneous neighborhoods
that are removed from the problems of the central city. In low-density, mid-
dle-class environments, life takes place with relative ease, and when residents wish
to relocate, they typically leave in better financial condition—the result of almost
certain housing appreciation in these locations."[29] In their view, attempts to control free market development through slow growth, sustainable growth, and smart
growth strategies adversely affect the nation's economic development and cause
urban housing prices to increase, placing a special burden on minority groups.[30]

Today, suburban areas often contain as many, and in some cases more, people,
industry, and cultural amenities than the nearby central city. This has created a
paradox for those interested in generating policies that benefit urban areas. Not
only do suburbs create a financial drain on central cities by providing the relatively
affluent an attractive alternative to call home, but their increasing political and
economic independence from the central city makes it difficult to generate policies
that address the entire metropolitan region. As one author put it: "The problem
then is to find a way to link the diverse communities of the central city and inde-

pendent-minded suburbs together so that problems of each metropolitan region as a whole can be tackled and alleviated."[31]

The suburbs' growing independence from cities is reflected in the emergence in recent years of what some scholars have termed edge cities. These small cities are located along highway corridors far removed from any large, urban center. Their economies are primarily technology-based, typically in either e-commerce (Internet transactions), telephone sales, or data entry (back-office) operations. In 1991, Joel Garreau of the *Washington Post* estimated that there were about 200 edge cities in existence at that time, a testament to the power of technology to change our economic lives and the importance of highways as a means to spatially link people to places.[32] Edge cities have come into existence because technology allows them to compete in the global economy, and highways and bridges provide them a means to connect their goods and people with the rest of the nation.

Policymakers, academics, and practitioners have debated for many years whether the national government's surface transportation policies should take into account their effect on cities and suburban sprawl. Those opposed argue that government should not use transportation funding to engage in "social engineering." In their view, if large, central cities are no longer viable economic entities, and people prefer to live in suburbs or smaller, edge cities, then government should not try to dissuade people from doing what they are convinced is in their best interest. Transportation policy should be about moving goods and people in the most efficient and cost-effective manner possible, not about the achievement of social objectives that may or may not be shared by the majority of American society.

Those arguing in the affirmative typically advocate the expenditure of additional revenue for urban mass transit projects and less for interstate and primary highways. In their view, those crafting the nation's transportation policies should be concerned with more than just the efficient movement of people and goods. They need to take a holistic approach that includes its total effect on American society. Because interstate and primary highway and bridge construction projects tend, in the aggregate, to adversely affect cities, policymakers should consciously attempt to mitigate the damage. Specifically, policymakers should carefully analyze the placement of highways to ensure that the cities' interests are taken into account. For example, several studies have indicated that limited-access beltways surrounding central cities have hastened suburban development to a greater extent than radial expressways that link the central city with its suburbs.[33] They also advocate additional funding for mass transit and commuter rail systems to reduce city traffic congestion and air pollution problems. This, in turn, enables cities to compete more effectively with suburbs as a place to live and conduct business. They also advocate increasing public participation in the decision-making process through such organizations as regional planning and zoning authorities and metropolitan planning organizations. In their view, expanding the range of inputs into the transportation decision-making process ensures that quality-of-life issues, such as air and noise pollution, are considered when developing plans for the use of public transportation funds.[34] They also note that Japan and several European nations, recognizing the negative effect that highways can have on cities, have established capital gains and inheritance taxes at almost confiscatory levels when land is sold or otherwise removed from agricultural use. The net effect is to limit suburbanization and inflate urban land values. This has encouraged people to live in cities where mass transit and rail service are purposively subsidized to provide a viable alternative to the automobile for commuting to work and for other travel purposes.[35] They also favor the European practice of congestion pricing, charging motorists a fee to drive during peak travel times, into congested areas, and for parking. Congestion pricing strategies encourage motorists to avoid driving during peak travel times, choose other destinations, share a ride, switch to mass transit or commuter rail services, and find other travel options. Advocates of congestion pricing strategies contend that, while these strategies disproportionately affect the impoverished, they make cities nicer places to live and work.[36]

As the next chapter demonstrates, advocates of slow growth/smart growth strategies were later able to incorporate several of these ideas into highway legislation. Their efforts were vigorously resisted by the highway lobby, largely because it recognized that in the absence of large funding increases these policy preferences diverted resources from highway construction.

HIGHWAYS AND MINORITY NEIGHBORHOODS

Liberals and other advocates of the poor, handicapped, and elderly residing in the nation's urban centers argued that these groups could not participate fully in American society without access to affordable and reliable transportation. They argued that the national government has a moral obligation to fund mass transit. Their argument was bolstered by the McCone Commission's findings concerning the causes of the 1964 race riot in Watts, a predominantly black neighborhood near the center of Los Angeles. It blamed the riot on the lack of employment in the area and the inadequate and expensive public transportation system that made it difficult for Watts' residents to take advantage of employment opportunities in other neighborhoods. The national government subsequently financed several demonstration projects to determine if increased bus service between urban areas experiencing high unemployment and suburban areas reduced unemployment in those urban areas. The results were disappointing, and the demonstration projects were abandoned during the early 1970s.[37] Nonetheless, liberals and other advocates for the urban poor continued to lobby for additional funding for both mass transit operating and capital expenses. During the 1960s, local mass transit systems unilaterally provided reduced fares for the elderly in an effort to increase ridership. In 1974, the national government made discount fares for the elderly virtually universal by requiring urban mass transit systems receiving national operating assistance to charge the elderly no more than half of the base fare of other riders. There was also a movement in Congress at that time to create rules and regulations to ensure that state and local governments receiving national funding for transportation projects accommodate the transportation needs of the physically handicapped. In

1973, the *Urban Mass Transportation Act* was amended to include funding for private, nonprofit agencies to provide door-to-door transportation for elderly and handicapped persons. Also that year, Section 504 of the *Rehabilitation Act of 1973* mandated that handicapped persons could not be discriminated against solely because of their handicap by any entity receiving national assistance. Most mass transit systems were subject to Section 504 because they received national assistance under the *Urban Mass Transportation Act*. In an effort to comply with Section 504, most mass transit systems instituted a supplemental, door-to-door, paratransit transportation system (typically vans on-call) for the elderly and handicapped. Advocates for the handicapped argued that this was insufficient and demanded that all conventional mass transit facilities (subway stations, subway cars, buses, etc.) be made handicapped-accessible. In 1978, the U.S. Department of Transportation issued regulations requiring bus and rail transit equipment to be handicapped-accessible. Among the regulations was one requiring new buses to be equipped with either a ramp or lift for wheelchair boarding and have the ability to kneel to within 18 inches of the road for easier boarding. Also, all rail transit and commuter railroad systems were to be retrofitted to accommodate people in wheelchairs within a 10- to 20-year period. The cost to local mass transit operators to make these changes was estimated at $1.5 billion, with the greatest expense for the installation of elevators in every subway station in the nation.

The new regulations were met with howls of anger from mass transit operators and city officials. They complained that the $1.5 billion cost estimate was far too conservative (they estimated that it would cost at least $6.8 billion) and that it would be more cost-effective to expand door-to-door, paratransit transportation services than retrofit equipment and facilities.[38] Local transit operators lobbied the U.S. Department of Transportation for regulatory relief. When those efforts proved ineffective, the operators' trade association, the American Public Transit Association, sued the U.S. Department of Transportation, arguing that its mandate exceeded the law's intent. The U.S. District Court upheld the mandate's legality, but the operators appealed to the U.S. Court of Appeals and won. The U.S. Department of Transportation then amended its regulations to apply only to the nation's "most important" subway and commuter rail stations (approximately 40 percent of all stations) and required mass transit operators to make a "special effort" to serve handicapped persons.[39]

The *Americans with Disabilities Act of 1990* rekindled the debate over handicapped access. It required mass transit systems to be handicapped-accessible and to provide the handicapped door-to-door, paratransit services that are at least comparable to the services provided nondisabled persons. The paratransit mandate applies unless it creates an undue financial burden on the public transit system. This language was included to reassure smaller mass transit operators who feared that these requirements could bankrupt them. Even with this language, it was estimated that mass transit operators would be forced to spend $35–$45 million annually for the purchase and maintenance of additional lift-equipped buses and between $500 million and $1 billion over 30 years to modify subway stations and other transit facilities.[40]

Another civil rights-related issue was the use of highway construction projects as a form of urban renewal. The national government's urban renewal program had its formal start as part of Title 1 of the *Housing Act of 1949*. It provided selected communities loans and capital grants to clear slums and pay for urban redevelopment projects. Its intent was to enable cities to replace its most dilapidated housing stock with affordable housing for the poor and nearly poor. In 1954, the law was amended to encourage cities to rehabilitate existing housing instead of focusing on clearance. The change was made because, in many instances, the cleared homes were not replaced. The *Housing Act of 1954* also allowed 10 percent of the program's funds to be used for commercial projects. That figure was increased to 20 percent in 1959 and to 30 percent in 1961. The urban renewal program, along with the 1966 Model Cities program that had a similar focus and intent, was folded into the Community Development Block Grant program in 1974.

The national government's urban renewal programs were criticized by many civil rights organizations for their failure to take into account the needs of the people who were living in the neighborhoods targeted for replacement. Residents were often forced to move from their homes and given little, if any, relocation assistance beyond the $100 minimum mandated by the national government. Moreover, many private lenders refused to finance housing projects on the land after it was cleared. As a result, many civil rights organizations called urban renewal "Negro removal." They claimed that white city officials used urban renewal to purposively break up African American and other minority neighborhoods. In their view, city officials recognized that their power base was being eroded by the suburban exodus of white, middle-class residents and used urban renewal as a weapon to solidify their political hegemony within the nation's cities. Their goal, they claimed, was not to improve city housing stock. It was to weaken the political clout of blacks and other minority groups by dividing and, in some instances, destroying their neighborhoods. They also claimed that many cities used urban renewal to wipe out viable housing stock occupied by minorities just to free up land suitable for other uses, especially commercial development.[41] City officials countered by arguing that their route selections were based on the advice of nonpolitically aligned traffic engineers whose primary goal was to alleviate traffic congestion. Civil rights leaders were not convinced. In their view, highways had become just another tool in the hands of city officials interested in promoting their own political agendas, and those agendas did not include the needs of the poor or minority populations.

TRUCKING DEREGULATION

As mentioned in Chapter 1, the national government began regulating the trucking industry in 1935 to prevent cutthroat price competition within the trucking industry and between the trucking industry and railroads. The Interstate Commerce Commission governed which routes were available for service, if existing routes could be discontinued, mergers within the industry, and shipping rates. It restricted the entry of new trucking firms to reduce price competition and approved rates that were based on what the market could bear rather than on the cost of transporting goods. In exchange, the trucking industry was forced to provide services on nonprofitable routes, typically within and between rural areas, to ensure that those communities were not economically isolated from the rest of the nation.[42]

Prior to the interstate highway system, the trucking industry's ability to provide door-to-door service gave it a competitive advantage over railroads in delivering goods on short hauls, particularly perishable items that needed to be cooled or delivered quickly to maintain freshness. As the interstate highway system took shape, the trucking industry became increasingly competitive with railroads at both mid- and long-distance freight hauling. Railroads continued to be the best choice for hauling very heavy items, like coal, over long distances. However, trucks were increasingly the first choice for many shippers. In an effort to capture as much of the freight-hauling market as possible, standard truck sizes were enlarged, almost doubling from 27 feet during the 1940s to 45 feet during the 1970s. By that time, the trucking industry had captured 70 percent of the nation's interstate freight revenue.[43]

The trucking industry's long-term economic prospects appeared fairly bright during the 1970s. The railroad industry's freight-hauling business was reduced to niche market status, and, as discussed in Chapter 4, its intercity passenger rail service operations were losing money, causing many railroads to experience significant financial hardships. While the trucking industry's economic prospects were looking good, the nation's economic prospects were not so bright. The Arab oil embargo of 1973 and a continuing national recession combined to create the misery index, a new economic phenomenon where unemployment and inflation increased simultaneously. As the misery index continued to rise, the American public demanded action. Consumer advocates and shippers nationwide complained that the national government's regulations protecting the trucking and airline industries from price competition were no longer economically justified. They argued that in an era of double-digit inflation, the nation needed more price competition in the transportation industries, not less. The assault on the economic regulation (protection) of the transportation industry began with the airlines, primarily because they were less politically powerful than the trucking industry. For example, the chairs of the committees and subcommittees with jurisdiction over trucking were all known to have developed strong ties to the trucking industry over the years.

Senator Edward Kennedy (D-MA) led the fight to deregulate the airline industry (see Chapter 5 for additional details). He conducted a series of hearings that drew national attention to the issue. The most persuasive evidence against the continuation of economic regulation came from the experiences of non-regulated, intrastate airline services offered in California and Texas. Price competition there had not caused any of the problems feared by the airline industry: none of the airlines went bankrupt, safety had not been compromised, and service to smaller communities had not been interrupted. Instead, fares were substantially lower than on comparable routes in regulated states, and unregulated markets were characterized by constant innovation, intensive advertising, and dramatic growth.[44] Faced with this evidence and under public pressure to do something about inflation, Congress passed the *Airline Deregulation Act of 1978*, and President Jimmy Carter (D, 1977–1981) signed it into law. Once the airlines were deregulated, Senator Kennedy and other national policymakers turned their attention to the trucking industry.

Under normal circumstances, government policies, such as the regulation of the trucking industry, that target benefits to well-organized and politically active groups and spread those benefits' costs to the general public are passed in the Congress with little fanfare. However, the misery index had changed the political environment. The trucking industry was now in the national spotlight, and national policymakers were faced with the difficult choice of doing nothing and facing the voters' wrath on Election Day or deregulating the trucking industry and facing the trucking industry's wrath on Election Day. In circumstances like these, Congress often delays action hoping that public interest in the issue wanes. Senator Kennedy, who was interested in running for the presidency and benefited from the media's coverage of the issue, and consumer advocates, like Ralph Nader, knew that many in Congress did not want this issue to come to a vote. They also knew that the press was interested in the issue because several studies had concluded that deregulating the trucking industry would save consumers up to $8 billion annually and reduce the nation's dependence on foreign oil by saving hundreds of millions of gallons of gasoline annually. The cost savings would be realized by eliminating or reducing the incidence of truckers returning to their point of origin with empty or nearly empty backhauls, circuitous routing, and unnecessary extra freight handling due to various regulatory policies and procedures. These rules resulted in needless wear and tear on equipment, inefficient use of gasoline, and unproductive use of drivers' time.

In an era when dependence on foreign oil threatened both domestic prosperity and national security, any proposal that saved fuel was considered newsworthy. However, technical reports and economic analyses have only limited appeal to reporters interested in garnering large audiences. They knew that trucking deregulation was important, but it lacked drama. That changed in 1977, when Interstate Commerce Commission auditors testified at congressional hearings that truckers and railroads routinely spent about $1.5 billion a year on gifts to shipping agents and government officials and passed these costs onto consumers. The auditors revealed that paid vacations to Las Vegas and the Caribbean, hunting trips, and other gifts were common practice in both trucking and rail industries.[45] These revelations made national headlines, and, with airfares falling following that industry's deregulation, inflation on everyone's mind, and Senator Kennedy and others pressing the issue, the deregulation of the trucking industry remained high on the national political agenda.

In an attempt to forestall congressional efforts to completely deregulate the trucking industry and, in the process, render it superfluous, the Interstate Commerce Commission announced in 1978 that it was unilaterally deregulating some aspects of the trucking industry. It abolished rules preventing companies that hauled their own goods from transporting goods for other shippers. This allowed these companies to load otherwise empty or only partially filled trucks on back-hauls. The American Trucking Association immediately attacked the new rule, calling it arbitrary, capricious, and unreasonable.[46] The Interstate Commerce Commission also limited future freight-rate increases to no more than 14 percent return on stockholders' equity. At that time, that was the average rate of return for all manufacturing industries in the United States. The American Trucking Association objected to that rule change because the average rate of return for regulated trucking companies at the time was 20 percent, meaning that future freight rate increases and profit margins were likely to be less than in the past.

Congressional deliberations on trucking deregulation featured a turf battle between Senator Howard Cannon (D-NV) and Senator Kennedy. Senator Cannon chaired the Senate Commerce Committee. It had jurisdiction over the Interstate Commerce Commission. Senator Kennedy chaired the Senate Judiciary Committee. It had jurisdiction over antitrust legislation. Senator Cannon was less eager than Senator Kennedy to deregulate the trucking industry, primarily because the Teamsters Union was very active in Nevada, and he did not have presidential aspirations. He wanted some deregulation, similar to the actions pursued by the Interstate Commerce Commission. As expected, Senator Cannon demanded exclusive jurisdiction over the legislation. Senator Kennedy sought joint referral. Recognizing that the referral fight was important, the trucking industry and its unions, particularly the 500,000+-member Teamsters Union, flooded congressional offices with mail demanding that the legislation be referred to the Commerce Committee exclusively. Some Senate offices received over 4,000 letters in a single week from industry and union members. In the end, Senator Cannon won the battle, with Senator Kennedy receiving the right of sequential referral, which included the right to review antitrust provisions and offer amendments on the Senate floor. The referral fight took a soap opera-like twist when the media learned that the Federal Bureau of Investigation was investigating Senator Cannon to determine if his relationship with a Chicago-based businessman with ties to the Teamsters Union constituted an illegal attempt to influence trucking deregulation legislation. The investigation centered on Senator Cannon's telephone calls to the businessman asking how he might purchase land owned by the Teamsters Union's pension fund. It turned out that Senator Cannon was representing his homeowners' association, which wanted to purchase land bordering his neighborhood to prevent it from being used for high-rise apartment and condominium development. Nevertheless, the investigation into potential wrongdoing made national news and brought critical attention to Senator Cannon's actions during both his committee's hearings and markup of trucking deregulation legislation.

During congressional deliberations, House and Senate leaders agreed to relax existing regulations but not end them altogether. They made entry easier for new trucking firms, relaxed shipping rate structures by allowing firms to set rates within 10 percent of specified levels, expanded the list of commodities exempt from regulation, and phased out antitrust immunity for single-line (but not joint-line) rate making beginning in 1983.[47] President Carter signed the legislation, the *Motor Carrier Regulatory Reform and Modernization Act of 1980*, into law on July 1, 1980. Later that year, he also signed the *Staggers Rail Act of 1980*. It deregulated the railroad industry, with provisions protecting captive shippers of coal and other commodities from monopolistic abuses by railroads lacking competition.[48] In both instances, senators and representatives from rural states and districts, respectively, opposed deregulation because they feared the loss of services. They were also not convinced that their constituents would realize any cost savings. The Interstate Commerce Commission's remaining regulatory powers were later rescinded in 1994, and the commission was dissolved in 1995. Its relatively few remaining functions were transferred to the U.S. Department of Transportation.

A 1990 study estimated that the *Motor Carrier Act of 1980* saved consumers about $10 billion annually, with producers and distributors saving at least six times that amount, primarily from productivity gains attributable to reductions in inventory expenses brought about by no longer having to deal with partially or totally empty backhauls. Also, freight rates fell, in both absolute and inflation-adjusted terms, benefiting both shippers and consumers. Moreover, competition encouraged technological innovation in the trucking industry. Many firms, for example, equipped portions of their fleets to haul containers, rather than trailers, to speed up the transfer of goods when interfacing with railroad and water transportation industries. In addition, the application of existing technologies, such as bar-coded package labels, satellite tracking of vehicles, database tracking of shipments, and computerized route selection, resulted in an increasingly sophisticated industry.[49]

While the airline, trucking, and railroad industries are no longer subject to national economic regulations concerning rates and routes, all three industries remain subject to national safety regulations and various national and state laws. Most states, for example, continue to regulate intrastate trucking. They restrict the entry of new firms, set freight rates, and establish routes for this subset of the trucking industry.[50] States also set weight and size restrictions on trucks to standardize highway clearances and minimize wear and tear on their highways. Prior to 1984, states did this without national government interference despite the trucking industry's complaints that different state standards forced them to load or unload at state lines, operate trucks at less than full capacity, and take longer routes to bypass certain states. This, in turn, raised costs, which they passed onto consumers.[51] They were particularly opposed to weight and length standards imposed by the three so-called barrier states of Illinois, Missouri, and Arkansas. Their relatively low weight and length standards created a midcontinental barrier for heavy trucks. In 1984, in exchange for the trucking industry's support for the 1982 increase in the national government's fuel taxes, national minimum weight standards were imposed that eliminated the midcontinental barrier.[52] In 1991, the national government once again overrode state authority to set truck weight and length standards by banning the spread of state laws allowing double- and triple-trailer combinations.

Another current regulatory issue of some importance to the trucking industry is the national government's driving time regulation. Noting that about 800 of the 5,203 truck-related fatalities in 1999 resulted from driver fatigue, the U.S. Department of Transportation proposed, on April 25, 2000, to change the hours-of-service rule, which regulates the number of hours that drivers of large trucks and buses can operate without resting. The rule required drivers to take 8 hours of rest after being behind the wheel for 10 hours, or 15 hours on duty. Under the rule, which was originally issued in 1935, modified in 1937, and last revised in 1962, drivers could drive up to 16 hours in a 24-hour day. The proposal, which generated considerable opposition from both the trucking industry and its unions, would have put all drivers on a 24-hour cycle, eliminated the distinction between being behind the wheel and on duty; reduced the number of hours that a driver can work in a given 24-hour cycle to no more than 12 hours; and required long-haul and regional drivers—drivers who do not report back to their home base of operations every day—to use electronic onboard recording devices to verify compliance with the new rules. The U.S. Department of Transportation argued that the rule changes would prevent approximately 2,600 crashes, 115 fatalities, and nearly 3,000 serious injuries annually. However, following a strong lobbying campaign by the trucking industry and its unions, the Transportation Department extended the comment period on its new rules twice, first from its initial July 31, 2000, closing date to October 30, 2000, and then to December 15, 2000.[53] It later dropped the proposed rule change altogether.

CONTEMPORARY DEBATES

Although minor, new construction projects continue to augment the mileage of the now 42,794-mile Dwight D. Eisenhower System of Interstate and Defense Highways each year, the interstate highway system was, as a practical matter, completed in 1991 at a total cost of approximately $129 billion. The national government provided over $114 billion of the total amount.[54] The interstate highway system's completion signaled for many a rare, historic opportunity to reevaluate the nation's highway and mass transit policies that had, for nearly an entire generation, focused almost exclusively on highway construction. One of those who took a special interest in this historic opportunity was Senator Daniel Patrick Moynihan (D-NY). Senator Moynihan chaired the U.S. Senate's Environment and Public Works Committee's Subcommittee on Water Resources, Transportation, and Infrastructure. It had jurisdiction over the national government's highway policy in the Senate. Senator Moynihan, a former member of Harvard's faculty, advocated the "balanced transportation system" viewpoint. He was convinced that the national government's surface transportation policies had caused needless environmental damage, excessive energy consumption, costly traffic congestion, too many deaths and injuries, and unsightly sprawl. As discussed in Chapter 3, he played a major role in developing the *Intermodal Surface Transportation and Efficiency Act of 1991*, landmark legislation that made wholesale revisions in the national government's highway and mass transit policies.

NOTES

1. Herman Mertins, Jr., *National Transportation Policy in Transition* (Lexington, MA: Lexington Books, 1972), pp. 37, 63, 66, 67.

2. Ibid., pp. 67, 68.

3. "Postwar Highway Program," in *Congress and the Nation, 1945–1964* (Washington, DC: Congressional Quarterly Service, 1965), pp. 535.

4. Robert Jay Dilger, *National Intergovernmental Programs* (Englewood Cliffs, NJ: Prentice-Hall, 1989), pp. 129–131.

5. James A. Dunn, Jr., *Driving Forces: The Automobile, Its Enemies, and the Politics of Mobility* (Washington, DC: The Brookings Institution Press, 1998), p. 37.

6. David R. Mayhew, *Congress: The Electoral Connection* (New Haven, CT: Yale University Press, 1974), pp. 52–61.

7. James A. Dunn, Jr., *Driving Forces*, pp. 35–39.

8. Ibid., pp. 40, 41.

9. Frank R. Baumgartner and Bryan D. Jones, *Agendas and Instability in American Politics* (Chicago: The University of Chicago Press, 1993), pp. 6–9.

10. Bruce McDowell, "Governmental Actors and Factors in Mass Transit," *Intergovernmental Perspective* 10:3 (Summer 1984): 7.

11. Milton Pikarsky and Daphne Christensen, *Urban Transportation Policy and Management* (Lexington, MA: Lexington Books, 1976), p. 96.

12. James A. Dunn, Jr., *Driving Forces*, p. 90.

13. "Transportation Policy," in *Congress and the Nation, 1969–1972* (Washington, DC: Congressional Quarterly Service, 1973), p. 147.

14. "Chronology of Action of Transportation and Communications," in *Congress and the Nation, 1981–1985* (Washington, DC: Congressional Quarterly Service, 1985), pp. 299–307.

15. Robert Jay Dilger, *National Intergovernmental Programs*, p. 141.

16. David R. Beam, "Washington's Regulation of States and Localities: Origins and Issues," *Intergovernmental Perspective* 7:3 (Summer 1981): 8–18.

17. Robert Jay Dilger, *National Intergovernmental Programs*, pp. 142–151.

18. Carol S. Weissert and Sanford F. Schram, "The State of American Federalism, 1995–1996," *Publius: The Journal of Federalism* 26:3 (Summer 1996): 25.

19. Terrance Rephann and Andrew Isserman, "New Highways as Economic Development Tools: An Evaluation Using Quasi-Experimental Matching Methods," *Regional Science and Urban Economics* 24:6 (1994): 723–751; and Hank Dittmar, "Highway Capital and Economic Productivity," Surface Transportation Policy Project, February 1999. Available on-line at: http://www2.istea.org/progress/febr99/hcep.htm; and Don Chen, "It's the Regional Economy, Stupid! Misinterpreting the Benefits of Highway Construction," Surface Transportation Policy Project, February 1999. Available on-line at: http://www2.istea.org/progress/febr99/region.htm.

20. Transportation Research Board, National Research Council, *The Costs of Sprawl—Revisited*. TCRP Report 39 (Washington, DC: National Academy Press, 1998), p. 1.

21. John D. Kasarda, "Urban Change and Minority Opportunities," in *The New Urban Reality*, ed. Paul E. Peterson (Washington, DC: The Brookings Institution, 1985), p. 36.

22. Etan Diamond, "Middle Class in Suburbs," in *Encyclopedia of Urban America: The Cities and Suburbs*, vol. 2, ed. Neil Larry Shumsky (Santa Barbara, CA: ABC-CLIO, 1998), pp. 461–463.

23. Mark. S. Foster, "Roads," in *Encyclopedia of Urban America: The Cities and Suburbs*, vol. 2, ed. Neil Larry Shumsky (Santa Barbara, CA: ABC-CLIO, 1998), p. 672.

24. Mark S. Foster, "Transportation," in *Encyclopedia of Urban America: The Cities and Suburbs*, vol. 2, ed. Neil Larry Shumsky (Santa Barbara, CA: ABC-CLIO, 1998), p. 798; and Mark S. Foster, "Automobiles," in *Encyclopedia of Urban America: The Cities and Suburbs*, vol. 2, ed. Neil Larry Shumsky (Santa Barbara, CA: ABC-CLIO, 1998), p. 54.

25. Mark S. Foster, "Roads," p. 673.

26. Michael Ebner, "Suburbanization," in *Encyclopedia of Urban America: The Cities and Suburbs*, vol. 2, ed. Neil Larry Shumsky (Santa Barbara, CA: ABC-CLIO, 1998), p. 760; and David G. Burwell, Keith Bartholomew, and Deborah Gordon, "Energy and Environmental Research Needs," in *Transportation, Urban Form, and the Environment* (Washington, DC: Transportation Research Board, 1990), pp. 91, 92.

27. Michael Ebner, "Suburbanization," p. 760.

28. Robert D. Putnam, *Bowling Alone: The Collapse and Revival of American Community* (New York: Simon & Schuster, 2000), pp. 204–215; Don Chen, "It's the Regional Economy, Stupid! Misinterpreting the Benefits of Highway Construction"; and April Petersen, "Sprawl: A Growing Political Concern," *Policy.com* (March 24, 2000). Available on-line at: http://www.policy.com/news/dbrief/dbriefarc534.asp.

29. Transportation Research Board, National Research Council, *The Costs of Sprawl—Revisited*, p. 39.

30. Ibid., pp. 9–40.

31. Richard H. Leach and Timothy G. O'Rourke, *State and Local Government: The Third Century of Federalism* (Englewood Cliffs, NJ: Prentice-Hall, Inc., 1988), p. 219.

32. Michael Ebner, "Suburbanization," p. 761.

33. Kenneth A. Small, "Transportation and Urban Change," in *The New Urban Reality*, ed. Paul E. Peterson (Washington, DC: The Brookings Institution, 1985), pp. 207, 208.

34. David G. Burwell, Keith Bartholomew, and Deborah Gordon, "Energy and Environmental Research Needs," p. 92.

35. Jeffrey A. Parker, "Does Transportation Finance Influence Urban Form?" in *Transportation, Urban Form, and the Environment* (Washington, DC: Transportation Research Board, 1990), p. 51.

36. National Research Council, *Curbing Gridlock: Peak Period Fees to Relieve Traffic Congestion* (Washington, DC: National Academy Press, 1994), pp. 1, 2.

37. John R. Meyer and Jose A. Gomez-Ibanez, *Autos, Transit and Cities* (Cambridge, MA: Harvard University Press, 1981), pp. 230, 231.

38. David R. Beam, "Washington's Regulation of States and Localities: Origins and Issues," *Intergovernmental Perspective* 7:3 (Summer 1981): 15.

39. Stephen L. Percy, "ADA, Disability Rights, and Evolving Regulatory Federalism," *Publius: The Journal of Federalism* 23:4 (Fall 1993): 98, 99.

40. Timothy J. Conlan, "And the Beat Goes On: Intergovernmental Mandates and Preemption in an Era of Deregulation," *Publius: The Journal of Federalism* 21:3 (Summer 1991): 45, 46.

41. June Manning Thomas, "Urban Renewal," in *Encyclopedia of Urban America: The Cities and Suburbs*, vol. 2, ed. Neil Larry Shumsky (Santa Barbara, CA: ABC-CLIO, 1998), pp. 827, 828.

42. Dorothy Robyn, *Braking the Special Interests: Trucking Deregulation and the Politics of Policy Reform* (Chicago: The University of Chicago Press, 1987), pp. 12–16.

43. Ibid., p. 15.

44. Ibid., p. 28.

45. Ibid., pp. 29, 30.

46. Ibid., p. 33.

47. Ibid., pp. 42, 45–56.

48. Larry Pressler, Democratic Senator from South Dakota, "Statement before the Subcommittee on Surface Transportation, U.S. Senate Committee on Commerce, Science, and Transportation," in *Staggers Rail Act of 1980*. Hearings before the Subcommittee on Surface Transportation, U.S. Senate Committee on Commerce, Science, and Transportation, 98th Congress, First Session (Washington, DC: U.S. Government Printing Office, July 26, 1983), p. 1; and Rail Shippers Association, "Statement before the Subcommittee on Surface Transportation, U.S. Senate Committee on Commerce, Science, and Transportation," in *Staggers Rail Act of 1980*. Hearings before the Subcommittee on Surface Transportation, U.S. Senate Committee on Commerce, Science, and Transportation, 98th Congress, First Session (Washington, DC: U.S. Government Printing Office, July 26, 1983), p. 154.

49. Cassandra Chrones Moore, "Intrastate Trucking: Stronghold of the Regulators," *Policy Analysis* 204 (February 16, 1994): 2, 3. Available on-line at: http://www.cato.org/pubs/pas/pa-204.html.

50. Ibid., p. 1.

51. Bruce D. McDowell, "Governmental Actors and Factors in Mass Transit," p. 342.

52. James A. Dunn, Jr., *Driving Forces*, p. 38.

53. Rodney E. Slater, Secretary of Transportation, "U.S. Transportation Secretary Slater Calls on Truck Safety Stakeholders to Discuss Driver Fatigue Safety Standard," press release (Washington, DC: U.S. Department of Transportation, August 9, 2000). Available on-line at: http://www.dot.gov/affairs/fmcsa1100.htm; and Rodney E. Slater, Secretary of Transportation, "Remarks as Prepared for Delivery, U.S. Secretary of Transportation Rodney E. Slater Notice of Proposed Rule Making on Hours-of-Service," press release (Washington, DC: U.S. Department of Transportation, April 25, 2000). Available on-line at: http://www.dot.gov/affairs/2000/042500sp.htm.

54. Office of Program Administration, U.S. Department of Transportation, "The Dwight D. Eisenhower Interstate System." Available on-line: http://www.fhwa.dot.gov/infrastructure/progadmin/Interstate.html. Viewed on February 28, 2000. Note: Including highways that were not financed by the national government, the interstate highway system had a total of mileage of 45,024.52 miles in 2000.

3

Highway and Mass Transit Policy Today: ISTEA and TEA-21, the Intermodal Solutions

American highway and mass transit policy took a sharp U-turn in 1991. Although the political organizations involved in the reauthorization of the *Federal Aid to Highway Act* in 1991 had not changed their respective arguments from previous years, the circumstances surrounding the program's reauthorization had changed a great deal. First, the interstate highway system was, for all practical matters, complete. This created a window of opportunity for those interested in altering the status quo. As one observer stated at the time, during the early years of the Federal Aid to Highway program the shared goal was to get the farmer out of the mud; from 1956 to 1991 the shared goal was to build the interstate highway system; but in 1991 there was no shared goal.[1] Second, despite the expenditure of hundreds of billions of dollars, America's highways and bridges were in relatively poor condition; traffic congestion, especially in the nation's largest cities, was getting worse, not better; pollution from automotive exhaust was getting worse, not better; and sprawl was rampant. These unresolved problems created an intellectual justification for considering major changes in the national government's highway and mass transit policies. Third, global competition for markets had made American companies very cost-conscious, replacing large inventories with just-in-time delivery systems that relied on the fast transportation of materials and finished products to manufacturers and distributors. Because materials and goods were often transported over multiple transportation modes (air, ground, and water) before arriving at their final destination, American companies, both large and small, needed all of the various modes within the national transportation system to work well together. They wanted the national government to create what numerous blue-ribbon panels and commissions had been recommending for years: an integrated, comprehensive, coordinated, and intermodal transportation system. Their participation in the reauthorization process was important because it provided additional political support for organizations, such as the U.S. Conference of Mayors and the American Transit Association, which had been advocating change for years. Fourth, the Surface Transportation Policy Project, a coalition of environmentalists, urban planners, bicycle enthusiasts, and various transportation consultants, developed a strong, working relationship with Senator Daniel Patrick Moynihan (D-NY), chair of the Senate's Environment and Public Works Committee's Subcommittee on Water Resources, Transportation, and Infrastructure. Senator Moynihan was convinced that change was necessary, and his subcommittee had jurisdiction over the Federal Aid to Highways program in the Senate. As a result, although the highway lobby was still active and intent on preserving the status quo, several factors converged in 1991 that created the possibility for significant change in the nation's highway and mass transit policies.

COMPETING VIEWS

The House, Senate, and White House took strikingly different approaches to resolving the nation's surface transportation needs during the 1991 reauthorization of the *Federal Aid to Highway Act*. President George Bush (R, 1989–1993) acknowledged that the nation's highways and bridges were in relatively poor condition. The U.S. Department of Transportation had previously reported that 42 percent of America's 575,000 highway bridges were structurally deficient (closed or restricted to light traffic) or functionally obsolete, 62 percent of the nation's paved roads needed to be rehabilitated or replaced, and highway delays in urban areas were escalating and had exceeded 2 billion hours annually, costing an estimated $34 billion in productivity losses each year.[2] Moreover, President Bush was aware of a National Governors' Association report that indicated that it would cost at least $1 trillion and perhaps as much as $3 trillion to bring the nation's highways and bridges up to an acceptable level over the next 20 years.[3] The governors and several other interest groups advocated a major funding increase for highways and mass transit, paid for, at least in part, by increasing the national government's excise tax on motor fuels. However, President Bush opposed significant funding increases for highways and mass transit because the national government's annual budget deficit had reached a then-record high of $221 billion in fiscal year (FY) 1990, and its cumulative deficit had reached a then-record high of $3.2 trillion. Also, he was adamantly opposed to another increase in the national government's fuel taxes. In 1990, he agreed to sign congressionally sponsored legislation that increased taxes $137 billion over five years to reduce the national deficit. The tax bill increased the national government's excise tax on motor fuels five cents per gallon (raising approximately $5 billion annually). Half of the proceeds from the motor fuels tax increase went to deficit reduction, and half went to the Highway Trust Fund. Conservative Republicans were outraged that the president violated his 1988 presidential campaign pledge of "read my lips . . . no new taxes." He subsequently apologized for accepting the compromise during the 1992 Republican presidential primaries and promised not to allow taxes to increase again.[4]

In February 1991, President Bush announced his five-year, $105 billion re-authorization proposal for the Federal Aid to Highways program. It included a 40 percent increase in funding for highways and a marginal increase for mass transit. He also announced that he would veto any bill that increased excise taxes on motor fuels or included highway demonstration projects. The expiring program had included $1.3 billion for 152 congressionally mandated highway demonstration projects. He opposed demonstration projects because they were not subject to critical review by national or state transportation officials and, in his view, could not be justified on any grounds other than political expediency.[5]

President Bush's proposal was guided by two fundamental principles: that state and local government officials should have a greater voice in project selection and governmental responsibilities and that financial support should reflect the program's geographic range-of-benefits. The geographic range-of-benefits argument (assigning governmental responsibility and financial support according to where the program's economic and/or social benefits accrue) was used in 1982 by President Ronald Reagan (R, 1981–1989) to justify his unsuccessful effort to devolve surface transportation programs to states. The concept resurfaced in 1987 and 1988 in a series of reports issued by the U.S. Advisory Commission on Intergovernmental Relations. President Bush used the argument to justify the consolidation of national highway programs into two programs: a $43.5 billion, 150,000-mile national highway system consisting of roads with significance for national defense or that carried goods and people across state lines; and a $22.2 billion, 716,000-mile urban and rural highway block grant for other nationally funded roads. Because the block grant consisted of roads lacking national significance, it would receive less funding than the national highway system, and its reimbursement rate would be lowered from 75 percent to 60 percent. The reimbursement rate for highways in the national highway system would remain the same, 90 percent for interstate highways and 75 percent for primary highways. Because mass transit's benefits accrue primarily within states and metropolitan areas, its funding would be increased only marginally, to $16.5 billion over the five years, and the national government's share of capital expenses would be reduced from 80 percent to 60 percent and for new starts from 75 percent to 50 percent. Operating assistance to 147 mass transit systems in regions with populations exceeding 1 million would be eliminated.[6]

Convinced that state and local government officials can make wise transportation decisions, President Bush's proposal allowed states to shift funds between urban and rural highways, from urban and rural highways to mass transit and, with the exception for new mass transit starts, from mass transit to urban and rural highways. He argued that this added flexibility would increase program effectiveness.

Senator Moynihan viewed the administration's proposal as a capitulation to the highway lobby. He worked with the Surface Transportation Policy Project to craft a radically new direction for the nation's highway and mass transit programs. His willingness to sponsor radial change in national surface transportation policy was rooted in his long-term advocacy of the "balanced transportation system" approach mentioned in the previous chapter. He was convinced that the national government's emphasis on highway construction to end traffic congestion had failed, primarily because of what traffic engineers referred to as latent demand. They discovered that when motorists noticed a reduction in traffic congestion during peak demand times, they changed the timing of their trips or made trips that they previously did not make, to take advantage of the added capacity. As a result, increasing highway capacity tended to have only a marginal, short-term, positive affect on mobility during peak traffic hours. Moreover, additional residential and commercial development usually followed the introduction of the added capacity, attracting even more traffic and congestion to the area in the long term. Between 1980 and 1991, major arterial highway capacity in the United States increased 25 percent, but traffic on those roads increased almost 60 percent, creating congested conditions throughout urban America.[7] The fact that Senator Moynihan was from New York, an urban state with a relatively high reliance on mass transit, also influenced his decision to challenge the status quo.

Senator Moynihan crafted a Senate reauthorization bill that reduced the national government's role in highway and mass transit policy to monitoring state maintenance of the interstate highway system. The bill allowed states to shift funding for the remaining 800,000+ miles of nationally funded highways to any surface transportation use of its choice. This added flexibility outraged the highway lobby but appealed to senators from urban states who wanted additional funding for mass transit and to senators from rural states who wanted additional funding for highways. Because Senator Moynihan was convinced that many state legislatures had an antiurban bias, the bill strengthened the role of metropolitan planning organizations in project selection.

To avoid a presidential veto, the bill was amended on the Senate floor to include funding for President Bush's 150,000-mile National Highway System and Surface Transportation Block Grant. The bill did not increase national gasoline taxes or include highway demonstration projects. However, it authorized funding at $123 billion, $18 billion more than the administration's proposal. It also increased mass transit funding to $21 billion over five years, $5 billion more than the administration's proposal, and continued mass transit operating assistance for all mass transit systems. It also set reimbursement rates at 80 percent for maintaining and improving transportation facilities, and 75 percent for new construction. The financial incentive to fund highways over mass transit was eliminated by giving mass transit and highways the same reimbursement rate. The financial incentive to fund new construction over maintenance was eliminated by giving maintenance a higher reimbursement rate than new construction. As mentioned previously, the bill enhanced the role of metropolitan planning organizations in project selection. At that time, most metropolitan planning organizations were advisory bodies, and their recommendations often were ignored. It was generally believed that they were more likely than state government officials to shift funding from highways to mass transit.[8]

The highway lobby urged the House Transportation and Infrastructure Committee, which was still working on its reauthorization bill, to retain the program's historic bias toward highway construction and repair. The committee did precisely that. Its bill authorized $151 billion for highways and mass transit over six years ($119 billion for highways and $32 billion for mass transit), $46 billion more than the administration's proposal and $28 billion more than the Senate's proposal. It also included $5.4 billion for 489 highway demonstration projects and financed its higher authorization level by spending down the $11 billion surplus that existed in the Highway Trust Fund at that time and extending through FY 1999 half of the previous year's nickel gasoline tax increase that was set to expire after FY 1995.[9] The House bill did not include the administration's proposed block grant. Instead, it authorized separate programs and funding levels for urban highways, rural highways, statewide highways, and bridges. However, the House did provide states added flexibility to spend urban, rural, and statewide highway program funds on any surface transportation project of their choice, including mass transit. It also accepted Senator Moynihan's level playing field argument by setting reimbursement rates at 80 percent for most programs and 90 to 95 percent for interstate construction and maintenance projects, with the larger reimbursement rate offered to states with large amounts of nationally owned land.[10]

ISTEA: THE GRAND COMPROMISE

During the congressional conference sessions, President Bush indicated his willingness to compromise on almost all contested issues because he did not want to be put into the politically embarrassing position of vetoing a bill that promised to provide thousands of jobs during a recession. The result was the *Intermodal Surface Transportation Efficiency Act of 1991*, known by its acronym ISTEA (pronounced ICE-TEA).

ISTEA included the House's position on the program's scope (six years) and cost ($151 billion). It also included 538 congressionally mandated special highway demonstration projects ($6.5 billion) and the House's position on the national government's share of project expenses (80 percent for most projects, 90 percent for interstate construction and maintenance, with up to 95 percent for states with large amounts of nationally owned land), financing (spend down the Highway Trust Fund and extend the motor fuels tax increase), state return on taxes paid (90 percent guaranteed), and funding for mass transit ($32 billion). The Senate's categories for highway programs were approved, but at authorization levels closer to those in the House bill, including $6 billion for a new Congestion Mitigation and Air Quality Improvement program, $7 billion to complete the interstate system, $16 billion for bridges, $17 billion for interstate maintenance and improvements, and $21 billion for a newly designated 155,000-mile national highway system. The U.S. Department of Transportation was given two years to designate which highways would be included in the national highway system. States could shift up to half of their national highway system's funds to other highway programs and mass transit, and states and localities with serious air pollution problems, designated as areas of "nonattainment," could shift all of their national highway system funds to mass transit with the approval of the U.S. Department of Transportation.

ISTEA also authorized $24 billion for the Surface Transportation Block Grant. Ten percent of its funds had to be set aside for transportation safety programs and another 10 percent for transportation enhancement activities, defined to include, among other activities, landscaping, the conversion of abandoned railway corridors to pedestrian or bicycle paths, and the control and removal of outdoor advertising. States could use the remaining funds for a wide range of transportation projects, including bicycle paths and pedestrian walkways, parking facilities, traffic management and monitoring, and planning. For most states, a complicated in-state allotment formula targeted at least 62.5 percent of the block grant's discretionary funds to urbanized areas with populations exceeding 200,000.[11]

Of particular interest to local government officials, ISTEA required approximately $9 billion of the Surface Transportation Block Grant's funds to be passed directly through to metropolitan planning organizations representing urban areas with populations of 200,000 or more. They were to consult with state officials prior to making final project selections, but, for the first time, they could make those selections without state approval. Also, statewide transportation plans were required for the first time, in addition to the metropolitan area plans that had been required since 1962. States had to devise both a long-range transportation plan and a shorter-range transportation improvement plan for all areas within the state. ISTEA also mandated a new style of performance planning for managing and monitoring highway pavement conditions, bridge maintenance, highway safety programs, traffic congestion mitigation, transit facility and equipment maintenance, and intermodal transportation facilities and systems.[12] The U.S. secretary of transportation was to issue regulations for these new management systems by December 18, 1993. States that failed to implement these management reforms by September 30, 1995, would forfeit up to 10 percent of their transportation funds.

In 1987, nine states (California, Colorado, Delaware, Florida, Georgia, Pennsylvania, South Carolina, Texas, and West Virginia) were granted waivers allowing them to use up to 35 percent of their Federal Aid to Highways funds on toll roads on new, or substantially new, noninterstate highways. As part of its effort to further decentralize highway and mass transit decision making, ISTEA expanded that option to all 50 states. It also authorized the expenditure of up to $150 million for up to five experimental demonstration projects involving congestion pricing strategies to reduce traffic congestion. In 1993, the San Francisco Bay Area Congestion Pricing Task Force, comprising various local government, environmental, and business groups, authored the first congestion pricing proposal approved for funding under ISTEA. Their proposal increased the toll on the San Francisco–Oakland Bay Bridge during peak demand times in an effort to divert traffic to mass transit.[13]

ISTEA'S LEGACY

ISTEA reflected the promotional politics of the past by increasing funding for both highways and mass transit. It also continued separate programs and administrations for highways, bridges, interstate maintenance, and mass transit. However, ISTEA also reflected the further disintegration of the highway lobby's policy monopoly that had dominated American surface transportation policy making so thoroughly during the construction of the interstate highway system. Although the highway lobby remained strong, as evidenced by the House Transportation Committee's acquiescence to nearly all of its positions, several organizations that had previously been on the outside looking in moved to the forefront of the policy-making process. For example, the Surface Transportation Policy Project, formed in 1990 to increase the political clout of its constituent groups, worked hand in hand with Senator Moynihan to craft a Senate bill that reflected their views. Although the House subsequently prevailed on most issues during the conference, ISTEA included several provisions that these organizations had been advocating for years. Specifically, ISTEA decentralized control over highway and mass transit decision making by creating a $24 billion Surface Transportation Block Grant; provided state and local government policymakers added flexibility to transfer funds from one program to another; strengthened the role of metropolitan planning organizations in project selection; revised reimbursement rates to create a "level playing field" for all transportation modes; required new planning styles for such things as traffic congestion management and pavement maintenance; and placed greater emphasis on intermodal transportation solutions to reduce traffic congestion, combat air pollution, and enhance economic productivity. In short, ISTEA was landmark legislation that was expected to divert significant amounts of national funding from highways to mass transit. However, that did not happen.

One of the reasons that states did not divert significant amounts of funding from highways to mass transit, at least initially, was their fear of national sanctions. The U.S. Department of Transportation took nearly two years to issue its planning regulations, and many states were reluctant to implement new planning procedures in the absence of those guidelines. Also, most highway and mass transit projects take several years to go from conception, to construction, to use. This meant that many states had committed funds to a large number of highway projects that were already "in the pipeline" when ISTEA went into effect. As a result, most states were not in a position to make significant changes in their funding patterns. In addition, most metropolitan planning organizations were not accustomed to playing a major role in project selection. Many of them lacked the staff, expertise, procedures, and political connections necessary to take on their new responsibilities.[14] Together, these factors prevented a major shift in highway and mass transit funding patterns during ISTEA's initial three years. In 1992, state and local governments spent nearly all (about 97 percent) of their flexible highway funds on highways.[15]

Between 1992 and when ISTEA's reauthorization process started in 1996, metropolitan planning organizations, particularly ones representing populations greater than 200,000, strengthened their staff resources, though often through the contracting out of services to planners in the private sector rather than hiring their own permanent staff. The national government's new planning procedures were also finally put into place.[16] Nevertheless, most of ISTEA's funding continued to be spent on highway construction and repair. State and local government officials "flexed" less than $3 billion of the more than $70 billion that could have been moved from highway construction to other transportation modes, and most of those flexed funds (55 percent) were in the $6 billion Congestion Mitigation and Air Quality Improvement program that specifically discouraged, with the exception of funding for high-occupancy vehicle (HOV) lanes, funding highways.[17]

In 1996, President Bill Clinton (D, 1993–2001) claimed that flexing nearly $3 billion in highway construction funds to other transportation modes was an indication that "state and local governments have responded enthusiastically to the increased flexibility in national programs."[18] Although the amount flexed under ISTEA increased each year, reaching nearly $800 million in 1996, flexing less than 4 percent of available funds, while noteworthy, was not a major policy shift. Moreover, most "flexing" occurred in just three states, New York, California, and Massachusetts.[19]

There are several reasons that highway and mass transit funding did not undergo a major shift under ISTEA. First and perhaps most important, the public did not demand change. Most Americans would rather drive to work or to do their shopping than ride a bus, board a train, walk, or ride a bicycle. Most passenger trips in the United States are made by automobile or privately owned truck (89 percent of daily trips and 92 percent of miles traveled). Bicycling or walking accounts for only 6.5 percent of passenger trips (0.5 percent of miles traveled), mass transit accounts for about 4 percent (3 percent of miles traveled), and rail accounts for less than 1 percent (less than 4 percent of miles traveled). Moreover, the trend is toward greater use of the automobile and truck and less for other transportation modes.[20] The public's preference for highway construction and repair projects was also reflected in the policies of 31 states that, at the time, restricted the use of state motor fuel tax revenue to highway projects. This created a bias in favor of highway construction and repair projects because most states use state fuel tax revenue to finance ISTEA's cost-sharing requirements. It appeared that state and local government officials recognized the public's preference for highway projects and were responding accordingly.[21]

Second, although ISTEA elevated the importance of metropolitan planning organizations, most of them continued to play an advisory role in project selection because all ISTEA funds had to be allocated in accordance with the state's transportation plans. Thus, states can veto metropolitan planning organizations' transportation improvement plans and prevent them from receiving their ISTEA funding. Metropolitan planning organizations can retaliate by vetoing transportation projects within their jurisdiction, including projects in the state transportation plan, but they were reluctant to exercise that power because states do not lose ISTEA funds in that circumstance. States can proceed with partial plans that bypass the metropolitan planning organization. Thus, despite mutual veto powers, state officials dominated state–local surface transportation decision making, though not to the degree as in the past. Because state Department of Transportation officials traditionally favored highway construction and repair over mass transit and other nonhighway uses, those funding patterns did not change much under ISTEA. As one study concluded, state Department of Transportation officials had developed an organizational culture through the years that not only favored highways over mass transit but also predisposed them to either resist or ignore national mandates to focus on intermodal solutions to traffic congestion.[22]

Although ISTEA did not have a large effect on the distribution of resources between highways and mass transit, it changed the process used to reach those funding decisions and, by changing that process, altered state–local relations in surface transportation policy. Instead of a national-state focus, highway and mass transit policy became more decentralized, with a greater focus on state control, coupled with increased local government input.[23]

TEA-21: IF AT FIRST YOU DON'T SUCCEED, TRY AGAIN

ISTEA's reauthorization process began informally early in 1996 as various surface transportation-related interest groups tried to convince the Clinton administration and key congressional members that ISTEA needed to be modified. Most of the lobbying dealt with the state-by-state distribution of funds. Hoping to appease everyone, many members of Congress wanted to increase the program's funding significantly. Although no one wanted to increase the Highway Trust Fund's taxes (18.4 cents per gallon of gasoline and 24.3 cents per gallon of diesel fuel), many advocated the repeal of the 1993 law that diverted revenue generated by 4.3 cents per gallon of the gasoline tax to the general revenue fund to offset the national budget deficit. They wanted that revenue, approximately $6.5 billion of the nearly $28 billion generated annually by the Highway Trust Fund at that time, used for highway and mass transit projects. Also, representatives from 18 "donor" states wanted ISTEA's funding formulas overhauled to give them a larger share of the program's funds. They complained that the return on the dollar contributed to the Highway Trust Fund in 1995 varied from 56 cents in South Carolina to $6.40 in Alaska. Although they conceded that some rural, low-population states lacked the population density necessary to finance their highway systems, they wanted ISTEA's funding formulas changed to ensure that the variation in the state-by-state return rate was narrowed considerably. Because many donor states were located in the Southeast, and Senator Daniel Patrick Moynihan (D-NY) was expected to play an important role in ISTEA's reauthorization, the reauthorization process had a strong regional overtone reminiscent of earlier Sunbelt-Snowbelt funding battles that had taken place during the 1970s and 1980s.[24] A key difference, however, was that since ISTEA's creation in 1991, the Democratic Party (in 1995) had lost its majority status in the U.S. Senate. Because he was a Democrat, Senator Moynihan no longer chaired the Senate's Water Resources, Transportation, and Infrastructure Subcommittee. Although he remained an influential member of the Senate, he was no longer in a position to dictate Senate action on highway and mass transit policy.

COMPETING INTEREST GROUPS

The STEP 21 Coalition (Streamlined Transportation Efficiency Program for the 21st Century), represented the states of Alabama, Arizona, Arkansas, Florida, Georgia, Indiana, Kentucky, Louisiana, Michigan, Minnesota, Mississippi, Missouri, Nebraska, North Carolina, Oklahoma, Oregon, South Carolina, Tennessee, Texas, Virginia, and Wisconsin. It wanted ISTEA's funding formulas altered to guarantee each state at least 95 cents per dollar contributed to the Highway Trust Fund, to consolidate ISTEA's programs into a national highway system (merging ISTEA's national highway system, interstate maintenance, and portions of its bridge program) and a new block grant, the Streamlined Surface Transportation Program. The block grant would receive approximately 60 percent of the program's total funding and could be used for all existing program activities. They argued that the Surface Transportation Block Grant's 10 percent set-asides for safety programs and transportation enhancement activities, coupled with ISTEA's separate programs for various transportation uses, such as the $6 billion Congestion Mitigation and Air Quality Improvement program, unduly restricted states' ability to meet their unique transportation problems. Although they applauded ISTEA's decentralization, they wanted even more decentralization, with states playing the primary role in project selection. Their proposals were endorsed by Senator John Warner (R-VA), the new chair of the Senate Environment and Public Works' Transportation and Infrastructure Subcommittee, and House Majority Whip Tom DeLay (R-TX).[25]

California, Ohio, South Carolina, Michigan, and several leading members of Congress, including Representative John Kasich (R-OH) and Senator Connie Mack (R-FL), advocated the devolution of highway and mass transit policy to states. They wanted to eliminate all but two cents of the national government's gasoline tax over three years. The funds from the remaining tax and from nonfuel-related excise taxes would be used for interstate maintenance and surface transportation programs for nationally owned lands, National Security Highways, and Emergency Relief. States would make all other highway and mass transit decisions, allowing them to determine their own transportation taxing and spending policies.

The American Association of State Highway and Transportation Officials raised the ire of local government officials by proposing that the 200,000 population threshold used to determine metropolitan planning organizations' eligibility for Surface Transportation Block Grant pass-through funding be increased to 1 million. This change would have increased the authority of state Departments of Transportation in project selection.

The Alliance for ISTEA Renewal (U.S. Conference of Mayors, National Association of Counties, National League of Cities, American Public Works Association, American Public Transit Association, Association of Metropolitan Planning Organizations, and Surface Transportation Policy Project) wanted to stop the redirection of gasoline tax revenue from the Highway Trust Fund, but, otherwise, recommended only minor changes to ISTEA. They strongly objected to the American Association of State Highway and Transportation Officials' proposal to increase the population threshold used to determine metropolitan planning organization's eligibility for pass-through funding. They also opposed the devolution proposal, fearing that it might result in less funding for mass transit and other nonhighway uses.[26] The National League of Cities, National Association of Counties, and U.S. Conference of Mayors also took the uncommon position of defending national mandates. They defended ISTEA's mandates concerning metropolitan planning organizations because those mandates enhanced local government authority at the expense of state government authority.[27]

Finally, the American Highway Users Alliance, representing oil, automobile, and trucking companies, advocated the merger of ISTEA's various programs into four national highway programs (National Highway System, Bridges, Safety, and Federal Lands), with at least $10 billion dedicated annually to the national highway system. Fifteen percent of ISTEA's funding would be turned over to states in a flexible block grant that could be used for either highways or mass transit. Their proposal was designed to increase the influence of state government officials in project selection, primarily because they viewed those officials as being more likely than metropolitan planning organizations to fund highway projects. They also wanted to stop the diversion of Highway Trust Fund revenue to offset the budget deficit. They wanted those revenues used for highways.[28]

NEXTEA

President Clinton's six-year, $175 billion reauthorization proposal was dubbed NEXTEA (*National Economic Crossroads Transportation Efficiency Act*). It retained and increased funding for virtually all of ISTEA's programs (see Table 3.1). As further proof of the highway lobby's loss of hegemony over highway and mass transit policy, NEXTEA included $4.7 billion for Amtrak and made it eligible for Surface Transportation Block Grant and national highway system funding. President Clinton included funding for Amtrak because it operated a number of commuter rail lines, similar to many light-rail mass transit systems. Also, Amtrak was experiencing serious financial problems (see Chapter 4). He argued that if mass transit deserved funding, so did Amtrak.

NEXTEA retained the 200,000 population threshold to determine which metropolitan planning organizations received pass-through funding and reduced the number of planning and program factors that states and metropolitan planning organizations must consider when developing transportation plans from 16 to 7 (economic vitality; safety and security; accessibility and mobility; environment,

Table 3.1
Transportation Funding (billions of dollars)

	ISTEA	NEXTEA	ISTEA II[a]	BESTEA	TEA-21[c]
National Highway System	$20.5	$26.1	$72.7[b]	$35.2	$28.5
Interstate Maintenance	16.5	26.4	—	28.5	23.8
Bridges	16.2	16.0	—	26.8	20.4
Appalachian Development Highways	—	2.2	1.9	2.2	2.7
Demonstration/High Priority Projects	6.5	—	—	9.0	9.0
Other, Primarily Highway Uses	35.2	26.0	48.5	28.9	41.3
Surface Transportation Block Grant	23.9	35.0	42.9	39.7	33.3
Congestion Mitigation and Air Quality Improvement	6.0	7.8	7.0	10.0	8.1
Mass Transit	32.2	35.5	41.3	36.7	36.3
Total	157.0	175.0	214.3	217.0	203.4

[a] Includes mass transit bill.
[b] $28.2 billion reserved for interstate maintenance and $8.6 billion for interstate bridges.
[c] An additional $10 billion will be made available if budgetary offsets can be found.

Sources: U.S. Department of Transportation web site (http://www.fhwa.dot.gov/reauthorization/index. htm); House Committee on Transportation and Infrastructure web site (http://www.house.gov/ transportation/bestea/besteai.htm); and the Surface Transportation Policy Project web site (http://www. istea.org/).

energy conservation, and quality of life; integration and connectivity; efficient management and operation; and preservation of existing transportation systems). Responding to complaints from rural officials that their state Department of Transportation often ignored their input during project selection, NEXTEA required state officials to consult with elected officials outside metropolitan planning areas when developing the statewide plan for those areas.

NEXTEA did not stop the redirection of gasoline tax revenue to offset the national budget deficit and made only modest revisions to ISTEA's state allotment formulas. Funding for most donor states was increased, and the range of return per dollar contributed to the Highway Trust Fund was narrowed (with a low of 82 cents per dollar contributed in Alabama, Florida, Georgia, North Carolina, and Tennessee to a high of $5.91 in Alaska), but not to the extent demanded by the STEP 21 Coalition.[29]

Bill Fay, president of the American Highway Users Alliance, called NEXTEA "the highway robbery announcement" because it increased funding for mass transit and the mass transit-friendly Congestion Mitigation and Air Quality Improvement program, added funding for Amtrak, continued the redirection of Highway Trust Fund money to offset the budget deficit, and only marginally increased highway funding. Representative Bud Shuster (R-PA), chair of the House Transportation and Infrastructure Committee, announced that he was disappointed in NEXTEA's funding (he wanted at least $180 billion over six years) and in the Clinton administration's refusal to move the Highway Trust Fund off-budget. He also objected to the redirection of Highway Trust Fund revenue to offset the budget deficit and the use of the $20 billion in unspent funds in the various transportation-related trust funds to mask the deficit's extent.[30]

THE BUDGET AGREEMENT

As the House and Senate Transportation Committees worked on their respective reauthorization bills, House and Senate leaders, chairs of the House and Senate Budget Committees, and White House representatives were busy negotiating an agreement to balance the national budget by FY 2002. In May 1997, they announced their final agreement. It allotted $125 billion over five years for highways and mass transit. The House and Senate Transportation Committees were outraged. Representative Shuster organized an all-out attempt to amend the budget agreement on the House floor to increase highway and mass transit funding to $137 billion. House Speaker Newt Gingrich (R-GA) opposed the amendment and viewed it as a personal affront to his authority. The amendment was voted on at 3:00 A.M. on May 21, 1997. It was defeated, 216–214, with the vote falling largely along party lines (Republicans opposed the amendment, 58–168, and Democrats supported it, 156–48). A similar bill was introduced in the Senate by Senators John Warner (R-VA) and Max Baucus (D-MT), the Senate Environment and Public Works Committee's ranking minority member. Their amendment also failed narrowly, 51–49.[31]

A NEW ERA FOR HIGHWAY POLITICS

NEXTEA and the two 1997 budget amendment votes were additional evidence that the relatively tranquil and predictable client and majoritarian politics that had dominated highway and mass transit policy during the construction of the interstate highway system had given way to the much more turbulent, partisan, and conflict-filled world of interest group politics. Organizations, like the Surface Transportation Policy Project, had broken the highway lobby's policy monopoly and were now winning concessions. Their success was aptly demonstrated by the renaming in 1991 of the *Federal Aid to Highway Act* to the *Intermodal Surface Transportation Efficiency Act*. The word highway no longer appears in the program's title. Moreover, the tax battles in 1997 demonstrated that the House and Senate Transportation Committees lost hegemony over highway and mass transit policy to the House and Senate Budget Committees. The Highway Trust Fund is now considered by many as just another pot of money that can be used to help balance the national budget. As a result, congressional debate over highway and mass transit policy is no longer focused primarily on how to best combat traffic congestion and enhance congressional reelection prospects by providing opportunities for claiming credit for highly visible construction projects. Congressional debate over highways and mass transit policy is now also embroiled in the highly partisan and conflict-filled debate over national fiscal policy.

SHORT-TEA

Following their failed attempt to amend the budget agreement, the House and Senate Transportation Committees became hopelessly deadlocked over formula allocation issues. Without additional funds, any changes in the funding formulas became a zero-sum game, and compromise became impossible. As the summer dragged on without any significant breakthroughs, the prospects of reauthorizing ISTEA before it expired on October 1, 1997, began to fade. In near desperation, both the House and Senate Transportation Committees passed reauthorization bills in September 1997 that exceeded the budget agreement's spending limits. The bills were expected to face significant opposition on both the House and Senate floors but were never put to a vote because the reauthorization process stalled in the U.S. Senate. At that time, the Senate was engaged in a protracted and highly partisan struggle over campaign finance reform legislation. Senate Democrats filibustered the Senate's reauthorization bill when it reached the Senate floor in an effort to force the Republican leadership to allow a vote on campaign finance reform. They knew that ISTEA and the congressional session were about to expire. After four failed cloture votes, Senate Majority Leader Trent Lott (R-MS) announced that a vote on campaign finance reform would take place in March 1998. He also announced that the Senate did not have enough time left in the session to deal with the reauthorization bill and all of the other legislative business still pending before the Senate. He then held several meetings with House and Senate leaders, and they subsequently agreed to extend ISTEA through May 1, 1998, and restart the reauthorization process during the next legislative session. The reauthorization bill, nicknamed Short-TEA (*Surface Transportation Extension Act of 1997*), was approved by the House and Senate without much debate, and President Clinton signed it into law on December 1, 1997.[32]

TEA-21

Following the holiday recess, the White House announced that the robust economy was bringing in more revenue than expected, and, for the first time since 1969, the national government was going to have a budget surplus. Although President Clinton asked Congress in his 1998 State of the Union Address not to touch the projected budget surplus until addressing Social Security, everyone involved in

ISTEA's reauthorization saw the surplus as the means to end the deadlock between donor and donee states.[33]

On March 2, 1998, Senator Lott and Senate Budget Committee Chairman Pete Domenici (R-NM) announced that they had agreed to increase highway funding to $173 billion over six years, a 38 percent increase over ISTEA's $124.8 billion for highway projects. Senators Lott and Domenici's announcement was telling. The chairs of the Senate's Environment and Public Works Committee and its Subcommittee on Water Resources, Transportation, and Infrastructure Subcommittee were not present at the announcement and played a minor role in the deliberations. They had lost control over highway and mass transit policy.

Most of the additional funding was used to guarantee each state at least 91 cents for each dollar that its highway users paid into the Highway Trust Fund. The increased revenue came from the general revenue account, not the Highway Trust Fund. This meant that the additional funding would have to survive the annual congressional appropriations process. Three days later, Senate Banking Committee Chairman Alfonse D'Amato (R-NY) and Senator Domenici announced that their committees had agreed to increase mass transit funding to $41 billion over six years. The additional $5 billion authorization was, like the additional highway funding, to come from general revenue and was not guaranteed.

After seven days of floor debate (with a total of 531 amendments filed), the Senate approved its reauthorization bill, ISTEA II, 96–4, on March 12, 1998. The six-year, $214 billion bill authorized $173 billion for highways, including $42.9 billion for the Surface Transportation Block Grant, $72.7 billion for the Interstate and National Highway System, $7 billion for the Congestion Mitigation and Air Quality Improvement program, and $41.3 billion for mass transit (see Table 3.1). States were required to spend at least $28.2 billion of their Interstate and National Highway System funds for interstate highway maintenance and at least $8.58 billion of those funds for interstate bridge construction and repair. It included the Clinton administration's proposals to reduce the number of planning factors used to select projects from 16 to 7 and strengthen the role of local elected officials in the designation of projects outside metropolitan areas. The Senate also approved, 62–32, an amendment to withhold national highway funds from states that refused to lower their drunken driving blood alcohol concentration level from .1 percent to .08 percent. States would lose 5 percent of their transportation funds if they did not enforce the .08 standard by October 2001 and 10 percent in subsequent years. Only 15 states had the .08 percent limit at the time of passage.[34]

The House approved its reauthorization bill, BESTEA (*Building Efficient Surface Transportation and Equity Act*), on April 1, 1998, 337–380. It authorized $181 billion for highways and $36 billion for mass transit and retained most of ISTEA's funding categories, including separate programs for bridges and interstate maintenance (see Table 3.1). Each state was guaranteed 95 cents for each dollar that its highway users contributed to the Highway Trust Fund. It also included the administration's proposals to reduce the number of planning factors that states and metropolitan planning organizations employ when selecting projects from 16 to 7 and to strengthen the role of local elected officials in the designation of projects outside metropolitan areas. Instead of mandating blood alcohol concentration levels for drunk driving, it authorized $260 million for Alcohol Traffic Safety Incentive Grants. States that established at least five of eight specified alcohol-impaired driving countermeasures were eligible for funding. One of the eight countermeasures was the acceptance of a prescribed list of penalties for driving under the influence and defining driving under the influence as any individual with a blood alcohol concentration level of .08 or greater.[35]

BESTEA generated considerable critical media attention for earmarking $9 billion for 1,467 construction projects located in 350 congressional districts. Representative Shuster defended these "high-priority" projects against allegations that they were political pork designed to attract support for the bill. He claimed that each project had survived a 14-point review process and were certified as a high priority by the state's secretary of transportation. Also, a group of fiscally conservative Republicans, led by Representative Kasich, criticized BESTEA for exceeding the budget agreement's spending caps. He offered an amendment to devolve highway and mass transit policy to states, but it was soundly defeated, 98–318.[36]

After weeks of negotiations, House and Senate conferees agreed to include in the *Transportation Equity Act for the 21st Century* (TEA-21) $167.1 billion for highways and $36.3 billion for mass transit over six years. This was approximately the amount of revenue expected to be generated by the Highway Trust Fund and was a symbolic victory for Representative Shuster, who had long advocated earmarking all such revenue for highway and mass transit uses. Conferees cut veterans' programs by $15.5 billion and social services programs by $1.8 billion to make up for the amount that the bill exceeded the budget agreement's spending caps. An additional $10 billion was made available ($6 billion for highways and $4 billion for mass transit) if other budgetary offsets could be found in the future (see Table 3.1). Each state was guaranteed at least 90.5 percent of the amount of revenue that its highway users paid into the Highway Trust Fund. ISTEA's basic structure was retained (the Bridge and Interstate Maintenance programs were kept as separate entities), the number of planning factors used when selecting projects was reduced from 16 to 7, and the role of local elected officials in the designation of projects in nonmetropolitan areas was strengthened. The House's $9 billion request for 1,467 demonstration projects was reduced to $7 billion, and $2 billion was added for Senate demonstration projects (increasing the total number of demonstration projects to 1,850). Language making Amtrak eligible for Surface Transportation Block Grant and Interstate and National Highway System program funding was deleted, but Amtrak was made eligible for Congestion Mitigation and Air Quality Improvement program funding. The Senate's drunk driving mandate was dropped. In its place, a $500 million Safety Incentive Grant was created. States that enforce the .08 blood alcohol concentration standard for determining when an individual is considered to be intoxicated while driving were eligible to receive funding from the new grant program.[37] This issue was revisited in 2000. Senator Frank Lautenberg (D-NJ), with the assistance of a persistent and highly visible lobbying effort by Mothers Against Drunk Driving, led an effort that resulted in legislation requiring states to adopt the .08 blood alcohol concentration standard by 2004 or lose 2 percent of their national highway funds. The crossover sanction increases to 8 percent by 2007. States that adopt the standard by 2007 would be reimbursed for any lost funds. At that time, 31 states had drunk driving blood alcohol concentration levels above the .08 threshold.[38]

THE 1990s: A DECADE OF MODEST CHANGE FOR HIGHWAY AND MASS TRANSIT POLICY OUTPUTS

ISTEA and TEA-21 provided state and local government officials more programmatic flexibility and created an opportunity for major, dramatic change in the distribution of highway and mass transit funding. However, an analysis of state and local government funding decisions made during the 1990s, representing more than 360,000 individual highway and mass transit projects, revealed that most state and local governments chose not to make radical changes in their funding decisions.[39] For example, between 1992 and 1999 state Departments of Transportation received almost $50 billion in "flexible" funds that could have been spent on any highway or mass transit project. They spent 87 percent of those funds on highway and bridge projects ($43.3 billion). Less than 7 percent of those funds was spent on alternative transportation modes, such as mass transit ($3.3 billion), and almost all (82 percent) of those funds were flexed by just five states (California, New York, Pennsylvania, Oregon, and Virginia). The remainder of the flexed funds were spent on administration and planning ($496 million), intelligent transportation systems ($191 million), and other projects ($2.6 billion).[40]

Although most states chose not to redirect significant amounts of funding to mass transit, they did redirect funding in other ways. Over the decade, the proportion of national funds spent on road repair and maintenance increased from 39 percent in 1990 to 47 percent in 1999, the proportion spent on new and widened highways and bridges declined from 35 percent to 28 percent, the proportion spent on mass transit declined from 21 percent to 17 percent, the proportion spent on safety declined from 5 percent to 4 percent, and the proportion spent on administration and planning increased from 1 percent to 3 percent. However, under TEA-21, the proportions spent on road repair and maintenance, new construction, and mass transit began to revert toward the proportions in place prior to ISTEA. The proportion of funds spent on road repair and maintenance fell from 49 percent in 1998 to 47 percent in 1999; the proportion spent on new and widened highways and bridges increased from 23 percent to 28 percent; and the proportion spent on mass transit declined from 19 percent to 17 percent.[41]

Mass transit advocates worried that the renewed emphasis on highway and bridge construction in 1999 and 2000 may signal the beginning of a trend away from mass transit and other alternative transportation modes. However, at least part of the escalation of highway spending in 1999 and 2000 resulted from a single project: Boston's Central Artery/Tunnel Project, known as the "Big Dig." This

7.5-mile highway project is replacing Boston's Central Artery, a six-lane elevated freeway through Boston's downtown. The new highway is an 8- to 10-lane underground expressway that includes a 14-lane, two-bridge crossing of the Charles River and a new tunnel under Boston Harbor. The project's cost has far exceeded initial estimates and is expected to exceed $13.6 billion. The trend toward highway and bridge construction could also be a reflection of pent-up demand. During the 1990s, over $100 billion in national funds was spent on road repair and maintenance (increasing from $5.8 billion in 1990 to $16 billion in 1999), compared to $57 billion for new and widened highways and bridges (increasing from $5.1 billion in 1990 to $9 billion in 1999).[42]

Government spent nearly $1 trillion on highways and bridges during the 1990s, with states contributing approximately $500 billion, local governments contributing about $250 billion, and the national government contributing nearly $200 billion. Yet, road conditions did not improve. The U.S. Federal Highway Administration ranks roads as being very good (roads with new or nearly new pavement), good (roads not requiring improvements in the near future), fair (roads likely to need improvement in the near future), mediocre (roads in need of improvement in the near future), and poor (roads in need of immediate improvement). In 1990, the U.S. Department of Transportation reported that 53 percent of nationally financed roads were in less than good condition. In 2000, that percentage had increased to 58 percent. Bridges fared better. In 1990, the U.S. Department of Transportation reported that 24 percent of the nation's bridges (137,865 of 572,205) were structurally deficient (in need of significant maintenance attention, rehabilitation, or replacement). In 2000, that percentage had been reduced to 15 percent (88,150 of 585,542).[43]

Government spent over $160 billion on mass transit during the 1990s, with state and local governments providing about 75 percent of the total (approximately $120 billion) and the national government providing about 25 percent (approximately $42 billion). The national government's mass transit spending nearly doubled during the 1990s, increasing from $3 billion in 1990 to nearly $6 billion in 1999, and reached $7 billion in 2002. State and local government mass transit spending also doubled during the 1990s, reaching nearly $14 billion in 1999. The increase in government funding for mass transit played a large role in halting the long-term decline in mass transit riders that had been taking place since the end of World War II. The turnaround began in 1997, when the number of unlinked mass transit passenger trips, which had declined from 8.5 billion trips in 1990 to 7.9 billion in 1996, started to increase. By the decade's end, the number of unlinked mass transit passenger trips had increased to 9.1 billion annually and in 2001 reached 9.5 billion. Mass transit's advocacy groups attributed the turnaround to improvements in the quality and extent of bus and commuter train service. During the 1990s, bus service mileage was increased 13 percent, and more than 300 additional miles of rail line was placed into service. Mass transit advocacy groups were quick to point out that from 1995 to 2000, mass transit use increased 21 percent while automotive use increased 11 percent. The only other times that mass transit use had grown faster than automotive use were during the recession years of the early 1980s, the Arab oil embargo of 1973, and World War II.[44]

Although national government funding for mass transit has increased dramatically, that increase needs to be placed into perspective. Between 1990 and 1999, national government spending on mass transit increased 75 percent. Over those same years, national government spending on highways and bridges increased 124 percent. Moreover, mass transit funding, as a percentage of national government funding for highway and mass transit projects, is less under TEA-21 (17 percent) than under ISTEA (21 percent).[45]

Two other new trends were evidenced during the 1990s. First, funding for administration and planning rose dramatically, from $257 million in 1990 to $893 million in 1999. The increased expenditures for planning and administration are directly attributable to ISTEA and TEA-21's mandate to develop state and local government short- and long-range planning documents that focus on intermodal solutions to traffic mobility and to broaden public participation in the decision-making process. Prior to ISTEA, the decision-making process was primarily limited to highway engineers, contractors, and a relatively limited number of appointed and elected government officials. Because states are not required to measure progress toward public participation goals, it is difficult to determine if additional funding for administration has had its intended effect. However, as mentioned previously, overall funding patterns have not changed much, suggesting that additional funds for planning and administration have not resulted in dramatic changes in the outcome of most decisions. However, anecdotal evidence suggests that public participation in the decision-making process improved in metropolitan areas served by metropolitan planning organizations. But, overall, public participation has not increased as much as ISTEA and TEA-21's advocates had hoped. In many areas, the public's participation in the decision-making process is often limited to invitations to public hearings that are held after many, if not all, final decisions have been made.[46] Second, although funding for bicycle lanes and pedestrian walking/jogging paths remains relatively small compared to highway and mass transit programs, funding for these purposes increased significantly, from $7 million in 1990 to $222 million in 1999. Moreover, these figures understate the amount spent on bicycle lanes and pedestrian walking/jogging paths because these projects are often part of larger highway and bridge construction projects that do not report expenditures on these projects separately. Although the spending figures are still relatively small, they represent a departure from the past, when expenditures on such projects were nearly nonexistent.

CONCLUSION

Although ISTEA and TEA-21 did not result in a revolutionary change in highway and mass transit spending patterns on a nationwide basis, they made it possible for states to make revolutionary changes. An analysis of state funding decisions conducted by the Surface Transportation Policy Project revealed that nine states,

Alaska, California, Connecticut, Illinois, New Jersey, New York, Rhode Island, Vermont, and Washington, made significant changes in their funding decisions during the 1990s. These nine states are more likely than others to spend a larger proportion of their funds on repairing highways and bridges than building new ones; spend more than one-third of their Congestion Mitigation and Air Quality Improvement program funds on projects that have long-term, as opposed to short-term, air quality benefits; flex funds from traditional highway and bridge programs to other transportation modes; and spend a relatively high proportion of their funds on mass transit and safety programs. The Surface Transportation Policy Project also praised Delaware and Hawaii for increasing spending on alternative surface transportation modes and on repairing highways and bridges.[47] Also, while spending outcomes may not have changed much, the decision-making process changed dramatically, especially in large metropolitan areas. They now have a broader range of participants in the decision-making process and greater emphasis on area-wide planning and intermodal solutions. This change is significant because those areas have the nation's worst traffic congestion problems.

Finally, highway and mass transit policy was transformed during the post-interstate highway era. The relatively tranquil and predictable client and majoritarian politics of the interstate highway construction era gave way to a more bellicose, partisan, and less predictable interest group politics. Importantly, the highway lobby lost its dominance over highway and mass transit outcomes, and the House and Senate Transportation Committees lost hegemony over highway and mass transit policy to the House and Senate Budget Committees. Surface transportation policy making is now much more open and less predictable than in the past.

NOTES

1. Richard Mudge, "ISTEA Legislation: The Promise versus the Reality," *Municipal Finance Journal* 64 (Winter 1994): 35.

2. U.S. Department of Transportation, *Moving America: New Directions, New Opportunities* (Washington, DC: U.S. Department of Transportation, 1990), pp. 23–25.

3. Governors' Task Force on Transportation Infrastructure, *America in Transition* (Washington, DC: National Governors' Association, 1991).

4. Robert Jay Dilger, "ISTEA: A New Direction for Transportation Policy," *Publius: The Journal of Federalism* 22 (Summer 1992): 69.

5. Mike Mills, "House Travels Favorite Road to Funding Local Highways," *Congressional Quarterly Weekly Report* (July 13, 1991): 1884–1888; and Mike Mills, "Lawmakers Lard Highway Bill with $6.8 Billion in Projects," *Congressional Quarterly Weekly Report* (July 27, 1991): 2063–2066.

6. Timothy J. Conlan and David B. Walker, "Reagan's New Federalism: Design, Debate, and Discord," *Intergovernmental Perspective* 8:4 (Winter 1983): 6–23; Rochelle L. Stanfield, "The New Federalism Is Reagan's Answer to Decaying Highways, Transit Systems," *National Journal* (June 12, 1982): 1040–1044; ACIR, *Devolving Selected Federal-Aid Highway Programs and Revenue Bases: A Critical Appraisal* (Washington, DC: ACIR, 1987), pp. 27–46; ACIR, *Local Perspectives on State-Local Highway Consultation and Cooperation: Sur-*

vey Responses From State Associations of Local Officials (Washington, DC: ACIR, 1987), pp. 1–25; ACIR, *State-Local Highway Consultation and Cooperation: The Perspective of State Legislators* (Washington, DC: ACIR, 1988), pp. 1–46; ACIR, *Devolution of Federal Aid Highway Programs: Cases in State-Local Relations and Issues in State Law* (Washington, DC: ACIR, 1988), pp. 1–53; and Mike Mills, "Administration Asks States to Carry the Transit Load," *Congressional Quarterly Weekly Report* (March 9, 1991): 599, 600.

7. National Research Council, *Curbing Gridlock: Peak Period Fees to Relieve Traffic Congestion,* vol. 1 (Washington, DC: National Academy Press, 1994), p. 20.

8. Mike Mills, "Senate Bill Would Alter Path of Nation's Road Policy,"*Congressional Quarterly Weekly Report* (April 27, 1991): 1054; Mike Mills, "Senate Panel Passes Overhaul of Federal Highway Policy," *Congressional Quarterly Weekly Report* (May 25, 1991): 1366–1368; Mike Mills, "Senate Endorsement Paves Way for a New Highway System," *Congressional Quarterly Weekly Report* (June 15, 1991): 1575–1577; and Mike Mills, "Surface Transportation," *Congressional Quarterly Weekly Report* (November 2, 1991): 3227–3234.

9. Mike Mills, "House Bill's Gas Tax Increase May Stall Highway Overhaul," *Congressional Quarterly Weekly Report* (July 20, 1991): 1973; Mike Mills and David S. Cloud, "House Dispute Over Gas Tax Puts Highway Bill on Hold," *Congressional Quarterly Weekly Report* (August 3, 1991): 2153–2155; and Mike Mills, "House Leaders Withdraw on Nickel for America," *Congressional Quarterly Weekly Report* (September 21, 1991): 2683.

10. Mike Mills, "Highway and Transit Overhaul Is Cleared for President," *Congressional Quarterly Weekly Report* (November 30, 1991): 3518–3522.

11. Ibid., p. 3519; Kirk Victor, "Skinner's Final Act," *National Journal* (December 14, 1991): 3016–3019; and Bruce D. McDowell, "Reinventing Surface Transportation: New Intergovernmental Challenges," *Intergovernmental Perspective* 18:1 (Winter 1992): 6–8, 18.

12. Robert Jay Dilger, "ISTEA," pp. 73, 74.

13. National Research Council, *Curbing Gridlock,* pp. 8, 36, 99.

14. Hank Dittmar, "Defining and Managing the Metropolitan Transportation System," in *ISTEA Planner's Workbook.* (Washington, DC: Surface Transportation Policy Project, 1996); and Robert W. Gage and Bruce D. McDowell, "ISTEA and the Role of MPOs in the New Transportation Environment: A Midterm Assessment," *Publius: The Journal of Federalism* 25:3 (Summer 1995): 133–154.

15. Robert W. Gage and Bruce D. McDowell, "ISTEA and the Role of MPOs in the New Transportation Environment," p. 138; U.S. General Accounting Office, *Transportation Infrastructure: Better Tools Needed for Making Decisions on Using ISTEA Funds Flexibly* (Washington, DC: GAO/RCED-94-25, October 1993), pp. 2–3; and Jonathan Walters, "The Highway Revolution That Wasn't," *Governing* 8:8 (May 1995): 30–33, 35–37.

16. W. M. Lyons, "The FTA-FHA MPO Reviews—Planning Practice Under the ISTEA and the CAA" (Washington, DC: U.S. Department of Transportation, 1995); and Surface Transportation Policy Project, "ISTEA Year Four" (Washington, DC: Surface Transportation Policy Project, 1995). Available on-line at: http://www.transact.org/yf/over.htm.

17. Donald H. Camp, "Transportation, the ISTEA, and American Cities" (Washington, DC: Surface Transportation Policy Project, 1996). Available on-line at: http://www.transact.org/mono/city.htm; U.S. Department of Transportation, "ISTEA Reauthorization Policy Statement and Principles" (Washington, DC: U.S. Department of Transportation, 1996). Available on-line at: http://www.dot.gov/ost/govtaffairs/istea/isteap&p.html; and American Public Transit Association, Testimony before the Senate Environment and Public Works Committee, Subcommittee on Transportation and Infrastructure (Washington, DC, March 13, 1997). Available on-line at: http://www. apta.com/govt/apatest/epwtea.htm.

18. Frederico Pena, "Statement before the House Committee on Transportation and Infrastructure Subcommittee on Surface Transportation" (Washington, DC, May 2, 1996). Available on-line at: http://www.dot.gov/affairs/1996/5296te.htm.

19. Jonathan Walters, "The Highway Revolution That Wasn't," 32–35.

20. U.S. Department of Transportation. *Transportation Statistics Annual Report 1999* (Washington, DC: U.S. Department of Transportation, 2000), p. 37. Available on-line at: http://www.bts.gov/programs/transtu/tsar/tsar99pt.html.

21. Robert Jay Dilger, "TEA-21: Transportation Policy, Pork Barrel Politics, and American Federalism," *Publius: The Journal of Federalism* 28:1 (Winter 1998): 54.

22. Transportation Research Board, National Research Council, *Institutional Barriers to Intermodal Transportation Policies and Planning in Metropolitan Areas* (Washington DC: National Academy Press, 1996), pp. 3–5, 3–6.

23. Robert Jay Dilger, "TEA-21," p. 55.

24. Robert Jay Dilger, *The Sunbelt-Snowbelt Controversy: The War Over Federal Funds* (NY: New York University Press, 1982).

25. Robert Jay Dilger, "TEA-21," p. 57.

26. Stephen Barlas, "States, Locals Battle for ISTEA," *The American City & County* 112 (March 1997): 12.

27. David Hosansky, "Web of Alliances and Interests Set to Snare Highway Funds," *Congressional Quarterly Weekly Report* 55:10 (March 8, 1997): 583.

28. Robert Jay Dilger, "TEA-21," p. 58.

29. David Hosansky, "Clinton Unveils Omnibus Bill to Mixed Reviews," *Congressional Quarterly Weekly Report* 55:11 (March 15, 1997): 623.

30. Ibid.; and Larry Williams, "Road Bill Faces Potholes," *Charleston Gazette*, March 13, 1997, p. 9A.

31. David Hosansky, "ISTEA Reauthorization Stalls Over Highway Funding," *Congressional Quarterly Weekly Report* 55:19 (May 10, 1997): 1066–1068; and David Hosansky and Alisa J. Rubin, "Shuster's Steamroller Stopped—For Now," *Congressional Quarterly Weekly Report* 55:21 (May 24, 1997): 1183.

32. Robert Jay Dilger, "TEA-21," pp. 62–65.

33. President William Jefferson Clinton, "1998 State of the Union Address," Washington, DC, January 27, 1998. Available on-line at: http://www.whitehouse.gov/WH/SOTU98/address.html.

34. William M. Welch, "Senate OKs $214 Billion Transport Bill," *USA Today*, March 15, 1998, p. 1A; and William M. Welch, "Extra $31B Paved the Way for Passage of Road Bill," *USA Today*, March 15, 1998, p. 11A.

35. Robert Jay Dilger, "TEA-21," pp. 66, 67.

36. Anick Jesdanun, "Panel Approves Transportation Bill," *The Charleston Gazette*, March 25, 1998, p. 3A; Ann Curley, "Fiscally Conservative Republicans Take Aim at Highway Bill," *allpolitics*, March 27, 1998. Available on-line at http://allpolitics.com/1998/03/27/highway.house/index.html; Brooks Jackson, "Proposed West Virginia Highway Under Fire," *allpolitics*, April 1, 1998. Available on-line at http://allpolitics.com/1998/04/01/jackson.highway/; and "House Oks $218.3 Billion Highway Bill," *allpolitics*, April 1, 1998. Available on-line at http://allpolitics.com/1998/04/01/highway.bill/.

37. "Transportation Equity Act for the 21st Century Sent to the President," Internet article (Washington, DC: Surface Transportation Policy Project, viewed on May 26, 1998). No longer available on-line.

38. Associated Press, "Congress Approves National DUI Law," *The Charleston Gazette*, October 4, 2000, p. 3A.

39. Barbara McCann, Roy Kienitz, and Bianca DeLille, *Changing Direction: Federal Transportation Spending in the 1990s* (Washington, DC: Surface Transportation Policy Project, 2000), pp. 5–7.

40. Ibid., p. 17.

41. Ibid., p. 5. Note: the percentages do not total to 100 because national transportation funds were also spent on other purposes (administration, safety programs, etc.).

42. Ibid., p . 21.

43. Ibid., pp. 21, 22; and American Society of Civil Engineers, *Renewing America's Infrastructure: A Citizen's Guide* (Washington, DC: American Society of Civil Engineers, 2001), p. 11.

44. Surface Transportation Policy Project, *Ten Years of Progress: Building Better Communities Through Transportation* (Washington, DC: Surface Transportation Policy Project, 2001), pp. 1–4.

45. Barbara McCann, Roy Kienitz, and Bianca DeLille, *Changing Direction*, pp. 13, 14.

46. Ibid., p. 31.

47. Ibid., p. 33.

4

AMTRAK:
ITS STRUGGLE FOR SURVIVAL AND RESPECT

Amtrak, the nation's intercity passenger rail service, began operations at 12:05 A.M. on May 1, 1971, when Clocker No. 235 departed New York's Penn Station bound for Philadelphia. Until then, private railroads provided the nation's intercity passenger rail service. However, declining ridership (falling from nearly 1 billion passengers a year in 1944 to less than 300 million in 1970) and mounting operating deficits (reaching nearly $.5 billion annually on a systemwide basis in 1970) forced many railroads to curtail passenger rail service and postpone needed infrastructure improvements. At the conclusion of World War II, there were over 6,000 intercity passenger trains operating in the United States. In 1970, there were only 400. Although many Americans held a romanticized fascination with railroads and rail travel, in most places in the United States intercity passenger trains could not attract enough riders to remain economically viable. People preferred the automobile's convenience when commuting relatively short distances to work, the airplane's speed when traveling long distances, and, when expense was a deciding factor, the relatively inexpensive bus when traveling either medium or long distances. Moreover, railroads could no longer count on the historically lucrative mail service to subsidize its passenger rail service. Some historians argued that the U.S. Post Office's decision in 1967 to remove first-class mail from passenger trains and ship them by truck and airplane was the final blow in a series of economic setbacks that doomed private intercity passenger rail service in the United States.

By the mid-1960s, nearly all railroad companies wanted to eliminate passenger rail services and focus on hauling freight. In fact, most passenger rail service outside of Chicago, the Boston–Washington, D.C., area, and southern California had become so unprofitable by 1970 that all other passenger rail service would have disappeared in the United States if it was not for the Interstate Commerce Commission. Railroads needed its approval to discontinue passenger rail service. The

Interstate Commerce Commission had, over the years, allowed railroads to shed their most nonprofitable intercity passenger rail routes. However, because it was committed to maintaining a national system of intercity passenger rail service, it required most railroads to continue operating at least some passenger trains as a condition of receiving a franchise to haul freight.[1]

By the mid-1960s, intercity passenger rail service in the United States was in a crisis situation. For many years, railroads covered passenger rail service losses with profits from hauling freight. However, they now faced stiff competition from both trucks and airplanes in the freight-hauling business, and their railroad freight-hauling profits narrowed considerably. Many railroads reported that unless the Interstate Commerce Commission allowed them to shed most, in some cases all, passenger rail services, they would go bankrupt. As Burlington Northern Railroad's chief operating officer, Louis W. Menk, stated in 1970, "Make no mistake about it. I want out [of the passenger rail business]."[2]

Some viewed the demise of intercity passenger rail service in the United States as an inevitable outcome of market forces weeding out an economically nonviable transportation mode. In their view, intercity passenger rail service was an obsolete technology that the vast majority of Americans neither wanted nor needed. Others believed that the national government's subsidy of highways and airports was at least partially responsible for the financial problems plaguing intercity passenger rail service. They argued that if intercity passenger rail service received equivalent subsidies, it would attract more passengers, especially in the nation's more urban and congested areas. Still others argued that intercity passenger rail service had to be saved because its demise would adversely affect the nation's environment because automobiles and airplanes require large tracts of land for their facilities and are significant sources of both air and, especially for airplanes, noise pollution. They also argued that the loss of intercity passenger rail service would adversely affect the nation's ability to move miliary personnel and goods during a national emergency.[3] They also cited numerous public opinion polls that indicated that the public wanted intercity passenger rail service to continue.

Railroad industry representatives pleaded with Congress to do something about intercity passenger rail service. Most of them wanted Congress to force the Interstate Commerce Commission to let them discontinue passenger rail operations. Others, including environmentalists and the railroads' unions, wanted the national government to give railroads enough public funding to continue providing intercity passenger rail services at then-current levels. The National Association of Railroad Passengers endorsed a compromise that originated in the U.S. Department of Transportation. It called for the creation of Railpax, a semipublic corporation that would operate a somewhat smaller system of intercity passenger trains than what was in place. Railpax would allow railroads to get out of the intercity passenger rail business while, at the same time, keep at least some intercity passenger rail services operating. Because the system would be smaller and run like a business, the U.S. Department of Transportation argued that it would require only a modest infusion of public funds.

As Congress debated these three alternatives, President Nixon (R, 1969–1974) sent mixed signals concerning Railpax. For example, the U.S. Department of Transportation announced on January 18, 1970, that it was about to send Congress a detailed Railpax proposal. The next day, the White House ordered the U.S. Department of Transportation not to submit the proposal. It soon became apparent that leading members of the White House staff opposed Railpax because of its potential cost and were urging President Nixon to kill it. As the debate within the Nixon administration continued, the Democratic Senate reported a bill out of committee that provided direct subsidies to railroads for operating intercity passenger rail service. Realizing that the Senate was about to enact legislation that was even more costly than Railpax, White House staffers relented and allowed the U.S. Department of Transportation to enter into negotiations with congressional leaders. Recognizing that the president was likely to veto a direct subsidy program, Senator Vance Hartke (D-IN), chair of the Senate Commerce Committee's Subcommittee on Transportation, and Senator Winston Prouty (R-VT), the ranking Republican on the subcommittee, negotiated a revised version of the original Railpax proposal. The Senate adopted it in May, and it received final congressional approval in October.

The *Rail Passenger Service Act of 1970* established the National Railroad Passenger Corporation as a quasi-public, for-profit enterprise under the provisions of the *District of Columbia Business Corporation Act*. Its mission is to provide modern, efficient intercity rail passenger service; help alleviate overcrowding of the nation's airports, airways, and highways; and provide an alternative to the automobile and airplane to meet the nation's transportation needs. It was to achieve these ends by consolidating existing private passenger train systems into a single, centrally managed unit. It was argued that this would reduce operating costs because redundant routes could be eliminated, equipment could be purchased at lower, bulk rates, and, on a systemwide basis, administrative overhead would be reduced significantly. The National Railroad Passenger Corporation's legal status was later changed by the *Amtrak Reform and Accountability Act of 1997* to a private corporation, although it remains subject to many operational constraints applicable to government-owned corporations.

Although it is difficult to pinpoint a single defining event that led to Amtrak's birth, Penn Central Railroad's request to discontinue all passenger rail service west of Buffalo, New York, and Harrisburg, Pennsylvania, in March 1970 and its subsequent bankruptcy in June 1970 signaled for many on Capital Hill that railroads were in serious financial trouble and that it was time for a change in national policy.[4] Also, the fact that President Nixon was a streetcar conductor's son and that his childhood ambition was to become a railroad engineer should not be overlooked. He knew that intercity passenger rail service was no longer economically viable, and many in his party adamantly opposed the bill because they believed that it was the first step to the railroad's nationalization. But he loved passenger trains and did not want to be remembered as the president who let them disappear. So, on October 30, 1970, he signed the bill into law. In deference to those within his party and administration who opposed the bill, he signed it without a formal signing ceremony.[5]

It is interesting to note that one of the law's goals was to alleviate traffic congestion both on the ground and in the air, yet it did not attempt to incorporate intercity passenger rail service into a larger, more integrated, intermodal solution to traffic congestion. For example, many European nations purposively place passenger rail stations at logical travel transfer points, such as airports and bus terminals, making it easy for passengers to move from one transportation mode to the other. This practice is the exception, not the rule in the United States, primarily because Congress decentralized its committee structure to expedite the handling of legislation. Because it acts on the various transportation modes separately and often at different times in different committees, Congress never even considered incorporating intercity passenger rail service into a comprehensive, integrated, intermodal solution to traffic congestion in the United States. Moreover, as will be shown, political expediency led Congress to focus on the survival of particular routes, rather than on the system's ability to efficiently move people and goods from place to place.

AMTRAK'S FORMATIVE YEARS: THE 1970S

The National Railroad Passenger Corporation was supposed to be administered by a 15-member Board of Directors (8 nominated by the president and approved by the Senate, 3 elected by common stockholders, and 4 elected by preferred stockholders) and a president selected by the board. Because preferred stock was not issued initially, the board actually operated with 11 members. They selected Roger Lewis, former vice president of Pan American World Airways and President of General Dynamics, to serve as Amtrak's first president. In 1981, Congress reduced the board to 9 members: a representative of organized labor, a governor, and a representative of the business community (all appointed by the President), two representatives of commuter railroads, two representatives of preferred stockholders, the U.S. secretary of transportation, and Amtrak's president. In 1997, Congress replaced the Board of Directors with a 7-member Amtrak Reform Board (each, except the Secretary of the U.S. Department of Transportation if a nominee, is nominated by the President and confirmed by the Senate). Representation of specific groups is no longer required. Instead, they must have technical qualifications, professional standing, and demonstrated expertise in transportation or corporate/financial management. Amtrak's president serves as a nonvoting, ex-officio member.

The company's legal name was, and continues to be, the National Railroad Passenger Corporation. However, it was initially called Railpax. Some board members worried that the public might make fun of the name, calling the company Railpox. Lippincott and Margulies, a New York City public relations firm, was retained to find the company a new name. The Board of Directors choose Amtrak (a contraction of the words American Travel by Track). Other names considered included Unitrak, Span, Trak, and Amtrax.[6]

The *Rail Passenger Service Act of 1970* allowed railroads to get out of the intercity passenger rail business by paying Amtrak half of their 1969 operating loss in cash, equipment (typically rolling stock), or services. In exchange, they could receive nonvoting, common stock in the company or write off their contribution as a tax loss. Although private railroads offering intercity passenger services were not required to join Amtrak, those that refused had to continue offering those services until at least January 1, 1975. Because nearly all intercity passenger rail service was losing money, most railroads offering intercity passenger rail service opted to buy into the system. Of the 20 railroads that bought into the system, only four, the Burlington Northern, Grand Trunk Western (now part of CN North America), Chicago, Milwaukee, St. Paul & Pacific (now part of CP Rail), and the trustees of Penn Central, choose to became stockholders. The rest wrote off their contribution as a tax loss.[7] As Southern Pacific President Benjamin Biaggini explained at the time, "We'll take the tax deduction instead of stock. We've had enough experience in the passenger business to know we don't want to own a piece of it. . . . [Amtrak] will be a losing enterprise throughout its entire life."[8]

Approximately 9.4 million shares of Amtrak common stock was issued at $10 each and remain outstanding today. Although Amtrak lists these shares as having a value of about $94 million, Biaggini's prediction was proven correct, as Amtrak's common stock is generally considered to have no market value. In 1997, the *Amtrak Reform and Accountability Act* required Amtrak to redeem its outstanding common stock at fair market value by October 1, 2002.

Thirteen of the 20 railroads that contracted with Amtrak (Atchison, Topeka & Santa Fe; Burlington Northern; Baltimore & Ohio-Chesapeake & Ohio; Milwaukee Road; Louisville & Nashville; Seaboard Coast Line; Missouri Pacific; Penn Central; Richmond, Fredericksburg & Potomac; Southern Pacific; Union Pacific; Gulf, Mobile & Ohio; and Illinois Central) transferred their intercity passenger operations to Amtrak. The remaining railroads that bought into the system had already discontinued intercity passenger rail service. They bought into the system to free themselves from the obligation of offering future intercity passenger rail service.

The *Rail Passenger Service Act of 1970* required Amtrak to issue preferred stock to the secretary of the U.S. Department of Transportation equal in par value to all national equipment and operating assistance received after October 1, 1981, and for capital and certain operating assistance received prior to that date. The stock was to accrue an annual dividend of 6 percent (the dividend was never paid and was discontinued by the *Amtrak Reform and Accountability Act of 1997*). The intent was to provide taxpayers a security interest in Amtrak's assets and a liquidation preference over common stockholders if Amtrak went bankrupt. In 1997, the liquidation preference and language providing preferred stockholders with voting rights on Amtrak's Board of Directors were eliminated. Amtrak was also encouraged to include employee ownership in any future stock issuance.

EQUIPMENT AND ROUTE SELECTION

Amtrak was required to establish a basic intercity passenger rail system that could be larger than existing routes, but only if it was economically prudent to do so. It was required to provide service on all routes in that basic system at least through June 30, 1973. It could reduce the system's size after that date, but any reductions had to be justified under strict cost-recovery criteria or result from a financial emergency. Amtrak could, and did, reduce the frequency of service on existing routes that were not profitable.

Amtrak began operations on May 1, 1971, with a basic system of 23,606 miles, less than half of the 54,000+ miles of intercity passenger rail service that existed immediately prior to its formation.[9] It started with $40 million from the national government, $66 million in entry fees from railroads (a total of $197 million was paid over three years), and authorization to borrow up to $100 million in nationally guaranteed loans. Initially, all of the tracks on which Amtrak trains operated were owned either by railroad companies that joined the system or by freight operators. Amtrak had compulsory access to freight operators' tracks and facilities but was required to reimburse them for using their tracks. As a result, when Amtrak started, it did not own any of the 23,606 miles of tracks on which its trains operated.

Amtrak did not have much choice when purchasing its initial stock of equipment. In an attempt to minimize their losses, most railroads at that time did not replace passenger cars and locomotives until they had reached the end of their useful lives. As a result, when Amtrak went shopping for its initial fleet, it had a difficult time finding appropriate equipment. It subsequently purchased 1,190 used passenger cars (coaches, diners, snack cars, sleepers, loungers, and observation cars) for $16.8 million from nine railroads. Nearly all of them (90 percent) were old, stainless steel models, averaging twenty-one years of service. It also purchased 447 cars from the Santa Fe Railroad system that were about 10 years old and 64 relatively new coaches, half of which were less than 6 years old, from the Union Pacific Railroad. These two purchases provided Amtrak with a nucleus of relatively new cars for its mainline service routes. It also bought 61 state-of-the-art, multiunit, high-speed, electric Metroliner cars for its Northeast Corridor (Washington, D.C. to Boston). Because the Northeast Corridor has the greatest population density in the nation, it was anticipated that Amtrak's most profitable routes would be located there.

Amtrak quickly discovered that it had a major problem with its passenger cars. At that time, there were no uniform industry design standards for passenger cars. Because of this, many of the cars that Amtrak purchased from one railroad were not compatible with those purchased from another. The lack of standardized equipment and the age of Amtrak's rolling stock resulted in numerous equipment failures that made it difficult for Amtrak to maintain its schedules. At any given time during its first four years of operation, as many as 35 percent of Amtrak's active fleet of passenger cars were out of service. Amtrak had an equally difficult time with its locomotives. It initially leased 286 diesel-electric and 40 all-electric locomotives from its predecessor railroads. During its first year in operation, Amtrak suffered 3,580 en route locomotive failures. The relatively poor condition of its tracks, especially in the Northeast Corridor, also contributed to Amtrak's inability to maintain its schedules. In some areas, steep curves and lack of track maintenance forced its trains to slow to less than 15 miles per hour.

Another problem was that most of Amtrak's passenger cars had steam heating and cooling systems. This was a throwback to the days when trains were pulled by steam locomotives. Most of Amtrak's locomotives were diesel-electric. As a result, many of Amtrak's trains had to be equipped with self-contained steam generators. These generators often failed, particularly on Amtrak's older trains because their steel wheels ran rough over the rails, and the jarring caused the heating and cooling systems to malfunction. Excessive or inadequate heat was one of Amtrak passengers' most frequent complaints during its initial years of service.[10]

Amtrak was purposively created as a nongovernmental agency to relieve it from political pressures to maintain unprofitable routes. However, from the start, several of Amtrak's route selections were questioned by journalists and others as politically motivated. The *Rail Passenger Service Act of 1970* directed Secretary of Transportation John A. Volpe to designate the system's endpoints. Placing that decision in the hands of an appointed political official instead of Amtrak's Board of Directors guaranteed that politics would play a role in route selection. Amtrak's Board of Directors selected routes between the endpoints.

Secretary Volpe issued a preliminary report on proposed endpoints to Congress on November 30, 1970. It named 21 pairs of cities for service, with routes generally following radial patterns emanating from Chicago and New York. Trains based in Chicago were to run to Seattle, San Francisco, Los Angeles, Houston, St. Louis, New Orleans, Miami, Cincinnati, Detroit, and New York. Trains based in New York were to run to Buffalo, Boston, Washington, New Orleans, and Miami. An additional route ran from Washington, D.C. to St. Louis.

Secretary Volpe's long-distance routes (e.g., Chicago to Seattle, Chicago to San Francisco, and Chicago to Los Angeles) were criticized by those who believed that long-distance passenger rail service could not compete with air service. They argued that these long-distance routes would never turn a profit and were selected only to enhance Amtrak's popularity in Congress by increasing the number of congressional districts that were serviced by at least one intercity passenger train. Still others complained about the lack of north–south routes outside the Northeast Corridor and the lack of service between southern California and the southern states. Secretary Volpe subsequently added routes between Seattle and San Diego, Los Angeles and New Orleans, and Norfolk and Cincinnati. He also extended the Washington, D.C. to St. Louis route to Kansas City.[11]

Amtrak's Board of Directors then selected the specific routes between endpoint cities. Most of their choices for the system's initial group of 184 passenger trains were based on the law's guidelines, which specified that they were to take into account such factors as current ridership and operating expenses, population densities served, physical terrain, and the condition of existing infrastructure. However, political considerations were clearly evident in several of their routing decisions. Routes passing through Montana, for example, were altered to accommodate Senate Majority Leader Michael Mansfield (D-MT), and an experimental route (later discontinued due to lack of passengers) was added between Washington, D.C. and Parkersburg, West Virginia, to accommodate Representative Harley O. Staggers (D-WV), chair of the House Commerce Committee (which had jurisdiction over Amtrak in the U.S. House of Representatives) and Senator Robert C. Byrd (D-WV). Senator Byrd was a leading member of the Senate and later was elected Senate Majority Leader. The frequency of service on routes also reflected political influence. For example, in 1972, Amtrak ran a train between Chicago and Los Angeles 7 times a week and between Chicago and Seattle, Washington, 10 times a week, even though more than 8 million people lived in the Los Angeles area, more than four times as many as the Seattle area. In addition, cities located along the Los Angeles route had much larger populations than those located along the Seattle route. However, trains running between Chicago and Seattle passed through Montana, represented in the Senate by Majority Leader Mike Mansfield, and finished their run in Washington, represented in the Senate by Warren G. Magnuson (D-WA), chair of the Senate Committee on Commerce. That committee had jurisdiction over Amtrak in the U.S. Senate.

Amtrak's Board of Directors were allowed to operate the trains directly or to contract their operations out to railroads that joined the system. It decided to contract with railroads, paying them 5 percent over "out-of-pocket" costs. Although the board's decision relieved them of the responsibility of dealing with large numbers of employees, it was later criticized on the grounds that the railroads' 5 percent over-cost guarantee did not provide the railroads an incentive to minimize expenses or improve the quality of services offered.[12] For example, the cost-plus financing system enabled railroad labor unions to negotiate more favorable contracts for its members with the 13 railroads that joined Amtrak. The railroads then shifted the added labor expenses onto Amtrak as part of their cost of providing services.[13] Although Congress later complained about Amtrak's inability to turn a profit, the shifting of labor expenses onto Amtrak did not receive much commentary during congressional hearings. One possible explanation for this was that both the House and Senate at that time were controlled by Democrats, and the Democratic Party was strongly allied with labor, relying on union support for both campaign contributions and other forms of campaign assistance. This also helps to explain why Amtrak's enabling legislation included language directing railroads to provide fair and equitable arrangements to protect employees adversely affected by discontinuances of intercity rail service caused by Amtrak's creation. The U.S. Department of Labor arbitrated disputes between Amtrak and its employees arising from such a discontinuance. At that time, the *Interstate Commerce Act* required railroads to provide employees laid off because of route restructuring with up to four years of compensation. The U.S. Department of Labor subsequently increased that amount to up to six years of full wages and benefits.

Finances

Given statutory constraints concerning the closure of nonprofitable routes, political influences over route selection, and prohibitions on contracting out most services, it was clear from day one that Amtrak was not going to be profitable. However, few suspected the extent of Amtrak's future financial woes (see Table 4.1).

From May to December 1971, Amtrak earned $22.6 million but spent $45.3 million, resulting in a loss of $22.6 million. Although troublesome to many on Capitol Hill, Amtrak was expected to have initial start-up problems. However, Amtrak's finances continued to deteriorate. In 1972, Amtrak had 16.6 million riders, with about half of them (8.1 million) in the Northeast Corridor. It had $163 million in revenue and $310 million in expenses, resulting in a loss of $147 million. In 1973, it lost another $143 million. Complicating matters, in 1973 the Interstate Commerce Commission ruled in favor of a complaint filed against Amtrak by the Penn Central Transportation Company. Amtrak's contract with its member railroads offered them the option of being reimbursed 5 percent over out-of-pocket expenses or according to a cost study. Penn Central was the only Amtrak member that opted to be reimbursed according to a cost study. Penn Central conducted the study, which, in summary, recommended additional compensation beyond what would have been provided under Amtrak's 5 percent over-cost formula. Penn Central argued that its depreciation costs were much higher than other railroads because, unlike other railroads, most (approximately 75 percent) of the traffic on its rails was from passenger trains. That meant that it did not have other substantial sources of revenue to provide necessary upkeep of its rails and roadbed, which were in relatively poor condition. Penn Central argued that Amtrak was causing its facilities to deteriorate faster than anticipated, and it needed additional money to deal with the problem. Amtrak disputed Penn Central's cost study, initially calling its cost estimates "incomplete."[14] Nevertheless, the Interstate Commerce Commission ordered Amtrak to pay Penn Central an additional $40 million annually in rent for using Penn Central's tracks. In return, Penn Central had to meet performance criteria related to schedule adherence, cleanliness, and other operational factors. Although the ruling resulted in better system performance, it increased Amtrak's operating expenses. Given Amtrak's competition for passengers from automobiles, buses, and airplanes and statutory prohibitions on reducing services on nonprofitable routes, Amtrak's management was in a no-win situation. If they did not increase fares to raise additional revenue, Amtrak was going to continue losing money. But, if they raised fares, Amtrak would lose ridership and still lose money. Lacking an easy solution, Amtrak decided to ask Congress for additional funding and greater authority to eliminate nonprofitable routes.

Congress praised Amtrak's management for centralizing ticketing and reservation procedures, creating working relationships with travel agencies, and equalizing fare structures nationally. However, it criticized Amtrak harshly for running a deficit and for poor service on nearly all routes. Only the new Metroliner service along the

Table 4.1
Amtrak's Finances, 1972–2001 (millions of dollars)

Year	Revenue	Expenses	Balance	Revenue/Expenses
2001	$2,203	$2,544	-$341	.86
2000	2,111	2,876	-765	.73
1999	2,011	2,660	-694	.75
1998	2,244	2,548	-304	.88
1997	1,669	2,359	-690	.70
1996	1,550	2,258	-708	.67
1995	1,490	2,257	-767	.66
1994	1,409	2,367	-958	.59
1993	1,400	2,113	-713	.66
1992	1,320	2,019	-699	.65
1991	1,347	2,067	-720	.65
1990	1,308	2,012	-704	.65
1989	1,269	1,935	-666	.66
1988	1,107	1,757	-650	.63
1987	974	1,672	-698	.58
1986	861	1,564	-703	.55
1985	826	1,600	-774	.52
1984	759	1,522	-763	.50
1983	664	1,469	-805	.45
1982	630	1,401	-771	.45
1981	612	1,443	-831	.42
1980	559	1,276	-717	.44
1979	496	1,113	-617	.45
1978	433	1,011	-578	.43
1977	415	945	-530	.44
1976	278	666	-388	.42*
1975	246	560	-314	.44*
1974	240	439	-199	.55*
1973	202	345	-143	.59*
1972	163	310	-147	.52*

Source: Amtrak, *Annual Report* (Washington, DC: National Railroad Passenger Corporation), various issues.

*calendar year; fiscal years (October–September) thereafter.

Northeast Corridor escaped scathing reviews concerning comfort and cleanliness, and nearly all of Amtrak's 250 trains operating at that time were criticized for failing to maintain schedules (see Table 4.2). In 1975, the Interstate Commerce Commission received over 8,000 letters of complaint from Amtrak passengers.[15] Ironically, among Amtrak's strongest and most persistent critics were intercity bus operators and their representatives in Washington, D.C. Bus operators claimed that they could provide intercity passenger services at a lower cost and with equivalent, if not superior, benefits for the environment and for promoting independence from foreign oil-producing nations (a major concern during and subsequent to the Arab oil embargo of 1973). The irony was that railroads played a major role in the formation of intercity bus travel. For example, railroads were once major stockholders in both Greyhound and Trailways.[16] The criticisms concerning Amtrak's financial performance and its lack of quality service became so strong that in early 1975 Amtrak's founding president, Roger Lewis, was replaced by Paul H. Reistrup (1975–1978). He promised better systemwide performance and embarked on an ambitious effort to upgrade Amtrak's fleet of passenger cars and continued his predecessor's effort to upgrade Amtrak's locomotives.

During 1975, Amtrak received 115 new, state-of-the-art Amfleet railcars and ordered 377 more that were delivered by 1977. These cars had specially designed suspension systems that provided added riding comfort, carpeted floors and walls to reduce noise, reclining seats with retractable tray tables, and electric heating and cooling systems. Amtrak also bought 30 new locomotives in 1975 and added 51 more in 1976. These purchases, coupled with the delivery of 110 new locomotives in 1974, and continued retirement of Amtrak's oldest passenger cars and locomotives reduced the average age of Amtrak's passenger cars from 24 years in 1974 to 20 years in 1977 and the average age of its locomotives from 14 years in 1974 to 11 years in 1977. Reistrup touted these purchases as the beginning of a new era for Amtrak. He subsequently launched an aggressive advertising campaign in 100 cities serviced by Amtrak, added several new routes, and expanded total route mileage to over 26,000 miles.

Reistrup's efforts were praised on Capitol Hill. However, the Ford administration had grown so upset with Amtrak's poor service record and budget deficits that, on January 29, 1976, Secretary of Transportation William Coleman announced that Amtrak passenger service was a waste of taxpayers' money, and if he had his way, it "would die tomorrow."[17]

Despite President Gerald Ford's (R, 1974–1977) opposition, Congress continued to increase Amtrak's operating subsidies (see Table 4.3). It also provided special, supplemental appropriations for maintenance, repairs, research and development, and capital improvement projects. For example, it provided $225 million for these purposes in 1973, $200 million in 1974, and $63 million in 1975. Amtrak's borrowing authority was also increased to $900 million. Amtrak used these additional funds and borrowing capacity to upgrade its rolling stock and continue rehabilitating its rail lines and other facilities. By 1980, the average age

Table 4.2
Amtrak System Characteristics and Performance, 1972–2001

Year	Route Miles	Passengers (millions)	Passenger Cars (number of)	Passenger Cars (average age in years)	Percent On-Time
2001	22,741	23.5	2,188	18	NA
2000	22,741	22.5	1,894	19	78
1999	22,616	21.5	1,992	22	79
1998	22,200	21.1	1,962	21	79
1997	24,300	20.2	1,728	20	74
1996	24,200	19.7	1,730	21	71
1995	24,700	20.7	1,722	22	76
1994	25,200	21.2	1,852	22	72
1993	25,200	22.1	1,853	23	72
1992	24,700	21.3	1,796	22	77
1991	24,100	22.0	1,786	21	77
1990	23,951	22.2	1,863	20	76
1989	23,800	21.4	1,742	18	75
1988	23,000	21.5	1,710	17	71
1987	24,000	20.4	1,705	16	74
1986	24,000	20.3	1,664	15	74
1985	24,000	20.8	1,523	14	81
1984	24,000	19.9	1,379	13	80
1983	23,500	19.0	1,480	15	82
1982	24,000	19.0	1,450	14	79
1981	24,000	20.6	1,436	13	77
1980	23,515	21.2	1,589	14	69
1979	27,000	21.4	1,607	20	57
1978	26,000	18.9	1,678	20	62
1977	26,000	19.2	1,806	20	62
1976	26,000	18.2	1,932	20	73
1975	24,800	17.4	1,882	25	77
1974	24,000	18.2	1,881	24	75
1973	22,000	16.9	1,717	23	60
1972	23,606	16.6	1,569	22	75

Source: Amtrak, *Annual Report* (Washington, DC: National Railroad Passenger Corporation), various issues.

Table 4.3
Amtrak's National Financial Assistance, 1971–2002 (millions of dollars)

Year	Operating Grants	Capital Grants	Northeast Corridor	Taxpayer Relief Act	Total
2002	$0.0	$521	0	$0	$521.0
2001	0.0	521	0	0	521.0
2000	0.0	571	0	0	571.0
1999	0.0	609	0	1,09	1,701.0
1998	202.0	0	250	1,092	1,544.0
1997	223.0	223	255	—	701.0
1996	285.0	230	115	—	630.0
1995	392.0	230	200	—	822.0
1994	351.7	195	225	—	771.7
1993	350.0	190	204	—	744.0
1992	330.0	175	205	—	710.0
1991	342.1	132	179	—	653.1
1990	520.1	83	24	—	627.7
1989	553.8	29	20	—	603.2
1988	532.3	46	23	—	601.5
1987	579.0	26	—	—	605.5
1986	587.1	2	—	—	589.1
1985	625.7	52	—	—	678.0
1984	614.9	98	—	—	713.2
1983	601.6	94	—	—	696.1
1982	555.5	176	—	—	732.1
1981	686.8	220	—	—	907.3
1980	650.4	191	—	—	841.4
1979	600.0	130	—	—	730.0
1978	536.0	130	—	—	666.0
1977	482.6	93	—	—	575.7
1976	462.0	139	—	—	601.2
1975	276.5	—	—	—	276.5
1974	146.6	2	—	—	149.1
1973	170.0	—	—	—	170.0
1971/72	40.0	—	—	—	40.0

Source: Amtrak, Annual Report (Washington, DC: National Railroad Passenger Corporation), various issues.

of Amtrak's passenger cars had fallen to 14 years, and the average age of its locomotives had fallen to 7 years.

The additional funding helped Amtrak's financial situation, but Congress continued to refuse to allow Amtrak to reduce expenses by eliminating nonprofitable
routes. Instead, it added several routes fancied by various congressional interests.
For example, three international routes (between St. Louis and Nuevo Laredo,
Mexico; Seattle and Vancouver; and Washington, D.C. and Montreal) and several
domestic routes were added by legislative mandate. Also, in 1976 Amtrak was directed to acquire the bankrupt Penn Central's 456-mile rail line extending from
Boston to Washington, D.C., a 62-mile rail line from New Haven, Connecticut, to
Springfield, Massachusetts, and 103-mile rail line from Philadelphia to Harrisburg, Pennsylvania. Amtrak paid Conrail (the national government agency over-
seeing Penn Central) $87 million for the trackage, payable over eight years. Thus,
for the first time, Amtrak was more than just a train operator. It now owned 621
miles of track. Unfortunately, the track was in terrible condition.

The national government initially appropriated $1.6 billion over a five-year pe-
riod to upgrade these tracks. These funds, plus more than another $1 billion after
the first five years' installment was spent, were used to replace 900,000 railroad ties,
install 420 miles of welded rails, realign over 50 curves, rebuild tunnels in New
York and Baltimore, replace or modify 600 rail bridges, improve existing electrification between Washington, D.C. and New Haven, Connecticut, and extend electrification from New Haven to Boston. Amtrak also acquired 83 miles of track in
Michigan and 12 miles of track in Albany, New York.[18]

The nation's trucking and water transportation industries opposed Amtrak's
purchase of Conrail's trackage and the national government's commitment to
fund the track's revitalization. Although Amtrak now owned the track, they were
still used by freight railroads. By improving those tracks, the national government
was helping the competition. The freight railroad industry argued that competition from inland waterway carriers and trucks had caused shipping rates to fall to
levels that contributed to the railroad's financial crisis. Therefore, it was only fair
that the national government help them during their time of need because it was
already subsidizing trucking and water transportation industries. As Stephen Ailes,
president of the Association of American Railroads, explained:

From 1947 through 1974, while Federal, state and local governments were spending $345
billion on constructing and maintaining highways and $4.3 billion on improving the inland
waterways, the percentage of total intercity freight ton-miles hauled by trucks rose from 10
to 22.9 percent and by barges from 3.4 to 10.5 percent. During the same period, only
insignificant amounts of government aid were provided for already bankrupt railroads such
as Penn Central, and the railroads's share of the freight market dropped from 65.3 to 38.9
percent.[19]

The Northeast Corridor's acquisition changed Amtrak. In 1972, it had 807 employees. In 1977, it had 18,400 employees represented by 13 unions. Although Am-

trak's track-miles increased only modestly during the 1970s, from 23,606 miles in 1971 to just under 27,000 miles in 1979, Amtrak was now recognized as a real railroad system. In addition to having more employees, Amtrak began to operate like other railroads. As part of Conrail's takeover, Amtrak was prohibited from contracting out any work other than food and beverage services if the contracting out adversely affected any unionized employee. As a result, Amtrak did its own work, such as refurbishing railcars, maintaining track, and switching from steam to electric heating and cooling systems. Amtrak also began to purchase existing rail stations along its tracks and built its own rail stations as well. However, despite these efforts, Amtrak's financial situation got worse, not better. By the decade's end, annual ridership had leveled off at 20–21 million passengers. Revenue had increased to approximately $500 million annually, but expenses had ballooned to over $1 billion. This created annual deficits exceeding $.5 billion. In 1979, Brock Adams, President Jimmy Carter's (D, 1977–1981) secretary of transportation, responded to Amtrak's rising tide of red ink by proposing that it reduce its intercity passenger rail network to about 15,700 miles. He recommended eliminating 16 long-distance routes, each passing through numerous congressional districts. His proposal reduced or eliminated Amtrak services in 40 states.

Congressional leaders strongly opposed the administration's plan. Harley Staggers (D-WV), chair of the House Commerce Committee, was particularly upset that it eliminated three of the four routes (the Shenandoah, Hilltopper, and Blue Ridge) that passed through his congressional district. Many congressional members recognized that Amtrak's financial woes were severe but, nonetheless, insisted that the routes passing through their districts should be saved. They argued that these routes were essential to the continued economic vitality of the communities served, especially following the 1978 deregulation of the airline industry. That reduced or eliminated air service in 184 communities. Many cities and towns slated to lose some or all Amtrak service had already lost some or all air service. They also cited public opinion polls indicating that the public supported funding Amtrak at current levels and asked why the Carter administration wanted to reduce services in an energy-efficient transportation mode during a national energy crisis. As Representative Wyche Fowler (D-GA) stated,

[T]he Administration's left hand does not know what the right hand is doing. One day it proclaims the high priority of mass transportation in helping to solve our energy program, while on the next it recommends a major curtailment in one of the main components of intercity mass transit. Therefore, it is up to Congress to take the initiative in providing for a balanced national transportation policy and not leave it up to the federal bureaucrats to decide for us.[20]

Even Rene Levesque, premier of the Canadian province of Quebec (Le Parti Québécois, 1976–1985) asked Congress not to eliminate Amtrak routes. He joined Richard Snelling, Governor of Vermont, and several other senators and representatives from New England states in urging Congress to save the Montrealer.[21]

Because no one was willing to step forward and volunteer their routes for elimination, and it was necessary to gather support from a majority of congressional
members to fund Amtrak, it became next to impossible to eliminate routes. Congressional politics mandated that Amtrak be a national system or no system at all.
As a result, eliminating the least cost-effective routes, principally the transcontinental routes, was not politically feasible. However, facing the possibility of a presidential veto, Congress recognized that something had to be done to improve
Amtrak's financial situation. It finally agreed to reduce Amtrak's mileage marginally, to 23,515 miles. It also gave Amtrak several performance goals, including 50
percent improvement in on-time performance within three years; a systemwide
average speed of 55 miles per hour; and revenue sufficient to cover at least 44 percent of operating expenses by the end of FY 1982 and at least 50 percent by FY
1985.[22]

THE 1980s

The 1980s were marked by strong disagreements between President Ronald
Reagan (R, 1981–1989) and Democratic Congresses over Amtrak's future. Facing
mounting national budget deficits, President Reagan wanted to eliminate Amtrak's operating subsidies and reduce funding for Northeast Corridor improvements. He also proposed selling Amtrak to the highest bidder. Congress, on the
other hand, continued to fund Amtrak, despite annual operating losses averaging
over $700 million; its inability to make scheduled payments in 1983 on nearly $1
billion in national government loan guarantees; and several contentious labor
stoppages over pay, benefits, and job security. The loan crisis highlighted Amtrak's
continuing fiscal difficulties. President Reagan resolved the crisis by ordering the
U.S. Department of Transportation to take title to the notes that were owned by
the Federal Financing Bank.[23]

Amtrak escaped the budget ax by improving its on-time performance from 69
percent at the beginning of the decade to 75 percent in 1989. It also improved its
"revenue to costs ratio" from 44 percent in 1980 to 66 percent in 1989 (see Table
4.1). Although this ratio excluded capital costs, Amtrak's management pointed to
them as indicators of their progress toward self-sufficiency. Amtrak's net loss per
passenger mile also declined, from 18 cents per mile in 1979 to 9 cents per passenger mile in 1989.

Amtrak also won congressional support by promising throughout the 1980s
that it would no longer need operating subsidies by 2000. Moreover, customer
complaints fell as Amtrak purchased newer, more comfortable passenger cars and
newer, more reliable locomotives. In 1983, it also met Congress's mandate to provide service between New York City and Washington, D.C. in two hours and 40
minutes. However, it did not meet Congress's mandate to provide service between
New York City and Boston in three hours and 40 minutes. The trip took about four
and a half hours in 1989. Also, Amtrak's on-time performance for long-distance
routes (over 400 miles) fell from 78 percent in 1985 to 54 percent in 1989.[24]

Amtrak's promise to end its need for operating subsidies was received warmly on Capitol Hill. The Reagan administration was not impressed. It argued that Amtrak's ridership had leveled off at 19–20 million passengers annually, limiting its ability to generate additional revenue. It also argued that Amtrak's labor costs were about to escalate because Congress refused to eliminate statutory limitations on Amtrak's ability to contract out services, and Amtrak was obligated to negotiate collective bargaining agreements with its employees' 13 unions. Moreover, Amtrak was in a very competitive labor market. Now that the nation's freight operators were no longer losing money on intercity passenger rail services, they were able to offer their employees higher salaries and competitive benefit packages. If Amtrak did not keep pace, it risked losing its best employees to private railroads. The administration was convinced that this meant that Amtrak was going to have a very difficult time keeping labor expenses under control. Given this and the statutory constraints on contracting out services, the administration argued that Amtrak would never end its need for national operating subsidies. Moreover, it noted that Amtrak's capital cost estimates, especially in the Northeast Corridor, were increasing at a rate far greater than inflation and had grown to more than $2 billion. In its view, Amtrak was always going to lose money, and, in an era of fiscal constraint, the national government could no longer afford it.

Many congressional members acknowledged that Amtrak was probably never going to turn a profit. They knew that passenger rail service was a labor-intensive enterprise, with very large, fixed, capital costs. They also acknowledged that passenger rail service was, with some exceptions, not an economically viable transportation alternative for most Americans. Nonetheless, Amtrak's advocates argued that Amtrak's economic difficulties were largely due to national subsidies to other modes of transportation, particularly automobiles. They pointed out that most European countries (e.g., France, Germany, Italy, Netherlands, and Switzerland) provided their passenger rail systems with massive government subsidies, funded, in part, by gasoline taxes. In their view, the Europeans had it right. They recognized that automobiles created a number of "hidden" costs on society, including automotive air and noise pollution, increased greenhouse gas emissions, time lost in traffic congestion, and expenses related to deaths and injuries on the nation's highways. The Europeans capture some of these hidden costs through increased gasoline taxes and use the funds to "even the playing field" by offering individuals an alternative to the automobile. Taking their cue from the Europeans, Amtrak's advocates argued that Amtrak's budgetary balance sheet did not take into account its positive effect on the nation's air quality and on the nation's health (rail death and injury rates per passenger mile are lower than for the automobile; in 2000, 41,821 people were killed and another 3,190,000 were seriously injured on the nation's highways, compared to 512 killed and 10,424 seriously injured on the nation's railroads). It also did not take into account Amtrak's role as an alternative to the automobile. They argued that if Amtrak ceased operations, the national government would have to pay for hundreds, perhaps thousands of miles of new highways to accommodate Amtrak passengers' transportation needs. Amtrak's advocates argued that when all of these benefits were taken into account, Amtrak was a good investment. They were particularly upset that the debate over Amtrak's future focused almost exclusively on Amtrak's "losing" money. In their view, this was unfair. No other transportation mode, including the automobile, was economically self-sufficient. The national government routinely supplemented revenue in the Highway Trust Fund to build and maintain the interstate highway system, but no one ever accused the automobile of "losing" money.

In addition to these arguments, the fact that Amtrak trains crossed 44 states and that its greatest level of service (nearly half of its passengers) was in the heavily-Democratic northeastern portion of the country also helped to explain why the Democratic Congress continued funding Amtrak. By the decade's end, the national government was providing Amtrak over $600 million annually in operating and capital grants.[25]

THE 1990s

President George Bush (R, 1989–1993) continued the White House's opposition to Amtrak operating subsidies. He shared the Reagan administration's view that the national government could not afford to subsidize passenger rail service. He was also concerned that the cost estimates for Amtrak's planned improvement of the Northeast Corridor (primarily for straightening curves, replacement and renovation of bridges/tunnels, and the electrification of the rails) were too low. The conservative Cato Institute voiced the concerns of many conservatives in the Administration and Congress when it attacked Amtrak's funding on the grounds that Amtrak (1) made only a negligible contribution to the nation's transportation system, representing just .007 percent of all daily commuter work trips and just .04 percent of all passengers making intercity trips; (2) had virtually no effect on reducing traffic congestion, pollution, or energy use; (3) unlike buses, catered primarily to comparatively affluent people, with only 13 percent of its passengers having incomes below $20,000; and (4) was the most highly subsidized form of intercity transportation, with an average subsidy of $100 per rider and over $1,000 per rider on some long-distance routes. The authors of another Cato Institute study claimed that it would be more cost-effective to close down Amtrak's long-distance routes and provide its long-distance passengers with cash to purchase round-trip airline tickets. Other critics noted that Amtrak's improvement in its costs-to-expense ratio and net operating loss per passenger mile during the 1980s was largely due to its deferring investment in new equipment, not a resurgence in public interest in intercity passenger rail service. They suggested that Amtrak purposively deferred purchasing new equipment to fend off the Reagan administration's effort to privatize Amtrak. Deferring equipment investment reduced Amtrak's operating costs, causing its costs-to-expense ratio and net loss per passenger mile figures to improve. Critics argued that while that saved Amtrak money in the short term, it significantly increased the average age of its rolling stock. The average age of Amtrak's locomotives increased from 4 years in 1982 to 11 years in

1989, and the average age of its railcars increased from 14 years in 1980 to 20 years in 1990. Critics noted that as Amtrak's equipment aged, maintenance expenses were likely to rise. They noted that the percentage of locomotives not available for service on an average day increased from 6.8 percent in 1985 to 13 percent in 1989. In their view, this was due to added maintenance needed on older machinery and was a harbinger of service problems to come.[26]

In 1990, Amtrak's fourth president, W. Graham Claytor Jr. (1982–1993), responded to these criticisms by going on the offensive. He told Congress that Amtrak would serve over 21 million passengers that year, the highest in its history. He also announced that Amtrak's total operating revenue would exceed $1.1 billion, another all-time high, and that Amtrak would no longer need any national government operating subsidies by 2000. Responding to criticisms concerning the age of Amtrak's equipment, in 1992 he announced that Amtrak was ordering 140 new Superliner II bilevel passenger railcars for $340 million. He also announced that Amtrak would spend $1 billion to improve the northern portion of the Northeast Corridor (New York City to Boston). Most of the money ($800 million) was used to improve the route's physical plant (e.g., straightening curves; replacing worn rails; building new, or renovating existing, bridges and tunnels) and the remainder ($200 million) to purchase new high-speed, electric trains for the route. He claimed that these improvements would enable Amtrak to reach the congressional mandate to provide service between Boston and New York City in three hours and 40 minutes.[27]

Amtrak's critics were quick to note that the expenditure of yet another $1 billion on the northern portion of the Northeast Corridor was ample evidence that the initial cost estimates for improving the Northeast Corridor were too low. They also repeated their assertion that Amtrak would never wean itself from national government operating subsidies and noted that Claytor purposively glossed over what, in their view, was Amtrak's seemingly insatiable appetite for capital subsidies.

Once again, Claytor responded to Amtrak's critics by taking the offensive. On February 26, 1992, he asked Congress to establish an Intercity Passenger Rail and Capital Improvement Trust Fund. It would be funded by one cent of the national government's gasoline tax. At that time, each cent of the gasoline tax generated about $1.3 billion annually. Claytor argued that the revenue from just one cent of the existing gasoline tax would enable Amtrak to meet all of its capital needs and was justified given Amtrak's diversion of cars from the nation's highways.[28] Although Claytor's proposal was not adopted, it altered the political debate. Instead of focusing almost exclusively on Amtrak's financial balance sheet, the debate shifted to why the national government was subsidizing automobiles more than mass transit and intercity passenger rail. This change in the nature of the debate and Amtrak's pronouncements concerning its ability to reach operational self-sufficiency led Congress to continue Amtrak's operating and capital subsidies during the early 1990s without much opposition.

Amtrak's survival was not an issue during President Bill Clinton's administration (D, 1993–2001). He shared the previous administration's concern about Amtrak's fiscal health, but he was committed to its survival. However, it soon became clear that, despite increasing its funding to over $700 million annually for operating subsidies and capital grants, Amtrak's financial situation was not improving, and its goal of being operationally self-sufficient by 2000 was not going to be achieved.

In 1995, the U.S. General Accounting Office released the first in a series of highly critical reports concerning Amtrak's financial situation. It noted that despite the infusion of nearly $19 billion in national assistance for operating subsidies and capital improvements between 1971 and 1995, Amtrak continued to lose money (recording deficits of $699 million in 1992, $713 million in 1993, $958 million in 1994, and $767 million in 1995). Moreover, Amtrak's capital needs had increased to nearly $5 billion (including $2.5 billion for the southern portion of the Northeast Corridor and another $1.6 billion for the northern portion), and, since 1987, it had accumulated an outstanding debt of nearly $1 billion. It also criticized Amtrak for deferring maintenance on train equipment in an attempt to reduce operating losses. The U.S. General Accounting Office pointed out that heavy equipment overhauls were overdue on nearly 40 percent of Amtrak's 1,900 cars and locomotives; that the average age of its cars in 1995 had risen to about 22 years, similar to what it was when Amtrak started operations in 1971; and that it would cost Amtrak at least $1.5 billion to overhaul its equipment. It also noted that Amtrak's expenses for using tracks owned by freight railroads (about $90 million annually) were likely to increase in the near future. The contracts for those leases were signed in 1971 and were set to expire in April 1996.[29]

The U.S. General Accounting Office's reports, coupled with the Republican Party's capture of a majority of seats in both the House and the Senate in the 1994 congressional elections, caused the debate over Amtrak's future to focus, once again, almost exclusively on its inability to generate a profit. Even Amtrak's most ardent supporters were convinced that something had to be done about Amtrak's finances. For example, Senator Max Baucus (D-MT) renewed the previously failed effort to redirect revenue from the Highway Trust Fund to Amtrak. His proposal to redirect revenue from one-half cent of the national gasoline tax to Amtrak was narrowly defeated in the Senate, 50–49, on May 25, 1995. Although the closeness of the Senate vote encouraged Amtrak's proponents, they knew that even if the proposal had passed, it had no chance of becoming law because Representative Bud Shuster (R-PA), chair of the House Committee on Transportation and Infrastructure, was vehemently opposed to any "raid" on the Highway Trust Fund by other transportation modes. Without his support, the proposal was not going to be reported to the House floor for a vote. Also, given Shuster's pivotal role in dispersing highway funds, even if the proposal somehow made its way to the House floor, it was very unlikely that it would pass over his objections.

While Congress deliberated the future of Highway Trust Fund revenue, Amtrak's management developed a series of strategic business plans to increase revenue and contain costs. Amtrak's new goal was to be free of national operating subsidies by 2002. Amtrak claimed that it could achieve that goal by reducing staff and frequency of service on its most nonprofitable routes and raising fares. As part of its cost-containment strategy, Amtrak also reduced the number of Heritage cars in its system from 437 in 1995 to 246 in 1996. Heritage cars were among those obtained by Amtrak in 1971. Because they averaged more than 40 years of service, they were more likely than other cars to malfunction and need costly repairs. Amtrak also asked Congress to provide it additional flexibility when negotiating labor matters such as severance pay, contracting, and work processes; exemption from national fuel taxes; and, to reduce interest expenses on its debt, authority to issue tax-exempt bonds.[30] It also renewed its request for a dedicated source of revenue for capital costs. For example, in 1996, it asked for the revenue generated by half of a cent of the national gasoline tax from 1997 through 2002.[31]

Amtrak's efforts to reduce operating costs and increase revenues in 1995 and 1996 had a marginal effect on its financial balance sheet. Revenue stayed about the same ($1.55 billion in 1996), primarily because the additional revenue from fare increases was offset by a decline in riders (from 20.7 million passengers in 1995 to 19.7 million in 1996). Amtrak's expenses also stayed about the same ($2.3 billion), primarily because savings from service reductions were offset by rising labor and equipment maintenance costs. As a result, Amtrak continued to lose money ($708 million in 1996).

Amtrak's political environment experienced a reversal of roles during the mid-1990s. Throughout the 1980s, the Democratic Congress opposed Republican presidents' efforts to reduce or eliminate Amtrak's funding. Now, the Republican Congress, led by Senator John McCain (R-AZ), chair of the Senate Commerce, Science, and Transportation Committee, and Senator Kay Bailey Hutchison (R-TX), chair of the Senate Commerce Committee's Surface Transportation and Merchant Marine Subcommittee, wanted to reduce Amtrak's funding, while the Democratic president wanted its funding increased and, as mentioned in the previous chapter, to make Amtrak eligible for highway and mass transit funding. The president's position was bolstered by polls indicating that the American public overwhelmingly supported funding Amtrak. For example, an October 27, 1997, national telephone poll indicated that 69 percent of Americans agreed that the national government should continue to fund Amtrak to ensure that the United States has a national train service, compared to 26 percent who agreed that the national government should stop funding Amtrak, even if that meant that train service could go out of business if it did not operate profitably on its own (1 percent said neither, and 4 percent said no opinion).[32] But, even President Clinton's patience concerning Amtrak's lack of progress toward operational self-sufficiency was wearing thin. He let it be known that his administration was ready to consider fundamental reform in the way that Amtrak operated. The result was the *Amtrak Reform and Accountability Act of 1997*. It provided Amtrak $2.9 billion for operating subsidies and $2.3 billion for capital expenditures through 2002. It also prohibited Amtrak from using national funds for operating expenses after 2002, except for expenses associated with Amtrak's liability for railroad retirement taxes that exceed the amount needed for employees' benefits (called excess contributions). To help Amtrak meet the mandate, the act included several cost-cutting provisions that Amtrak's management requested but had been denied for years. The statutory prohibition on contracting out services (other than for food and beverages) was phased out over two years and made a negotiable item in its collective bargaining agreements with its 13 unions. The statutory requirement providing laid off employees or those required to move more than 30 miles from their home with up to six years of severance pay was also eliminated and made a negotiable item with its unions. Also, Amtrak's liability exposure was limited to $200 million per accident. This reduced Amtrak's projected insurance expenses. Importantly, Amtrak's mandate to operate the basic system of routes inherited from private railroads in 1971 was eliminated. Amtrak now has the authority to eliminate nonprofitable routes.

The *Amtrak Reform and Accountability Act of 1997* replaced Amtrak's Board of Directors with the Amtrak Reform Board. Its job was to ensure that Amtrak was "operationally self-sufficient" by December 2, 2002. In addition, a special independent body, the Amtrak Reform Council, was created to monitor Amtrak's progress toward meeting the operationally self-sufficient mandate. If, at any time after December 2, 1999, the Reform Council determined that Amtrak was not going to meet the operationally self-sufficient mandate by December 2, 2002, it was required to inform Congress and submit an action plan for meeting the mandate. In that circumstance, Amtrak had to submit a plan for its own liquidation. If Congress did not approve a restructuring plan within 90 days after receiving one from the Reform Council, the Senate was required to introduce and act on a resolution to liquidate Amtrak.

Congress also approved the *Taxpayer Relief Act of 1997*. It provided Amtrak nearly $2.2 billion for capital improvements deemed necessary to eliminate the need for further operating subsidies. About two-thirds of these funds were used for capital improvements, including nearly $400 million for Amtrak's high-speed rail program in the Northeast Corridor. The remainder was used to replace or upgrade older equipment (reducing maintenance costs) and install automating functions (reducing labor costs).[33]

The infusion of national government assistance reduced Amtrak's red ink to $304 million in 1998, but it then incurred deficits of $694 million in 1999 and $765 million in 2000. Amtrak's cash flow situation deteriorated to the point that it was forced to borrow money on several occasions to meet its payroll. Moreover, in 1999 Amtrak announced that its capital needs in the Northeast Corridor had increased to approximately $12 billion.

To meet those capital needs, Senator Frank Lautenberg (D-NJ) renewed Amtrak's previous request for authority to issue tax-free bonds. He introduced legislation in 2000 to allow Amtrak to issue $10 billion in tax-free bonds over a 10-year period. The funds would be used to make improvements necessary to provide high-speed train service, primarily in the Northeast Corridor. The proposal's advocates noted that this was less than the $13.6 billion projected cost of Boston's

Central Artery Tunnel Project, know as the "Big Dig." They argued that it did not make sense for Congress to appropriate billions of dollars for a single highway project whose benefits fall largely within a single state while, simultaneously, refusing to provide Amtrak authority to borrow funds that had a high probability of being repaid and benefits many states. Nevertheless, Lautenberg's bill was never reported out of committee. In 2001, a similar 10-year, $12 billion railroad bond bill was introduced in the Senate by Senator Joseph Biden (D-DE), but Senator McCain used his authority as chair of the Senate Commerce Committee to prevent the committee from voting on it.

Although Amtrak continued to lose money, it insisted that it could meet the operationally self-sufficient mandate by December 2, 2002. In 1999, Amtrak's Board of Directors announced a series of initiatives to increase Amtrak's revenue. The most significant was the introduction of Amtrak's Acela high-speed rail service between Boston and Washington, D.C. The first new, high-speed trains began limited service on January 31, 2000. They reduced travel time between Boston and New York City from four and one-half hours to four hours. They also provided passengers a number of amenities, such as redesigned café cars and bathrooms, conference tables, larger overhead bins, more comfortable seats, and readily available electrical outlets and audio controls. Amtrak claimed that Acela would attract more passengers, especially as the continued improvements in the Northeast Corridor reduced travel times, making rail travel more competitive with commuter airline services. It was hoped that these improvements would enable Acela to meet the congressional mandate of offering service between Boston and New York City in less than 3 hours and 40 minutes by 2002. Amtrak estimated that Acela would generate at least $400 million in additional revenue for the company by 2002.[34] Unfortunately, the delivery of Acela equipment was delayed, causing the timetable for its planned expansion in the Northeast Corridor to be pushed back. Regular Acela service did not begin until the fall of 2000, and the number of Acela trains in operation in 2001 was below initial expectations. The delay raised serious concerns about Amtrak's ability to meet the operationally self-sufficient mandate by December 2, 2002. Also, the Amtrak Reform Council questioned Amtrak's accounting methods in determining the threshold for meeting the operationally self-sufficient mandate. Amtrak argued that the threshold should exclude funding for several expenses, including depreciation, that were estimated to total $567 million in FY 2002. Amtrak asserted that these expenses have been, and continue to be, funded by capital grant funds, even though they are included as operating expenses in Amtrak's financial statements. The American Public Transportation Association supported Amtrak's position, arguing that public transit agencies rarely use operating revenue to purchase equipment. Amtrak's Reform Council disagreed. It reported to Congress that treating depreciation as a capital expense was inappropriate.[35] The widening rift between the Reform Council and Amtrak's management was further demonstrated by the Reform Council's recommendation on March 20, 2001, that Amtrak divest itself of its rail and rail station maintenance functions and concentrate on providing passenger rail service. The Reform

Council also recommended that Congress privatize the divested services instead of creating another quasi-governmental agency to oversee them.

As debates over accounting methods and privatization proposals continued, Amtrak's President, George Warrington, announced on July 6, 2000, the implementation of Amtrak's Satisfaction Guarantee program. Designed to improve customer loyalty and ridership, it allows any passenger who believes that he or she did not receive a safe, comfortable, and enjoyable trip to claim a voucher good for future Amtrak travel of equal cost by calling a toll-free number and explaining the difficulty. Warrington also announced the implementation of an employee bonus program to encourage Amtrak's employees to treat passengers well. The program offered employees a monthly bonus equal to the average fare (about $50) if at least 99.9 percent of riders that month did not request a service guarantee voucher.

SEPTEMBER 11, 2001, AND THE PUSH FOR PRIVATIZATION

Amtrak's ridership and ticket revenue received a short-term boost following the tragic events of September 11, 2001, when hijackers crashed two airliners into the World Trade Center in New York City, and another into the Pentagon. A fourth airliner, target unknown, crashed into a field in Shanksville Township, Pennsylvania, east of Pittsburgh, following an attempt by several passengers to regain control of the aircraft from the terrorists. Immediately following these events, millions of Americans, concerned about air safety, altered their travel plans. Many postponed trips or canceled them. Others used Amtrak and intercity bus services to reach their destinations. This was especially true in the Northeast Corridor due to the prolonged closure of Reagan National Airport in Washington, D.C. During the last two weeks of September 2001, nearly 1 million passengers used Amtrak, 10 percent higher than the number recorded for that same time period the previous year. Amtrak's ridership moderated in October, and by mid-November passenger levels had returned to the levels experienced prior to September 11. Nevertheless, Amtrak ridership for 2001 was the highest in its history, and its supporters hailed Amtrak's performance during the crisis. They argued that the events of September 11, 2001, proved that the national government's funding of Amtrak was a worthwhile investment that not only improved national mobility during times of peace but also ensured the nation's mobility during times of war. Amtrak's critics countered that intercity bus ridership also surged to record highs following the events of September 11. They argued that an investment in intercity bus service would provide even more mobility than Amtrak during a time of crisis and that the investment required was only a fraction of Amtrak's cost.

The tragic events of September 11, 2001, contributed to a record increase in Amtrak ticket revenue, but those events did not have a lasting effect on Amtrak's financial situation. Although both the number of passenger trips and ticket revenue increased to record levels during 2001, Amtrak's expenses continued to escalate, causing a severe cash-flow problem. During the last quarter of 2001, Amtrak was forced to mortgage a portion of New York City's Penn Station for $300 million to avoid running out of cash, and, according to figures released by the inspector general of the U.S. Department of Transportation, Amtrak recorded a deficit of $1.1 billion in FY 2001, the largest in its history (this resulted in a loss of $585 million after the national government's $521 million annual operating subsidy was factored in). Although Amtrak's accounting practices suggested a somewhat smaller deficit in 2001 (see Table 4.1), Amtrak's president, George Warrington, admitted that Amtrak's fiscal situation was precarious. On October 31, 2001, he informed Congress that Amtrak could not meet the operationally self-sufficient mandate. As he put it: "With the economy contracting and public expectations about security and safety rising, the self-sufficiency deadline will force us to choose very soon between two evils. Those are: cutting back on service to save money, or keeping service with better security, only to lose more money and risk liquidation."[36]

After carefully examining Amtrak's financial situation, Amtrak's Reform Council voted 6–5 on November 9, 2001, to formally report to Congress that Amtrak was incapable of meeting the December 2, 2002, deadline for achieving operational self-sufficiency. The vote's closeness resulted from a disagreement among the Amtrak Reform Council's members concerning the report's timing, not the finding relating to Amtrak's inability to meet the deadline. Under the law, the vote required Amtrak's Reform Council to devise a restructuring plan for Amtrak within 90 days and Amtrak to prepare a plan for its own liquidation.

Amtrak's Reform Council submitted its restructuring plan to Congress on February 7, 2002. Hailed by congressional Republicans and panned by congressional Democrats, the Reform Council's plan emphasized the introduction of competitive bidding processes and privatization to reduce Amtrak's expenses and improve service quality and customer satisfaction. Specifically, it recommended that Amtrak be divided into three units, each with a separate Board of Directors and accounting system. The first unit would administer and oversee freight railroad rights-of-way, provide train operator's insurance, divest non-Northeast Corridor assets, such as train stations, and preserve the national reservations system and joint ticketing operation. The second unit would provide train service, including the mail and express business, passenger and commuter operations, and equipment and repair shops. After a 2–5-year transition period designed to allow Amtrak time to become more efficient and competitive, all train services would be opened to a competitive bidding process, which would allow the private sector and individual states as well as groups of states to compete with Amtrak for the right to operate trains on specific routes and to provide specific services, such as railcar repair and maintenance. The third unit would be responsible for infrastructure. Noting that Amtrak estimated in 2001 that it needed $73.6 billion over the next 20 years for capital costs (including $28 billion for improvements to the Northeast Corridor), the Amtrak Reform Council recommended that, after a suitable transition period, maintenance on the Northeast Corridor be opened to competitive bidding. Also, if additional operating subsides were not forthcoming, it recommended that all long-distance trains (over 400 miles) be eliminated. The Amtrak Reform Council noted that long-distance trains carry only 18 percent of Amtrak's riders but are responsible for 75 percent of Amtrak's operating loses. It estimated that the elimination of long-distance passenger train service would save at least $270 million annually.[37]

Anticipating the Amtrak Reform Council's push for privatization and in recognition of its continuing cash-flow problem, Amtrak's president, George Warrington, announced on February 1, 2002, that Amtrak would reduce annual expenses by $285 million by laying off 1,000 of its 24,600 employees; reduce or freeze travel, marketing, advertising, and other assorted office-related expenditures; and defer $175 million in planned capital improvements. He also requested that annual funding be increased to $1.2 billion, instead of allowing it to drop from $521 million to zero in FY 2003, as mandated by the *Amtrak Reform and Accountability Act of 1997*. Most of the appropriation request ($840 million) was to provide for basic and mandatory capital investments, $200 million to subsidize unprofitable long-distance service, and $160 million for excess railroad retirement taxes. He also cautioned Congress that Amtrak needed another $5.8 billion for capital improvements necessary to improve service, promote safety, and reduce trip times. If Congress failed to appropriate the $1.2 billion, Amtrak would be forced to eliminate 18 unprofitable long-distance routes at the opening of the new fiscal year on October 1, 2002.[38]

Congressional Republicans generally viewed Amtrak's announcement that it was not going to meet the operating self-sufficiency mandate as proof that it was time to give privatization a chance. On February 15, 2002, Senator McCain was the first member of Congress to introduce legislation to privatize Amtrak. However, Senator McCain was no longer chair of the Senate Commerce, Science, and Transportation Committee. The Republican Party had lost control of the Senate to the Democratic Party in 2001. The Commerce Committee's new chair, Senator Ernest Hollings (D-SC) announced that he opposed the Amtrak Reform Council's privatization plan because it was unfair to criticize Amtrak for operating a deficit when it had to compete with the federal highway system and its over $30 billion in national subsidies and with air service and its $13 billion in national subsidies. Instead of breaking Amtrak into three parts and contracting out much of its services to the private sector or to states, he advocated increasing Amtrak's funding to meet its operating expenses and providing Amtrak with bonding authority to deal with its capital asset needs.[39]

Amtrak's financial problems received national media attention when Amtrak's new president, David L. Gunn, announced in June 2002 that Amtrak did not have enough cash to finish the fiscal year. A systemwide shutdown of all Amtrak services nationwide, which was to commence on July 1, 2002, was averted following the Department of Transportation's decision to provide Amtrak with a $100 million loan. Although Amtrak's immediate funding crisis was resolved, Gunn noted that Amtrak was going to lose a record $1.1 billion in FY 2002 and needed a substantial increase in funding to continue operating in the future.

Congressional deliberations on Amtrak's budget were still in progress when this volume went to press. Congress is unlikely to liquidate Amtrak. However, the Amtrak Reform Council's push for privatization, the Bush administration's interest in privatizing at least some nonprofitable routes, Amtrak's failure to meet the operationally self-sufficient mandate, and new projections that place Amtrak's capital needs at over $70 billion over the next 20 years suggest that even if the operationally self-sufficient mandate is lifted and additional funding is provided, Amtrak's financial difficulties will continue to dominate the policy-making process for many years to come.

CONCLUSION

For nearly 30 years Amtrak's management was in a no-win situation. For most of its existence, Amtrak was evaluated by Congress and the White House as if it were a business, yet Amtrak's management was not provided the authority to act as a business. Congressional mandates concerning route structure, procurement procedures, labor relations, and a host of other issues prevented Amtrak's management from running Amtrak like a business. In 1997, Representative Bud Shuster characterized Amtrak's situation well:

Amtrak's current condition is due in part to chronic federal interference by statute. Congress has specified almost every aspect of Amtrak's finances: where it should operate, when it is allowed to reduce or eliminate service, who its directors are, what kind of stock it may issue, restrictions on its borrowing and capital formation, what benefits it must pay employees, when it can contract with private-sector railroads and businesses, who must audit its books, which law governs all of its contracts, and even who can get reduced-fare transportation on Amtrak trains.[40]

Although Congress subsequently repealed most of Amtrak's operational mandates, Amtrak's management is not entirely free to behave in a businesslike manner. Amtrak is still statutorily required to enter into collective bargaining agreements with its 13 unions, and, importantly, even if it was to become operationally self-sufficient, it depends on government subsidies for capital expenses. Because congressional power is geographically based, especially in the Senate, where each state has two senators, Amtrak's funding is predicated on the establishment of a national passenger rail system. Although a regional system, focusing on the nation's most highly populated corridors (e.g., the Northeast Corridor and southern California), would create the highest probability of being profitable, limiting itself to regional service would likely cause it to lose congressional support needed for the continuation of capital subsidies. As a result, Amtrak is in the difficult position of having to balance the need to generate political support by providing service to as many congressional districts and states as possible with the necessity of shedding services that are least likely to generate enough revenue to cover costs.

The congressional debate over Amtrak's future highlights culture's influence on expectations in the political process. In most instances, Europeans take for granted passenger rail's role as an integral part of their national transportation system. As Table 4.4 demonstrates, on a per capita basis, the United States' financial support for passenger rail service ranks among the lowest in the industrialized world. Europeans are not comfortable with the American notion of judging passenger rail's success or failure primarily on the basis of its making or losing money. They are also puzzled by America's infatuation with the automobile and the political necessity of keeping national gasoline taxes and overall prices for gasoline relatively low. For example, when gasoline prices in the United States spiked to over $1.70 a gallon for regular, unleaded gasoline in March 2000, Congress seriously debated temporarily eliminating the 4.3 cent per gallon increase in the national government's excise taxes on gasoline, diesel, and aviation fuel that was approved in 1993. The stated objective was to provide relief to consumers.[41] Although some dismissed the debate as a political maneuver by congressional Republicans to bring attention to their party's opposition to taxes, such a debate would be unthinkable in many European countries, where, at that time, gasoline sold for nearly $5 a gallon.

Traffic congestion in Europe represents an economic loss equivalent to about 2 percent of the European Union's annual gross domestic product. The traditional response to this economic loss, especially in the United States, would be to construct new or expand existing highways and bridges to meet demand. However, in Europe, there is an emerging consensus of opinion that increasing the supply of roads and bridges only leads to increased travel demand. The growing emphasis there is on reducing the need to travel and promoting alternative modes of travel, such as the use of bicycles, mass transit, and passenger rail. Among the alternatives given serious consideration there and routinely dismissed in the United States is placing physical, psychological, or financial controls on access to city centers. The use of physical measures, such as gated entrances, to control traffic access, and the use of informational campaigns to encourage people to use alternative modes of transportation to reduce traffic congestion are commonplace across Europe. There is also a growing movement (especially in Norway) to engage in a process called road charging, by which traffic congestion is reduced by imposing charges (gasoline taxes, parking fees, tolls, etc.) to discourage automobile use. The pricing strategy can be used to deter all automotive use (e.g., through higher fuel taxes) or can be targeted to specific problem areas or during specific peak travel times (e.g., through toll fees that vary during the day).[42]

The European experience is often touted by those advocating government subsidies for Amtrak. However, the American public's "love affair" with the automobile and the highway lobby's political influence are powerful deterrents to enacting policies that reduce demand for road usage. That is not to say that the United States has not moved in this direction at all. For example, HOV (high-occupancy vehicle) lanes, where access to some highway lanes are restricted at certain hours to those with at least two or three passengers, are eligible for national funding. But American culture and politics are different from those in Europe. What is seen as an appropriate response to traffic congestion in Europe is less readily acceptable and less politically possible in the United States.

Table 4.4
National Financial Assistance for Mainline Passenger Rail Service, Selected Countries, 1995 (U.S. dollars)

Country	Per Capita
Luxembourg	$228.65
Austria	226.35
Switzerland	215.24
Belgium	166.42
Sweden	157.33
France	77.17
Denmark	62.07
Britain	58.16
Italy	46.63
Ireland	40.72
Spain	33.83
Norway	23.99
Czech Republic	15.34
Finland	9.66
Slovakia	9.21
Portugal	8.61
Poland	7.57
Canada	6.72
Japan	6.03
South Africa	5.61
Greece	4.86
Estonia	4.45
United States	**3.97**
Tunisia	3.76
Hungary	1.65
Saudi Arabia	1.20
Bulgaria	.11

Source: National Association of Railroad Passengers, "World Rail Funding," May 7, 1999. Available on-line at: http://www.narprail.org/pc.htm.

NOTES

1. Frank N. Wilner, *The Amtrak Story* (Omaha, NB: Simmons-Boardman Books, Inc., 1994), pp. 33–35; and David C. Nice, *Amtrak: The History and Politics of a National Railroad* (Boulder, CO: Lynne Rienner Publishers, Inc, 1998), pp. 4, 5.

2. "The Unloved Passenger," *Time* (January 5, 1970): 48.

3. David C. Nice, *Amtrak*, pp. 3–5, 100, 101.

4. Frank N. Wilner, *The Amtrak Story*, pp. 41, 42.

5. Ibid., pp. 42, 43.

6. Ibid., pp. 43, 44.

7. George W. Hilton, *Amtrak: The National Railroad Passenger Corporation* (Washington, DC: American Enterprise Institute, 1980), pp. 15–16.

8. "Now the Railpax Row Will Begin," *Business Week* (November 28, 1970): 38; cited in Frank N. Wilner, *The Amtrak Story*, p. 46.

9. Roger Lewis, President of Amtrak, "Statement before the Subcommittee on Surface Transportation, U.S. Senate Committee on Commerce," in *Administration's Request for Additional Funding for Amtrak*. Hearings before the Subcommittee on Surface Transportation, U.S. Senate Committee on Commerce, 92nd Congress, First Session (Washington, DC: U.S. Government Printing Office, October 26, 1971), p. 36; Anthony Haswell, Chairman of the National Association of Railroad Passengers, "Statement before the Subcommittee on Surface Transportation, U.S. Senate Committee on Commerce," in *Amtrak Oversight and Authorization*. Hearings before the Subcommittee on Surface Transportation, U.S. Senate Committee on Commerce, 93rd Congress, First Session (Washington, DC: U.S. Government Printing Office, May 16, 1973), p. 38; and James C. Miller, "An Economic Policy Analysis of the Amtrak Program," in *Perspectives on Federal Transportation Policy*, ed. James C. Miller, III (Washington, DC: American Enterprise Institute, 1975), p. 158. Reprinted in *Criteria and Procedures for Making Route and Service Decisions by Amtrak*. Hearings before the Subcommittee on Surface Transportation, U.S. Senate Committee on Commerce, 94th Congress, Second Session (Washington, DC: U.S. Government Printing Office, March 3, 1976), pp. 144–162.

10. George W. Hilton, *Amtrak*, pp. 16–17; and Frank N. Wilner, *The Amtrak Story*, pp. 62–64.

11. George W. Hilton, *Amtrak*, pp. 18–20.

12. Ibid., p. 20.

13. Roger Lewis, "Statement before the Subcommittee on Surface Transportation," pp. 38–40.

14. Roger Lewis, "Letter to Honorable Vance Hartke, Chairman, Surface Transportation Subcommittee, U.S. Senate Committee on Commerce, dated November 23, 1971," in *Administration's Request for Additional Funding for Amtrak*. Hearings before the Subcommittee on Surface Transportation, U.S. Senate Committee on Commerce, 92nd Congress, First Session (Washington, DC: U.S. Government Printing Office, October 26, 1971), p. 111; and Stephen Ailes, President, Association of American Railroads, "Statement before the Subcommittee on Surface Transportation, U.S. Senate Committee on Commerce," in *Amtrak Oversight and Authorization*. Hearings before the Subcommittee on Surface Transportation, U.S. Senate Committee on Commerce, 93rd Congress, First Session (Washington, DC: U.S. Government Printing Office, May 16, 1973), pp. 124–127.

15. George N. Stafford, Chairman, Interstate Commerce Commission, "Letter to Honorable Vance Hartke, Chairman, Surface Transportation Subcommittee, U.S. Senate Committee on Commerce, dated March 17, 1976," in *Criteria and Procedures for Making Route and Service Decisions by Amtrak: Additional Articles, Letters, and Statements*. Hearings before the Subcommittee on Surface Transportation, U.S. Senate Committee on Commerce, 94th

Congress, Second Session (Washington, DC: U.S. Government Printing Office, March 3, 1976), pp. 113–116.

16. Frank N. Wilner, *The Amtrak Story*, pp.17, 18.

17. Vance Hartke, Chair, Surface Transportation Subcommittee, U.S. Senate Committee on Commerce, "Statement before the Subcommittee on Surface Transportation, U.S. Senate Committee on Commerce," in *Criteria and Procedures for Making Route and Service Decisions by Amtrak*. Hearings before the Subcommittee on Surface Transportation, U.S. Senate Committee on Commerce, 94th Congress, Second Session (Washington, DC: U.S. Government Printing Office, March 3, 1976), pp. 27, 28.

18. George W. Hilton, *Amtrak*, pp. 21–30.

19. Stephen Ailes, President of the Association of American Railroads, "Statement before the Subcommittee on Transportation and Commerce, U.S. House Committee on Interstate and Foreign Commerce," in *Railroad Revitalization*. Hearings before the Subcommittee on Transportation and Commerce, U.S. House Committee on Interstate and Foreign Commerce, 94th Congress, First Session (Washington, DC: U.S. Government Printing Office, July 23, 1975), pp. 568, 569.

20. Representative Wyche Fowler, Democratic Representative from Georgia, "Statement before the Subcommittee on Transportation and Commerce, U.S. House Committee on Interstate and Foreign Commerce," in *Amtrak Fiscal Year 1980 Authorization and Amtrak Route Restructuring*. Hearings before the Subcommittee on Transportation and Commerce, U.S. House Committee on Interstate and Foreign Commerce, 96th Congress, First Session (Washington, DC: U.S. Government Printing Office, April 3, 1979), p. 106.

21. Richard Snelling, Governor of Vermont, and Rene Levesque, Premier, Province of Quebec, Canada, "Letter to James L. Florio, Chair, Subcommittee on Transportation and Commerce, U.S. House Committee on Interstate and Foreign Commerce," in *Amtrak Fiscal Year 1980 Authorization and Amtrak Route Restructuring*. Hearings before the Subcommittee on Transportation and Commerce, U.S. House Committee on Interstate and Foreign Commerce, 96th Congress, First Session (Washington, DC: U.S. Government Printing Office, April 3, 1979), p. 20.

22. George W. Hilton, *Amtrak*, pp. 29–31; and David P. Baron, "Distributive Politics and the Persistence of Amtrak," *Journal of Politics* 52 (August 1990): 883–913.

23. "Amtrak Authorization," *Congressional Quarterly Almanac, 1983* (Washington, DC: Congressional Quarterly, Inc., 1983), p. 561.

24. U.S. General Accounting Office, *Amtrak's Northeast Corridor* (Washington, DC: U.S. Government Printing Service, April 1995), pp. 22–29; and David C. Nice, "Financial Performance of the Amtrak System," *Public Administration Review* 51:2 (March/April 1991): 138–144.

25. Seth Payne, "Why Amtrak Won't Stop to Let the Taxpayer Off," *Business Week* (January 30, 1989): 90; Eloise Salholz, "Bush Proposes to Eliminate Amtrak," *Newsweek* 113 (January 16, 1989): 26, 27; Howard Gleckman, "Reagan's Budget Won't Wash—But Can Congress Do Better?" *Business Week* (January 19, 1987): 32; Monroe W. Karmin, "Hanging a 'For Sale' Sign on Government," *U.S. News and World Report* 100 (January 13, 1986): 18, 19; Susan Dentzer, "Amtrak's Struggle to Stay on Track," *Newsweek* 105 (June 3, 1985): 50; Tom Morganthau, "A New War on Spending," *Newsweek* 104 (December 17, 1984): 45, 46; and Jean Vivier, "Urban Transport Pricing," *Public Transport International* (May 1999): 28–35.

26. Jean Love, Wendell Cox, and Stephen Moore, "Amtrak at Twenty-Five: End of the Line for Taxpayer Subsidies," Cato Policy Analysis No. 266 (Washington, DC: The Cato Institute, December 19, 1996); and David C. Nice, "Financial Performance of the Amtrak System," pp. 143, 144.

27. "Claytor Insists Amtrak Will Not Need Operating Subsidies by 2000," *Traffic World* (July 9, 1990): 223; "How Is Amtrak in 1990? Busy," *Sunset* (February 1990): 68, 69; and Robert Roberts, "New Direction for Amtrak," *Railway Age* (June 1991): 59, 60.

28. Kevin G. Hall, "Lawmaker Wants Amtrak Trust Fund to Be Paid for with Fuel-Tax Dollars," *Traffic World* (March 2, 1992): 13; and "Two-Year Reauthorization for Amtrak Clears," *Congressional Quarterly Almanac 1992* (Washington, DC: Congressional Quarterly Inc., 1993), 201.

29. U.S. General Accounting Office, *Intercity Passenger Rail: Financial and Operating Conditions Threaten Amtrak's Long-Term Viability* (Washington, DC: U.S. Government Printing Office, February 1995), pp. 6–10; and U.S. General Accounting Office, *Amtrak's Northeast Corridor: Information on the Status and Cost of Needed Improvements* (Washington, DC: U.S. Government Printing Office, April 1995).

30. U.S. General Accounting Office, *Intercity Passenger Rail: Financial and Operating Conditions Threaten Amtrak's Long-Term Viability*, p. 12.

31. U.S. General Accounting Office, *Intercity Passenger Rail: Amtrak's Financial Crisis Threatens Continued Viability* (Washington, DC: U.S. Government Printing Office, April 1997), pp. 8–10.

32. "Public Strongly Supports Continuing Government Subsidies for Amtrak," *The Gallup Poll*, October 27, 1997. Available on-line at: http://trainweb.com/crocon/poll.html.

33. U.S. General Accounting Office, *Intercity Passenger Rail: Amtrak Needs to Improve Its Accountability for Taxpayer Relief Act Funds* (Washington, DC: U.S. Department of Transportation, February 29, 2000), p. 4.

34. U.S. General Accounting Office, *Intercity Passenger Rail: Amtrak Faces Challenges in Improving Its Financial Condition* (Washington, DC: U.S. Government Printing Office, October 28, 1999), pp. 1–7.

35. William Miller, President, American Public Transportation Association, "Statement before the Committee on Commerce, Science, and Transportation's Subcommittee on Surface Transportation and Merchant Marine" (Washington, DC, February 23, 2000). Available on-line at: http://www.amtrakreformcouncil.gov/testimony.html; and Gilbert E. Carmichael, Chairman, Amtrak Reform Council, "Statement before the Committee on Commerce, Science, and Transportation's Subcommittee on Surface Transportation and Merchant Marine" (Washington, DC, February 23, 2000). Available on-line at: http://www.amtrakreformcouncil.gov/testimony.html.

36. Melissa B. Robinson, "Lawmakers Debate Amtrak's Future," Associated Press Release (November 1, 2001).

37. Amtrak Reform Council, *An Action Plan for the Restructuring and Rationalization of the National Intercity Rail Passenger System* (Washington, DC: Amtrak Reform Council, February 7, 2002). Available on-line at: http://www.amtrakreformcouncil.gov/finalreport.html.

38. National Railroad Passenger Corporation, "Amtrak Announces $285 million in Cuts and Federal Appropriations Request of $1.2 billion," press release (Washington, DC: National Railroad Passenger Corporation, February 1, 2002).

39. Reuters News Service, "Key Senator Opposed to Amtrak Breakup Plan," press release (February 11, 2002); Laurence Arnold, "House Railroad Panel Debates Proposal to Break Up Amtrak," *The Charleston Gazette*, February 15, 2002, p. 12A; and Associated Press, "Bill Would Abolish Amtrak," *The Charleston Gazette*, February 16, 2002, p. 6A.

40. Bud Shuster, "Chairman Shuster, Chairwoman Molinari Applaud Committee Approval of Amtrak Reform Bill," press release (Washington, DC: U.S. House Committee on Transportation and Infrastructure, July 30, 1997).

41. Bud Shuster, James L. Oberstar, Thomas Petri and Nick J. Rahall, II, "The Impact of Reducing the Federal Fuel Tax on Transportation Programs." Dear Colleague Letter (Washington, DC: U.S. House Committee on Transportation and Infrastructure, March 4, 2000).

42. The European Local Transport Information Service, "Demand Management and Pricing." (Brussels, Belgium, viewed on-line on May 1, 2000). Available on-line at: http://www.eltis.org/en/index.htm; and Commission of the European Communities, "White Paper on Fair Payment for Infrastructure Use: A Phased Approach to a Common Transport Infrastructure Charging Framework in the EU" (Brussels, Belgium, July 22, 1998). Available on-line at: ftp://ftp.ttr-ltd.com/cupid/white_paper.pdf.

5

THE CIVILIAN
AIR TRANSPORTATION SYSTEM

On the morning of September 11, 2001, America and its civilian air transportation system were changed forever as hijackers crashed two airliners into the World Trade Center in New York City and another into the Pentagon. A fourth hijacked plane crashed in Shanksville Township, Pennsylvania, east of Pittsburgh, following an attempt by passengers to regain control of the airplane from the terrorists. Thousands of lives and America's sense of security were lost forever. As the horrific events of that fateful morning unfolded, the U.S. Federal Aviation Administration (FAA) ordered all airports in the United States closed and all airborne civilian aircraft to land immediately at the closest airfield. For the first time in American aviation history, the skies over America were empty, save for military fighter jets patrolling the New York and Washington D.C. skylines.

At the time of this great national tragedy, air traffic congestion was the number one issue facing the civilian air transportation system in the United States. Congressional debate focused on how to address the public's seemingly insatiable demand for additional flights. Airline delays exceeding 15 minutes hit a record high of 450,289 in 2000, and several airlines aired television commercials nationwide apologizing to the traveling public, asking for their patience. Several analysts warned that the United States was vulnerable to acts of air terrorism, particularly the placing of bombs in aircraft cargo bays. They argued that airport security measures were lax and needed improvement. But, it had been nearly a decade since an airliner was hijacked in the United States, and most policymakers believed that the introduction of X-ray machines for carry-on luggage, magnetometers for passengers, canine bomb detection teams, and other measures, such as the matching of baggage with passengers, were sufficient deterrents to air terrorism. They were wrong.

The civilian airline industry was shaken by the tragic events of September 11, 2001. It was already experiencing economic difficulties. In the months immediately preceding the attacks, the national economy had weakened, causing tourist and business travel, which accounts for nearly three-quarters of airline revenue, to decline. Several smaller carriers sought bankruptcy protection and, systemwide, the airline industry, which generated a $7 billion profit in 2000, was on pace to lose over $2 billion in 2001. The mandated two-day shutdown of the nation's airspace following the terrorist attacks cost airlines hundreds of millions of dollars in lost revenue. When the airports reopened, the airlines experienced more economic hardship as commercial airplanes were less than half full. Many Americans avoided flying, worried that another round of hijacks might occur. At least for the short term, the most important issue facing the civilian airline industry was no longer air traffic congestion but economic survival. Within days of the attack, the nation's major airlines announced massive employee layoffs and reduced flight schedules by a third. More than 100,000 airline employees were laid off, with American Airlines and United Airlines laying off 20,000 employees each. In addition, anticipating that orders for new airplanes would fall, Boeing laid off 30,000 of its 93,000 commercial airline workers. The airline industry's economic troubles (they ended up losing $4.3 billion in 2001), the negative economic consequences for related industries, the World Trade Center's destruction, and a dramatic drop in consumer confidence sent the stock market plummeting.

Anticipating the possibility of an economic panic, the American stock exchange ceased trading on September 11, 2001, as news of the terrorists' attacks spread across the globe. When the stock market reopened on September 17, 2001, the Dow Jones Industrial average plunged 684 points, its largest single-day loss in American history, and lost another 600 points over the next four days. To calm investors' nerves, President George W. Bush (R, 2001–) announced that the national government would provide $40 billion in emergency spending for New York City and $15 billion for the airline industry, $5 billion in direct relief and $10 billion in loan guarantees.

The $15 billion bailout of the civilian air transportation industry in 2001 reflects its central role in the American economy. It is a large system that includes 19,281 airports, 21 air route traffic control centers, 195 terminal radar approach control facilities, 496 airport traffic control towers, 75 flight service stations, 355 air surveillance radar facilities, 712 remote center air–ground facilities, 1,733 remote communications outlets, and 4,753 air navigation facilities. These facilities support 91 civilian air carriers, 217,500 active civilian aircraft, and 616,342 certified pilots. In 2001, even in the aftermath of the events of September 11, 2001, there were over 200,000 landings and takeoffs at civilian airports each day, and nearly 700 million people paid to board a commercial airplane in the United States (see Table 5.1). In addition, the civilian aviation industry employs more than 1.1 million people directly and another 9 million people in related industries. The industry also moves more than 14 billion ton-miles of freight shipments each year.

On September 11, 2001, air security surpassed air traffic congestion as the most important issue facing the civilian air transportation system. In the months immediately following September 11, no one in the industry worried about air traffic

Table 5.1

The Civilian Air Transportation System, Selected Years, 1930–2001

Year	Airports	Aircraft (active)	Certified Pilots	Passengers (millions)	Fatalities
2001	19,281	217,500	616,342	681.3	536
2000	18,770	219,400	625,581	698.7	582
1995	18,224	195,500	639,000	547.8	727
1990	17,490	218,900	703,000	465.5	762
1985	16,318	215,400	710,000	382.0	945
1980	15,161	214,800	827,000	302.8	1,239
1975	13,770	196,300	728,000	205.0	1,252
1970	11,261	134,500	733,000	169.9	1,310
1965	9,547	97,741	480,000	102.9	1,029
1960	6,881	78,760	348,000	62.2	787
1955	6,839	60,432	643,201	45.0	158
1950	6,403	60,921	525,000	19.1	144
1945	4,026	37,789	296,895	7.1	115
1940	2,331	17,128	69,829	3.2	35
1938	2,374	11,159	22,983	1.4	32
1934	1,900	6,339	13,949	.6	NA
1930	1,344	7,354	15,280	.4	NA

Sources: U.S. Department of Transportation, Federal Aviation Administration, *Administrator's Handbook* (Washington, DC: U.S. Government Printing Office, February, 2002); U.S. Department of Transportation, The Office of Airline Traffic Data, *Historical Air Traffic Data, 1981–2000* (Washington, DC: U.S. Government Printing Office, 2000); U.S. Department of Transportation, The Office of Airline Traffic Data, *Historical Air Traffic Data, 1954–1980* (Washington, DC: U.S. Government Printing Office, 2000); and U.S. Bureau of the Census, *Statistical Abstract of the United States* (Washington, DC: U.S. Government Printing Office, various years).

congestion. They were busy trying to convince the American public that it was safe to resume flying. After dropping almost in half immediately following the events of September 11, air passenger traffic increased slowly, week by week, as the initial shock of those horrific events and the massive media attention provided to the attacks and the cleanup of New York City began to lessen. Some analysts predicted that air passenger traffic would be back to nearly normal levels by Thanksgiving, but on November 12, 2001, American Airlines' flight 587 crashed shortly after takeoff from New York's Kennedy International Airport. All 260 people onboard and 9 people on the ground were killed. Although the crash was not terrorist-related, it rekindled the public's anxiety over air safety. Air passenger traffic remained at lower than 2000 levels for the remainder of the year, and, for the first time, air passenger traffic fell from the previous year, from 698 million enplanements in 2000, to 681 million in 2001. Nevertheless, air traffic congestion will reemerge as a major issue. The crash of American Airlines flight 587 extended the timetable for that to occur, but most analysts believe that air passenger traffic will, once again, be establishing new records in the near future.

The security measures implemented in the aftermath of the terrorist attacks on the World Trade Center and Pentagon, such as increased identification checks, allowing only ticketed passengers into boarding areas, forbidding curbside check-in at many domestic airports, and random baggage searches, while justified, increase the time necessary to board passengers and load cargo. As a result, although the terrorist attacks temporarily eliminated the civilian air system's traffic congestion problem, in the long run, it will exacerbate it.

WHO'S TO BLAME FOR THE DELAYS?

For years, the airline industry blamed government for the nation's air traffic congestion problem. They argued that government environmental policies made it very difficult to build additional runways, and Federal Aviation Administration safety regulations prevented airplanes from altering established flight paths once airborne. They wanted environmental laws changed to expedite the construction of additional airfields and runways and the Federal Aviation Administration's ground-based, radar air traffic control technologies replaced by a satellite-based navigation system to enable aircraft to travel more direct routes to destinations and outside established air lanes when necessary.

In June 2001, the Federal Aviation Administration announced that it would spend $11 billion to shift to a satellite-based Global Positioning System by 2010. It also reduced the required minimum vertical space separation distance between airborne aircraft from 2,000 to 1,000 feet and allowed airplanes to take off for cities experiencing bad weather if forecasts predict that the storms will be over by the time the airplane is scheduled to arrive at its destination. It also allowed pilots to steer through storms rather than fly around them and to use previously restricted Canadian and military airspace to avoid storms. It also reduced the minimum space separation distance between airborne aircraft from five to four miles. These changes enable aircraft to fly more optimum routes and save fuel. They also increase airspace capacity, though, some argued, at the expense of passenger safety. Federal Aviation Administration officials defended the changes, noting that, by themselves, they would not solve the nation's air traffic congestion problem but were necessary given expectations concerning the continued growth of air passenger traffic over the next decade. As one airline official noted shortly after the rules changes were announced, the changes were expected to increase air capacity by about 10 to 15 percent by 2009, but air travel was expected to increase by at least 30 percent over that same time.

The airline industry argued that government needed to do more, especially concerning the construction of additional runway capacity. Federal officials countered by pointing out that they were already spending nearly $14 billion annually on air transportation. They argued that airlines needed to do more. They noted that many flight delays were caused by airlines purposively overbooking peak travel hours. For example, in 2000, 15 of the 31 busiest airports in the United States could not handle all flights scheduled during peak travel hours even under ideal weather conditions. Also, because of the way that airlines schedule flights, when bad weather causes flight delays at one airport, especially at one of the airlines' major hubs, the effect spreads, domino-style, throughout the entire civilian air transportation system. They also noted that continued labor unrest in the airline industry contributed to the problem.[1]

As will be shown, concern over air traffic congestion is a relatively recent phenomenon. However, concern over air safety is not new. Air safety has been a key issue for the civilian air transportation system since its inception in 1914.

THE EARLY YEARS: CONQUERING THE FEAR OF FLYING

On December 17, 1903, Wilbur and Orville Wright made their historic flights on a sandy knoll near Kitty Hawk, North Carolina. Eleven years later, in 1914, the St. Petersburg–Tampa Airboat Line started the first, regularly scheduled commercial airline passenger service in the United States. Tickets were five dollars for its 18-mile run between the two cities.[2] At that time, there were relatively few pilots in the United States, and safety concerns kept most potential passengers away. It was not surprising that the first regularly scheduled commercial flight, other than those offered on an ad hoc, for-hire basis, was an airboat service. Most people were afraid to fly over land. The fledgling nature of aviation in the United States was reflected in the number of military pilots at the outset of World War I. When the United States formally entered World War I in 1917, it had 83 Signal Corps, Navy, and Marine Corps pilots and 109 military aircraft. By the war's end in 1919, the military had trained more than 27,000 pilots and had purchased 10,500 airplanes. Once the war was over, many pilots purchased surplus military airplanes and tried to start their own airlines. Although there were some successes, such as Aero Limited's service between New York City and Atlantic City, New Jersey, most efforts failed because most people were afraid to fly. At that time, the public's safety concerns were justified. In 1918, the U.S. Post Office inaugurated airmail service. By 1925, 31 of the first 40 pilots hired by the U.S. Post Office had died in crashes.[3]

THE 1920S: THE BEGINNING OF GOVERNMENT SUBSIDIES

The early and mid-1920s were marked by record-setting exploits by pilots chasing large cash prizes for distance, time, and altitude records. Charles Lindbergh's historic solo, nonstop 3,610-mile transatlantic flight from New York to Paris on May 21, 1927, in the *Spirit of St. Louis* and Amelia Earhart's record-shattering exploits captivated the nation's attention and admiration. However, the commercial airline industry struggled for public acceptance as a safe and reliable alternative to railroads for mid- and long-distance travel. Commercial airline operators looked enviously at their European counterparts, who, at that time, received relatively generous government subsides ($2.5 million in Germany and France and $1.75 million in England in 1925) and had uniform, government-enforced safety regulations. They appealed to congressional leaders for similar assistance and, after considerable debate over constitutional provisions concerning government's role in mail delivery, Congress approved, and President Calvin Coolidge (R, 1923–1929) signed into law the *Kelly Airmail Act of 1925*. Named for its sponsor, Representative Melville "Clarence" Kelly (R-PA), it required the U.S. Post Office to contract out its airmail services to private airlines.

The *Kelly Airmail Act* provided an economic boost to the commercial airline industry. Airlines fortunate enough to win a government airmail contract were provided the cash flow necessary for economic survival. Unfortunately, intense competition for airmail contracts led to behavior that almost destroyed the airline industry. In 1934, Postmaster General Walter Brown and executives from four newly created airlines, American, Eastern, United, and Trans World, were charged by a U.S. Senate investigation committee, chaired by Hugo L. Black (D-AL, later appointed to the U.S. Supreme Court) with bypassing the competitive bidding process for awarding airmail contracts and colluding to monopolize the nation's airways. On February 19, 1934, President Franklin Roosevelt (D, 1933–1945) rescinded all existing airline airmail contracts and ordered the secretary of war to take over airmail delivery. The Army Air Corps began delivering airmail almost immediately but stopped on March 10, 1934, following a series of crashes that resulted in the deaths of 10 pilots. The army resumed flights on March 19 and continued delivering the mail until June 1, 1934. At that time, airmail contracts were rebid. Commercial airlines charged with collusion were, supposedly, ineligible. However, the four charged airlines discovered and exploited a legal loophole. By changing their corporate names, by added Inc. or changing Airways to Airlines, they became eligible to submit bids. After the bidding process concluded, the nation's then-three transcontinental air routes were, once again, won by United, American, and Trans World, and the East Coast route was won by Eastern. Those four airlines subsequently retained almost exclusive rights on those air routes for another 40 years.[4]

The airmail scandal and questions surrounding the rebidding process subjected the civilian aviation industry and the U.S. Postal Service to intense investigation and critical scrutiny. Several bills calling for the creation of an independent governmental agency to award airmail contracts were introduced in Congress. A presidential commission went even further. It recommended that an independent government agency be created to award airmail contracts, regulate airfares, and issue air safety regulations. Concerned that cutthroat competition in the airline industry contributed to its relatively poor safety record, the commission also recommended that airmail contracts be considered a subsidy, with payments purposively exceeding costs. In exchange for receiving the subsidy, the airline industry would be regulated like a public utility, with passenger fares and shipping rates controlled by the national government. It was argued that this would assure the industry's financial future, improve its safety record, and preclude the concentration of ownership.[5]

The civilian airline industry welcomed the imposition of uniform safety regulations, primarily because they were convinced that their industry would never reach its full economic potential unless the public was convinced that it was safe to fly. They were unable to impose uniform safety regulations on their own, primarily because adding safety features increased costs, and, in a very competitive environment, both within the aviation industry and with other transportation modes, few airline operators were willing to take the risk of adding safety features that could price them out of the market. As a result, the aviation industry looked to the national government to do the job for them.

The *Air Commerce Act of 1926* gave the U.S. secretary of commerce the responsibility to foster air commerce, issue and enforce air traffic rules, license pilots, certify aircraft, establish airways, and maintain and operate aids to air navigation. An aeronautics branch (renamed the Bureau of Air Commerce in 1934) was formed within the U.S. Department of Commerce to oversee the aviation industry. It initially focused on issuing safety rules and certifying pilots and aircraft. It also assumed, from the U.S. Post Office, responsibility for building and operating the nation's system of lighted airways and introduced radio beacons to assist air navigation during inclement weather and at night.[6]

THE 1930s: GOVERNMENT REGULATION OF THE AIRLINE INDUSTRY EXPANDS

The commercial airline industry, as did most other industries in the United States, suffered economic setbacks during the Great Depression (1929–1938). The Bureau of Air Commerce's efforts to improve the commercial airline industry's safety standards, primarily through periodic inspections, had a positive affect on air safety (the death rate per mile flown improved from one in 1.4 million miles in 1927 to one in 13 million miles in 1937), but the weak national economy reduced both business and vacation travel, which, in turn, prevented the industry from expanding during the 1930s. Also, the crash of a Trans World Airlines Sky Chief near Atlanta, Missouri, on May 6, 1935, claimed the life of U.S. Senator Bronson Cutting (R-NM) and four others. The crash set off a series of congressional hearings on air safety that were generally critical of the Bureau of Air Commerce. Republicans argued that the Bureau provided Democrats preference when hiring new inspectors, and Republicans and Democrats questioned the professionalism and competence of the bureau's inspectors and criticized its radio beacons for not being accurate and subject to heavy static during bad weather. Moreover, its personnel disagreed publicly over the use of the bureau's funds, and many criticized the bureau for not opposing the civilian airline industry's policy of basing pilot salaries on their record of completing flights regardless of weather conditions. Later that year, on August 15, 1935, famed aviator Wiley Post and movie star Will Rogers were killed in a airplane crash at Walakpi, Alaska. These two crashes and several others received extensive press coverage that made it difficult for airlines to convince the general public that it was safe to fly.

In 1936, the Bureau of Air Commerce, still smarting from criticisms received before Congress, encouraged the nation's airlines to establish air traffic control centers to help pilots avoid midair collisions. The first three centers, at Chicago, Cleveland, and Newark, became operational in July 1936. Initially, they were operated by the airlines. The Bureau of Air Commerce assumed operational control over the centers later that year and began to systematically expand the air traffic control system across the United States. By the end of 1936, air traffic control centers were also operating in Detroit, Los Angeles, Oakland, Pittsburgh, and Washington, D.C. At that time, air traffic controllers used maps, blackboards, and mental calculations to ensure the separation of aircraft traveling along designated routes between cities. Pilots relied on beacon lights to assist them in landing and taking off during the day and in fair weather and on the bureau's radio beacons at night and in poor weather conditions.

Congressional discontent with the Bureau of Air Commerce's progress in enhancing air safety, the perception that politics influenced its hiring practices and impeded efforts to create and enforce appropriate safety rules, and anger over the Post Office's handling of airmail contracts led them to adopt the *Civil Aeronautics Act of 1938*. It created an independent agency, the Civil Aeronautics Authority, to replace the Bureau of Air Commerce. Its independence from the executive bureaucracy was supposed to free it from political pressure to "go easy" on the airline industry when enforcing safety violations and crafting safety regulations. It was also supposed to prevent partisan considerations when hiring inspectors and other personnel and serve as a symbolic gesture recognizing the aviation industry's importance to the nation. In addition to assuming the Bureau of Air Commerce's functions, the Civil Aeronautics Authority regulated airline fares, determined air routes (a "grandfather clause" allowed airlines to continue flying existing routes), approved or disapproved airline consolidations and mergers, and awarded airmail contracts.

The commercial airlines did not oppose these economic regulations. At that time, competition for relatively scarce air passengers had driven down ticket prices and profits, and many in the industry, especially smaller airlines, feared bankruptcy. By imposing relatively uniform fares, government regulation stopped the price wars that were reducing profits and putting many smaller airlines out of business. Also, many in the aviation industry believed that the Civil Aeronautics Authority would make it easier for consolidations and mergers to take place because it would create routines and procedures for those actions, taking away much of the guesswork and "reinventing of the wheel" that, at the time, surrounded those actions.

Famed aviatrix Amelia Earhart testified at congressional hearings that the new government agency might stifle competition by preventing new airlines from entering into the marketplace. Congressional Democrats, led by Senator, later President, Harry S. Truman (D-MO), dismissed the arguments of those, like Earhart, who worried that the agency would become a captive of existing airlines. As Truman put it, "My God, you have to trust someone, don't you?"[7] However, Earhart's premonition came true. The rate-making authority within the Civil Aeronautics Authority, later named the Civil Aeronautics Board, did not allow another new, major scheduled airline to enter the marketplace for another 40 years. Also, the *Civil Aeronautics Act of 1938* provided the existing 18 airlines with permanent rights to fly on the routes that they already held. That had a dramatic affect on the civilian airline industry in the United States. It gave those airlines a distinct economic advantage over any new start-ups and was a key factor that enabled American, United, Trans World, and Eastern to maintain their hegemony over the civilian airline industry for the next 40 years.[8]

In 1940, the Civil Aeronautics Authority was replaced by two agencies, the Civil Aeronautics Administration and the Civil Aeronautics Board. The Civil Aeronautics Administration provided air traffic control, certification of pilots and aircraft, safety enforcement, and airway development. The five-member Civil Aeronautics Board issued safety rules, investigated accidents, and regulated the airline industry. Although both agencies were part of the U.S. Department of Commerce, the Civil Aeronautics Board reported directly to Congress, bypassing the U.S. secretary of commerce. The intent was to insulate it from the political process, particularly decisions concerning the economic regulation of the airline industry.[9]

The Civil Aeronautics Administration focused initially on improving safety by lighting airfields, increasing the number of beacon lights, expanding air traffic control operations (there were 14 centers in service in 1941), and introducing a radio-based instrument landing system consisting of a runway localizer range (very high frequency) course for lateral guidance, a glide path or landing beam for the path of descent, and two marker beacons for showing the progress of approach to the landing field. In 1941, instrument landing systems were operating at Chicago, Cleveland, Fort Worth, Kansas City, Los Angeles, and New York. The Civil Aeronautics Administration also become increasingly involved in planning and developing airports.

The *Civil Aeronautics Act of 1938* was a turning point in the national government's role in planning and developing the nation's system of airports. Although the airline industry obviously involved interstate commerce, prior to the Great Depression the spirit of laissez-faire government and states' rights led national government policymakers to purposively leave airport planning and funding to state and local governments. They, in turn, typically issued revenue bonds, supported by various fees and taxes on airlines and passengers, to pay for airport construction and improvements. However, the Great Depression's enormous economic upheaval convinced the Roosevelt administration that the national government had to spend money to "jump-start" the national economy. Among its many spending programs was $33 million for airport construction and repair projects. These funds were a stopgap measure to combat the nation's unemployment problem. They did not represent a fundamental reordering of governmental responsibility for planning and constructing airport facilities. The money was used to improve over 1,200 airports. Also, the Works Progress Administration assisted in the construction of 373 new airports during the 1930s, including Washington (now Reagan) National Airport. Nevertheless, the aviation industry's continued growth convinced Congress that it was time to help state and local governments plan, build, and improve airports.

The *Civil Aeronautics Act of 1938* authorized $560 million over six years to build up to 4,000 additional airfields, nearly tripling the number of airfields in the United States (see Table 5.1). However, as discussed shortly, Congress appropriated only $40 million of this amount. Although relatively insignificant amounts were appropriated for airport development, the *Civil Aeronautics Act of 1938* was important because it established the precedent for the expansion of national government funding for airports.[10]

THE 1940s: THE MILITARY INFLUENCE

From America's entry into World War II following the Japanese surprise attack at Pearl Harbor, Hawaii, on December 7, 1941, until the war's end in 1945, the nation's airspace and airfields were, for all practical matters, under military control. For example, during World War II, the military accounted for over 80 percent of the nation's air traffic. Initially, Civil Aeronautics Administration controllers retained authority over altitude and air route assignments for both military and civilian flights, but military pilots routinely ignored civilian traffic control operators instructions, even in highly congested areas. In 1942, President Roosevelt issued an executive order granting the military authority to take over any civilian aviation system that it deemed necessary. To reduce the possibility of midair collisions, all airspace above 17,000 feet, on and off established air routes, was reserved for military use. The Civil Aeronautics Administration also took several actions to increase air safety. It improved lighting at the nation's airfields, installed instrument landing systems at airports across the nation, and greatly expanded its Civilian Pilot Training Program to replace pilots who either volunteered or were drafted into military service.

In 1943, an Interdepartmental Air Traffic Control Board was created to coordinate military and civilian airspace issues. It subsequently reduced the width of civilian air routes from 20 to 10 miles (giving the military more airspace), ordered the military to stop training activities along and within civilian air routes, and allowed the military to continue to fly during daylight hours without civilian approval of a flight plan (a source of constant agitation for civilian flight controllers). In 1945, the Air Traffic Control Board was replaced by the Air Coordinating Committee. It included representatives from the Army, Navy, Air Force, U.S. Post Office, Department of the Treasury, Department of Commerce, the Civil Aeronautics Board, and the Federal Communications Commission. It established a number of subcommittees, panels, and boards to foster communication among the various aviation groups (private, commercial, and military) and develop guidelines concerning airspace management and implementation of air traffic control systems.

However, consensus on many issues was not achieved. For example, the military and civilian aviation communities opted to employ different air traffic control devices, and agreements over who got what airspace were both time-consuming and contentious, with the military often refusing to relinquish its primacy over much of the nation's airspace.[11]

In 1939, the Civil Aeronautics Administration determined that in the event of a national emergency none of the nation's 2,374 airports at that time were large enough to accommodate all existing military aircraft. Based on that study, the secretaries of war, navy, and commerce asked Congress to appropriate funds to improve the nation's civilian airfields, primarily to lengthen existing runways. As mentioned earlier, the *Civil Aeronautics Act of 1938* authorized $560 million over six years to build nearly 4,000 additional airfields, but Congress had not appropriated any funds for that purpose. Given the joint request by the secretaries of war, navy, and commerce, Congress appropriated $40 million in 1940 that was used to expand runways and make other improvements at 193 airports. The construction work was done by the Works Progress Administration.[12] During the war, the military extended runways and made other improvements at many of the nation's larger civilian airports to accommodate its needs.

After the war, most congressional members believed that their failure to fund civilian airports in the past had harmed the nation's military preparedness and were now convinced that they had a responsibility to fund the expansion of civilian airports to keep pace with military needs during an emergency. With President Harry S. Truman's (D, 1945–1953) support, Congress approved the *Federal Airport Act of 1946*. It created the Federal-Aid to Airport intergovernmental grant program, providing state and local governments $234 million over the next decade (1947–1956) on a 50-50 matching basis for airport development projects consistent with needs identified in a new, mandated, annual national airport plan prepared by the Civil Aeronautics Administration. Although eligibility requirements varied somewhat over the years, funding was typically available only for construction of landing areas and safety-related facilities, such as runways, taxiways, aprons, lighting installations, and control towers. Funding was usually paid directly to local airport authorities, but many states required local airport authorities to receive state government approval before applying for, and receiving, grant funds. An allocation formula, similar to the one used for the distribution of highway funding, ensured that all states and most congressional districts received funding (25 percent was allocated from a discretionary account based solely on "need" as defined in the annual airport plan, and 75 percent was allocated according to an area/population formula—half according to the state's proportion of the total national population and half according to the state's proportion of the total national land area). Although some complained that the allocation formula prevented the Civil Aeronautics Administration from targeting the program's funds to those airports most in need (primarily those located in the nation's urban areas), the formula enhanced the program's political appeal within Congress, especially in the U.S. Senate, where each state is represented by two senators regardless of population. The program's justification as a means to enhance national defense also attracted support from conservative Democrats and Republicans, who ordinarily opposed such funding as a violation of states' rights.[13] The Federal-Aid to Airports program provided approximately 65 percent of the amount spent on improvements and construction of publicly owned airports during this period, with local airport authorities contributing about 30 percent and states contributing about 5 percent. As Table 5.1 demonstrates, the Federal-Aid to Airports program was instrumental in increasing the number of civilian airports in the United States from 4,026 in 1945, to 6,839 in 1955.

THE 1950S: THE FAA IS BORN

On June 30, 1956, two civilian airliners collided over the Grand Canyon, killing all 128 people onboard the two aircraft. The accident drew nationwide media attention, much of it critical of both the airline industry and government regulators. At that time, pilots relied on visual sightings to avoid midair collisions when flying in less-congested airspace.

The national government responded to the accident and to the negative press, by increasing funding for air traffic control facilities (from approximately $3 million annually prior to the accident to $16 million in 1956, $75 million in 1957, and $146 million in 1958) and creating the Airways Modernization Board to reexamine the nation's air traffic control safety measures. Then, on May 14, 1957, President Dwight D. Eisenhower (R, 1953–1961) endorsed the creation of an independent Federal Aviation Agency to replace the Civil Aeronautics Administration and assume some of the Civil Aeronautics Board's responsibilities. The new agency was the brainchild of President Eisenhower's special assistant for aviation matters, General Edward P. Curtis. Importantly, except during times of war or national emergency, the new agency would coordinate both civilian and military air traffic.[14]

Two fatal, midair collisions between civilian and military aircraft, one over Las Vegas, Nevada, on April 21, 1958, and another over Brunswick, Maryland, on May 20, 1958, once again attracted nationwide media attention. Sixty-one people were killed in the two accidents. Worried that the negative publicity about air safety could jeopardize their industry's future and recognizing the need to coordinate civilian and military air operations, the airlines urged Congress to endorse President Eisenhower's recommendation for a centralized government agency to oversee air traffic control and other safety issues. Other aviation groups, including the Air Traffic Control Association, Air Transportation Association of America, Aircraft Owners and Pilots Association, Airline Stewards and Stewardesses Association, Air Line Pilots Association, Airport Operators Council, American Association of Airport Executives, National Association of State Aviation Officials, National Aviation Trades Association, and National Business Aircraft Association, also urged Congress to create a centralized agency to oversee air traffic control. They argued that the nation's airspace had become dangerously overcrowded. In addition to the two, dramatic midair crashes that year, there were 971 near misses between aircraft in 1957. They also argued that the introduction of civilian jet aircraft, continuing growth in air traffic, and the unresolved dispute between the military and the Civil Aeronautics Administration over which air traffic control device was best had created an untenable situation that had to be resolved. As E. Thomas Burnard, executive director of the Airport Operators Council, stated at the time: "The need for a better and more comprehensive system of controlling air traffic has been emphasized to us all again in recent weeks by tragic accidents. It will become more and more imperative as jet-propelled aircraft are placed in operation in civil air commerce. The establishment of a Federal Aviation Agency as provided in S. 3880 with power to control both civil and military air traffic will be a major step forward."[15]

The Civil Aeronautics Board was the only organization that opposed the proposal. It argued that shifting the board's safety responsibilities to a new agency located within the U.S. Department of Commerce would politicize aerospace policy making, enhance presidential authority at Congress's expense, and enhance the influence of those with political clout (the inference was aimed at the commercial airline industry) at the public's expense.[16]

Faced with a restless public worried about air safety, the media's demand for action, especially from city newspaper editors, support from the various aviation interest groups, and the president's endorsement, Congress passed the *Federal Aviation Act of 1958*. It created the Federal Aviation Agency (renamed the Federal Aviation Administration in 1966). It was to promote air safety and aviation's general development; manage the nation's navigable airspace; prescribe regulations concerning pilots' competence, and the airworthiness of aircraft and air traffic control systems; operate air route traffic control centers, airport traffic control towers, and flight service stations; and issue rules concerning the design, construction, maintenance, and inspection of navigation, traffic control, and communications equipment. The Civil Aeronautics Board continued to investigate accidents, regulate airlines, and issue monthly and quarterly financial and traffic data for certified air carriers.

President Eisenhower appointed the chair of the Airways Modernization Board, former General E. R. "Pete" Quesada, to head the Federal Aviation Agency. During his relatively brief two years in office, the Federal Aviation Agency issued over 400 safety rules and regulations and processed 8,822 reported violations of agency rules and regulations (the average was 2,000 a year prior to his assuming office). He raised the ire of the Air Line Pilots Association and the Aircraft Owners and Pilots Association by intensifying training programs, requiring pilots to undergo physical examinations by Federal Aviation Agency-designated physicians, forcing retirement of civilian transport pilots at age 60 (age 55 for jet aircraft), and tightening up rules concerning cockpit discipline. He offended many in Congress for recommending that the politically popular Federal-Aid to Airports program be phased out. Quesada argued that airports were local assets that should be financed by state and local governments. Congressional leaders insisted that airports were vital to the continued expansion of the national economy and that national financial assistance was justified under the interstate commerce clause.[17] Also, although it was never mentioned during congressional hearings, most congressional members supported Federal-Aid to Airports because it enhanced their reelection prospects by providing them an opportunity to claim credit for providing highly visible benefits to constituents.[18] To this day, congressmen rarely miss a ribbon-cutting ceremony dedicating the construction or expansion of the local airport or forget to issue a press release announcing their role in securing a grant for the expansion or improvement of the local airport.

When President John Kennedy (D, 1961–1963) entered office, he nominated Najeeb E. Halaby, a civilian pilot and lawyer, to replace Quesada. The appointment demonstrated in vivid fashion that while the Federal Aviation Agency was an independent agency, it was not free from political influence. Halaby subsequently established a number of committees and boards to review the Federal Aviation Agency's rules and, reflecting the Democratic Party's alliance with labor, included on those committees representatives from both the Air Line Pilots Association and Aircraft Owners and Pilots Association. Also, under his leadership, the Federal Aviation Agency focused less on issuing rules and more on expanding air traffic control and navigational aides to promote air safety.[19]

The *Federal Aviation Act of 1958* also extended Federal-Aid to Airports through 1963 and increased its authorization to $100 million annually. Congress subsequently appropriated $63 million annually from 1957 through 1961 and $75 million annually in 1962 and 1963. The funds were used to improve existing publicly owned airports, primarily to lengthen and strengthen existing runways in larger airports to accommodate jet traffic, and to build new airports. Because funding was limited, smaller airports received relatively little funding, and private airports were not eligible. Although their complaints were ignored, some congressional members from rural areas opposed targeting funds to the nation's largest airports.

THE 1960s: HIJACKERS, AIRPORT FUNDING, AND NOISE CONTROLS

On April 17, 1961, the United States sponsored the ill-fated invasion of Cuba at the Bay of Pigs. The invasion was an attempt to oust Fidel Castro. Two weeks later, on May 1, 1961, Puerto Rican-born Antuilo Ramirez Ortiz hijacked a commercial flight en route from Miami to Key West, Florida, forcing the pilot at gunpoint to divert to Havana, Cuba. Ortiz was granted asylum and hailed as a hero in Cuba. Two months later, another commercial airplane enroute over Florida was hijacked and forced to divert to Havana. A third hijacking to Cuba was attempted on August 2 by a father and his 16-year-old son aboard a flight en route from Phoenix to Houston. The pilot convinced the hijackers that the airplane was running low on fuel. They allowed him to land at El Paso, Texas. While on the ground, President Kennedy ordered the airline not to allow the airplane to be taken to Cuba. When the pilot taxied into position to take off, the airplane's tires were shot flat, forcing the pilot to abort the takeoff. The hijackers later surrendered. A few days later, a French Algerian passenger on a Pan American flight over Mexico hijacked the airplane, forcing the pilot to divert to Havana.[20]

The national government responded to the hijacks by enacting legislation in September 1961 that made air piracy punishable by death or imprisonment for not less than 20 years. When Antuilo Ramirez Ortiz returned to Miami in 1975, he was arrested and convicted of air piracy and sentenced to 20 years in prison. Interfering with flight crew members or flight attendants in the performance of their duties was also made a criminal offense.

On May 22, 1962, a commercial airliner en route from Chicago to Kansas City exploded over Iowa, killing all 37 passengers and eight crew members onboard. Ironically, it was the same airplane that had its tires shot out in El Paso. After examining the wreckage, it was determined that the explosion was caused by dynamite in a washroom. The Federal Aviation Agency then launched an extensive study of the feasibility of using X-rays, fluoroscopes, moisture analysis, microwaves, chemical techniques, and biological techniques to discover bombs. This led to the modern practice of using X-ray machines to screen both passengers and baggage for weapons and bombs and for using specially trained dogs to check baggage for bombs and other contraband, particularly illegal drugs.

In an effort to deter air piracy, on September 14, 1963, the United States became one of the first signatories to the Tokyo Convention. The convention's signatories agreed to return hijacked airplanes and passengers to the home county and prosecute the alleged hijackers. By 1969, 41 countries had signed the Tokyo Convention, and 172 more agreed to abide by its rules. Cuba was not among them.

In 1965, the Air Line Pilots Association asked Congress to ban flight insurance vending machines in airports after it was determined that two explosions that killed 88 people that year were linked to individuals who had purchased insurance at such machines. Although Congress refused to ban the machines, the following year it lowered the maximum allowable trip insurance at vending machines to $50,000.[21] It also passed the *Transportation Act of 1966*. This historic legislation created the U.S. Department of Transportation. Among the new law's many provisions was one removing the Federal Aviation Administration's independent status and placing it under the jurisdiction of the Department of Transportation. This meant that the head of the Federal Aviation Administration reported to the secretary of the U.S. Department of Transportation instead of Congress. There was relatively little said during congressional hearings on the *Transportation Act of 1966* concerning the potential that this change had for politicizing the Federal Aviation Administration, primarily because air safety was not a highly charged partisan issue, and, other than creating a National Transportation Safety Board to investigate accidents, the legislation did not result in any major changes to the Federal Aviation Administration's funding or functions. However, President Lyndon Baines Johnson (D, 1963–1969) quickly took advantage of the change. He wanted the Federal-Aid to Airports program's allocation formula changed to provide a larger portion of the program's funding to the nation's largest airports. He argued that they deserved more because, unlike smaller airports, they serve a national purpose by carrying significant volumes of commercial, interstate air traffic. He instructed his secretary of transportation to make that feeling known to the head of the

Federal Aviation Administration and Congress. Congress was not interested in changing the allocation formula. Spreading the program's funding to as many congressional districts as possible served their reelection needs very well. As a result, despite President Johnson's efforts, the program's allocation formula funding was not changed (one-quarter of the money was allocated according to greatest "need" as defined by the Federal Aviation Administration's Annual Five-Year National Airport Plan and three-quarters according to a population/area formula that dispersed funds widely across the nation).

The civilian aviation industry's interest groups were more concerned with the amount of Federal-Aid to Airports funding that was available than in how those funds were distributed among airports. They argued that $75 million annually was woefully inadequate given the nation's increasing air traffic and the introduction of jumbo jets that required both longer and stronger runways. They pointed out that passenger enplanements in the United States had increased from 70.7 million in 1963 to 126.4 million in 1967, and passenger miles flown over that period had increased from 45.9 billion miles to 83.3 billion miles.[22] Given this growth, they argued that the program's funding should be increased to at least $100 million annually, the level recommended by congressional authorizing committees. They also wanted a $1 billion low-interest revolving loan program to assist local governments build and expand airports.[23]

The Johnson administration opposed additional funding for airport development and most other domestic activities because it worried about rising costs associated with the Vietnam War. Recognizing that it lacked the political clout necessary to override a presidential veto, the civilian aviation industry shifted tactics and lobbied for the creation of an Airport Trust Fund financed by user fees, similar to the Highway Trust Fund, to pay for airport construction and improvements. The Air Transport Association recommended a 2 percent tax on airline passenger tickets and a two-dollar-per-head tax on airline passengers departing on international flights to pay for up to 75 percent of the principal and interest on securities issued by local governments to finance airport development.[24]

The Johnson administration initially opposed the creation of an aviation trust fund for airports. It argued that most of the economic benefits from airports accrue locally, making airports primarily a local government responsibility. However, in 1967, it did endorse the use of user fees to finance the automation of the Federal Aviation Agency's air traffic control system. In a letter to his secretary of transportation, Alan S. Boyd, dated September 20, 1967, President Johnson wrote that the rapid growth of commercial and private flying justified a substantial expansion and improvement in the nation's air traffic control system. Because the national government managed air traffic control, it should help devise a means to pay for the system's expansion and improvement. However, the aviation industry and the flying public should pay for most of the cost to improve the air traffic control system because they benefited most from its improvement. As he put it, "I do not believe that the general taxpayer should be asked to shoulder this burden."[25]

During congressional hearings on the creation of the Airport Trust Fund, Secretary of Transportation Boyd added that it would be improper to use general revenue to subsidize airport construction and improvement because the national government should promote a balanced transportation system. He argued that the national government's investment in one transportation mode as opposed to another should be dictated by that mode's efficiency. In his view, travelers should make transportation choices based on the full cost of the services offered. Therefore, the national government should not use general revenue to subsidize airport construction and improvements because that would distort the public's transportation choices by artificially reducing the customer's cost of flying.[26]

The aviation industry countered Boyd's argument by noting that the national government routinely supplemented revenue in the Highway Trust Fund. They argued that providing additional resources for airport development helped even the playing field with surface transportation projects that had for many years received significant subsidies from the national government.

Although the Johnson administration endorsed it, bickering over the proposal's details, especially the inclusion or exclusion of eligibility for airport construction and improvement projects, coupled with time constraints imposed by the impending 1968 congressional and presidential campaigns, precluded congressional action on an Airport Trust Fund at that time. However, the question was no longer if an Airport Trust Fund would be created. Now firmly on the political agenda, the questions were: When would the Airport Trust Fund be created?, How would its funds be generated?, How much funding would it have?, and Who was going to get the money?

Although it did not generate a great deal of attention at the time, in 1968, the Federal Aviation Administration was empowered to regulate aircraft noise. Facing billions of dollars in lawsuits over property damages and alleged depreciation of property values from the introduction and spread of jet aircraft, local government officials lobbied the national government to force airlines to use quieter jet engines and alter air routes to avoid residential areas. They also wanted money to purchase properties affected by aircraft noise. In November 1969, the Federal Aviation Administration established noise standards for new turbo jet engines (called Part 36). However, it refused to require airlines to retrofit existing jet aircraft or to alter air routes. Its reluctance to issue more stringent noise regulations became a regularly discussed topic at congressional hearings. Senator John Tunney (D-CA) was particularly concerned about aircraft noise and the future of Los Angeles International Airport. It faced more than $4 billion in aircraft noise-related lawsuits. The airline industry argued that stringent noise regulations were not necessary because they were already replacing older, noisier aircraft with newer, more quiet jet aircraft. As Clifton F. van Kann, senior vice president of the Air Transport Association of America, the trade and service organization representing airlines, testified before the Senate Commerce Committee's Subcommittee on Aviation on March 30, 1973:

Existing fleet aircraft will be modified to comply with currently recognized and achievable noise limits as proven hardware that is noise effective and cost effective becomes available and as financial realities permit. Clearly, the cost of such modifications is substantially beyond the economic capacity of the airline industry. Therefore, major hardware changes of this scope can be accomplished only with some form of public subsidy.[27]

THE 1970s: *FEDERAL AIRPORT ACT OF 1970*, AIRCRAFT NOISE, AND DEREGULATION

President Richard Nixon (R, 1969–1973) shared President Johnson's view that airports were primarily a state and local government responsibility because most airport economic benefits accrue locally. However, he knew that many state and local governments lacked the fiscal capacity to keep up with the demand for additional airport capacity. Therefore, in addition to advocating the use of user fees to pay for the automation and improvement of the air traffic control system, he also supported their use in helping to finance airport construction.

The *Federal Airport Act of 1970* replaced Federal-Aid to Airports with the Airport Development Program and increased national funding for airport construction and improvements from $75 million annually to $250 million annually from FY 1971 to FY 1980. It also created the Airport and Airway Trust Fund to finance the Federal Aviation Administration's other activities, including the automation of its air traffic control system. The trust fund's revenue was generated by increasing the existing passenger ticket tax from 2 percent to 8 percent; imposing a $3 per head tax on passenger tickets for most international flights departing the United States; creating a 5 percent tax on airfreight waybills; increasing fuel taxes from two cents per gallon to seven cents per gallon on gasoline and kerosene used by noncommercial aviation (commercial aviation was exempt from this tax because they were subject to the passenger ticket tax); and creating other assorted fees. Annual trust fund revenue exceeded $1 billion in 1970, $1.2 billion in 1975, $2.2 billion in 1980, $4.9 billion in 1990, and $11 billion in 2000.[28]

The Airport Development Program continued to limit eligibility to publicly owned airports with demonstrated needs identified in the Federal Aviation Administration's Annual Five-Year National Airport Plan and projects that either improved existing publicly owned airports, primarily lengthening and strengthening existing runways in larger airports to accommodate jumbo jet traffic, or assisted in the construction of new airports. Parking facilities and construction of airport buildings, other than those directly related to improving airline safety, were ineligible. The program's allocation formula was changed. Instead of allocating 25 percent of funds according to "need" and automatically allocating 75 percent of funds according to a congressionally mandated area/population formula, 63 percent was allocated according to "need," and 37 percent was allocated according to the area/population formula. Although some worried that this would further politicize the awarding of airport aid, the Nixon administration insisted on the change, primarily to ensure that funding was targeted to airports serving a national purpose (i.e., those carrying substantial amounts of interstate and/or international air traffic).[29]

The *Federal Airport Act of 1970* required airports receiving national government financial assistance to use those funds on environmentally sound projects. This provision was included to encourage new airports to be built on much larger tracts of land than existing ones. The idea was to create a noise and safety buffer zone between jet aircraft and high-population land uses. Two years later, tired of waiting for the Federal Aviation Administration to take a more proactive position concerning aircraft noise, Congress passed the *Noise Control Act of 1972*. It required the Federal Aviation Administration to issue regulations controlling aircraft noise that is presently, or will in the future, affect public health and welfare. The Federal Aviation Administration subsequently ordered airlines to use lower power settings and higher altitudes during initial landing approaches to reduce ground noise levels. It also ordered minimum flying altitudes increased, especially over hospitals and schools, and expanded a collaborative research and development effort with the National Air and Space Administration to find cost-effective means to retrofit existing aircraft with sound-absorbing materials to make them quieter.[30]

Congressional debates concerning the national government's role in airport construction and noise abatement were contentious but paled in comparison to the acrimony exhibited during congressional debate concerning the national government's economic regulation of the airline industry. By the mid-1970s, academics and consumer interest groups, such as Ralph Nader's Aviation Consumer Action Project, were calling for an end to the Civil Aeronautics Board's economic regulations that, in their view, kept ticket prices artificially high by limiting the airline's ability to offer air services wherever they wanted and by imposing fares well above what the airlines would charge in an open marketplace. Because the chairs of the congressional committees with jurisdiction over airlines were sympathetic to the airline industry, the effort to deregulate the industry came from congressional members who were not on those committees. Their champion was Senator Edward M. Kennedy (D-MA), chair of the Senate Subcommittee on Administrative Practices and Procedures.

Senator Kennedy's effort to deregulate airlines began in 1974, when his legislative assistant, Stephen Breyer, a Harvard law professor with expertise in antitrust law, noticed a short article in the *Washington Post* concerning a meeting that was to be held later that day between the secretary of transportation, Claude Brinegar, and representatives of Pan American and several other airlines. The airlines were having financial difficulties stemming from the quadrupling of oil prices in the aftermath of the 1973 Arab oil embargo and the resulting recession's adverse affect on the number of transatlantic air passengers. The article indicated that the airlines were going to ask the secretary of transportation to convince the Civil Aeronautics Board to increase minimum fares on flights to Europe. The airlines' request was targeted at charter flights, which, at the time, were the airlines' primary source of price competition. Breyer knew that fare agreements had to be approved in public hearings. He decided to attend the meeting as an uninvited guest. During the meeting, he was asked to leave when the discussion turned to specific proposals. Bryer then reported to Senator Kennedy that the meeting was, in his opinion, illegal. Senator Kennedy then held hearings on what consumer advocates later called the charter rate scheme. Senator Kennedy claimed jurisdiction over the matter because it involved the Civil Aeronautics Board and its administrative procedures. The airlines protested, claiming that their actions were part of the normal lobbying process. During the hearings, Keith Clearwater, a Justice Department official, testified that the plan agreed to at the meeting in the secretary of transportation's office and subsequently approved by the Civil Aeronautics Board was illegal. His testimony received nationwide media attention, including a front-page story in the *New York Times*. Senator Kennedy, still smarting from negative publicity surrounding the drowning death of Mary Jo Kopechne in a car that he was driving at Chappaquiddick, Massachusetts, in 1969, had found an issue that not only put him back into the nation's spotlight but put him in the enviable political position of being the champion of consumers in an era of soaring oil prices and inflation.[31]

Over the next two years, Senator Kennedy held a number of hearings concerning Civil Aeronautics Board rulings. During congressional hearings in 1976, he assailed the Civil Aeronautics Board's "procedural irregularities" and "violations of fundamental principles of due process," its allowing, through mergers, the number of trunk carriers (major airlines) to fall from the original 16 to 10, and its refusal since 1938 to approve any of the 79 applications to provide additional trunk services. He also pointed out that California and Texas airfares on air routes not regulated by the Civil Aeronautics Board were 30 to 50 percent less than those charged by regulated airline carriers over comparable routes. The airlines and Civil Aeronautics Board argued that the fare differences were due to differences in weather, traffic density, and a host of other factors not related to government regulation. However, Senator Kennedy was convinced that the Civil Aeronautics Board's fare regulations had created a situation where lack of competition from new entrants had caused airlines to fly with artificially high fares in "half-empty planes and using timely and frequent departures, along with extraneous frills, as the carrot to lure the thinning ranks of air travelers to their planes."[32]

Senator Kennedy's reference to extraneous frills referred to what the media called the airlines' "sandwich wars" that began during the late 1960s. Intent on improving market share but forbidden to engage in price competition, the major airlines added onboard frills, such as fancy sandwiches and picnic baskets, to lure passengers from other airlines. At one point, the Civil Aeronautics Board had to rule on a complaint filed by Delta Airlines accusing Northwest Airlines of false advertising because Northwest Airlines' steaks were allegedly not "cooked to order" as its advertisements promised but simply reheated.[33]

Senator Kennedy also complained that the Civil Aeronautics Board's fare regulations were geared "not to the average American, but to the well-to-do. . . . It's no wonder that more than 50 percent of all air travel is business travel. . . . Although, historically, airfares since 1938 have fallen in real dollar terms, the trend under recent regulation has been reversed. Since November 1974 airfare increases have outpaced the rate of inflation."[34] President Jimmy Carter (D, 1977–1981) shared Senator Kennedy's views on this issue. In 1975, he endorsed legislation to provide airlines with greater flexibility to reduce airfares, ease Civil Aeronautics Board's regulations on trunk entry, and made it easier, with some protections for small communities, for airlines to eliminate nonprofitable routes.[35]

The airline industry strongly opposed the relaxation or elimination of national government rules concerning entry and exit of air routes and passenger ticket prices. During congressional hearings, they testified that head-to-head competition might cause ticket prices to fall, but it would also bankrupt many smaller airlines, leading to the concentration of airline service into just a few large carriers that could, conceivably, control the marketplace and impose even higher fares on passengers than before deregulation took place. For example, Robert Six, chairman of the board and chief executive officer of Continental Airlines, Inc., testified before the U.S. Senate Commerce Committee that "deregulation will not lead to a more competitive situation. Rather, it is liable to result in a period of initial chaos and ultimately in a situation in which most of our air transportation system will be in the control of a few industry giants."[36]

The aviation industry also argued that deregulation would cause service reductions and, in some instances, complete elimination of service along many less profitable air routes, particularly those serving rural states and small-population cities. They also worried that deregulation would frighten investors, making it more difficult for them to finance badly needed equipment and facilities. For example, Edward E. Carlson, chairman and chief operating officer of United Airlines, Inc., testified:

Revenue bonds for airport construction, aircraft leases, airline property leases, credit instruments of all kinds hang on the integrity of the operating rights held under the certificate of public convenience and necessity. If we impair the value of this essential foundation in an industry which is cyclical by nature, we will create a high degree of risk for financial institutions which could bring new investment in the industry to a halt.[37]

They also warned that deregulation would adversely affect air safety because price competition would force airlines to defer maintenance and keep airplanes in service as long as possible. The industry's labor unions also opposed deregulation. They feared that increased price competition might make it more difficult for them to win wage and salary concessions at the bargaining table.[38]

While Congress debated deregulation's pros and cons, Alfred Kahn, President Carter's choice to head the Civil Aeronautics Board, was sworn into office on June 10, 1977. He systematically altered the Civil Aeronautics Board's regulatory behavior to allow airlines to fly as many routes as possible and at the lowest fares that they could afford. As airfares fell across the nation, Kahn received extensive and very positive media coverage. Although Congress was probably going to deregulate airlines regardless of Kahn's actions, the favorable publicity concerning Kahn's efforts signaled to many on Capitol Hill that it would be political suicide to fight airline deregulation.

President Carter signed the *Airline Deregulation Act of 1978* into law on October 24, 1978. It phased out the Civil Aeronautics Board's control over domestic service entry, with the virtual elimination of those regulatory powers on December 31, 1981. The only remaining requirement that applicants had to meet to enter a market was to be "fit, willing, and able." Airlines were allowed, with some limitations, to exit any market that they chose. Initially, airlines were allowed to raise or lower fares within a specified percentage range. The Civil Aeronautics Board's authority over fares was phased out, with almost complete deregulation of airfares starting on December 31, 1982. Finally, the Civil Aeronautics Board itself was phased out. It ceased operations on January 1, 1985.[39]

THE 1980S AND 1990S: DEREGULATION AND THE FAA'S MODERNIZATION PROGRAM

The commercial airline industry's deregulation had a profound affect on the aviation industry. Soon after deregulation was put into place, new start-ups, such as Air Chicago, New York Air, People Express, Air Florida, and others, challenged established airlines. Airfares were lowered on most routes and raised on others. Customers soon became accustomed to seeing ticket prices change, sometimes day to day, as commercial airlines tried to fill their airplanes with as many passengers as possible. Bargain discounts for frequent flyers and for those willing to buy tickets in advance became commonplace. However, in 1981, an unanticipated event made it difficult for new start-ups to compete with larger, established airlines. On August 1, 1981, the 13,000-plus-member Professional Air Traffic Controllers Association walked off the job. Their union contract had expired in mid-March 1981, and their demands for a shorter workweek and higher pay had been continuously rejected by the Federal Aviation Administration. President Ronald Reagan (R, 1981–1989), noting that the controllers did not have the right to strike, ordered them back to work within three days or lose their jobs. Most did not return to work, and President Reagan carried through on his promise and fired them. With most of its air traffic control personnel dismissed, the Federal Aviation Administration ordered airlines to temporarily ground one-third of their aircraft. The large airlines had excess seating capacity, and were able to handle the unexpected reduction without much financial difficulty. The smaller start-ups, on the other hand, had very little excess seat capacity and suffered large financial losses. Several of them appealed to the Federal Aviation Administration for an exemption, but their appeals were refused. The Federal Aviation Administration also restricted the number of landing slots at the nation's then-four busiest airports, New York's LaGuardia and Kennedy Airports, Chicago's O'Hare Airport, and Washington D.C.'s National Airport. The restrictions prevented start-ups from accessing several of the nation's most lucrative air markets. The restrictions continued for several years as the Federal Aviation Administration slowly rebuilt its air traffic control staff to prestrike levels.[40]

Sensing an opportunity to destroy its new competition, the larger airlines systematically reduced passenger airfares on routes also flown by the new start-ups. The practice was called predator pricing. The idea was to outlast the new start-ups and later recoup losses by raising passenger airfares after the start-ups were driven out of business. The strategy worked for Northwest Airlines. Its discount pricing forced People Express to abandon its Newark to the Twin Cities route. Northwest Airlines' hub was at the Twin Cities Airport. However, in most instances, predator pricing resulted in economic losses for all airlines. Eastern Airlines, for example, lost so much money trying to kill off World Airlines' coast-to-coast routes that it was forced to withdraw from transcontinental service altogether. Also, United Airlines nearly went bankrupt trying to kill off People's Express.[41] By the late-1980s, predator pricing and other factors forced many start-ups into bankruptcy and many others to merge with other airlines. Overall, deregulation increased the number of air carriers (there were 43 air carriers in 1978, 76 in 1993, and 91 in 2000), but American, Delta, and United (referred to by industry analysts as the Big Three) continued their dominance over the U.S. market.

Deregulation changed the basic nature of air service in the United States. Before deregulation most airlines exchanged passengers freely at major airports, a practice called interlining. After deregulation, airlines tried to keep their passengers to themselves. They discovered that it was more profitable to provide nonstop passenger air service between several major hubs instead of offering point-to-point, nonstop air service to numerous communities across the nation. They then provided deplaning passengers flights to their final destination, but only if the number of passengers was sufficiently large to be profitable. Smaller, regional airlines, such as Dallas-based Southwest Airlines, using smaller jet aircraft, tried to fill this new market niche. They competed head-to-head with the larger airlines to transport the larger airlines' deplaning passengers to their final destinations. They also offered air service to airports abandoned by major carriers. By the decade's end, about two-thirds of domestic airline passengers traveled through a major hub airport before arriving at their final destination. The strategy was an economic success for the larger airlines. More than 8 out of 10 passengers who changed flights at these hubs remained with the same airline. However, passengers with destinations outside major urban areas are now much more likely than before deregulation to have to change airplanes to reach their final destination.[42]

Deregulation resulted in generally lower airfares, but not everyone was pleased with the new emphasis on less expensive, low-frills flying. As one author put it, "Today's airline passengers face illogical airfares, cramped and suffocating cabins, and cattle-car treatment at hub airports that do to humans what postal sorting centers do to our mail."[43] Deregulation also altered the structure of the airline business, with the emergence of a three-tiered civilian aviation system. The Big Three currently serve international markets and heavily traveled domestic routes between major hubs. Smaller commuter/regional carriers provide service from major hubs to smaller communities. Midsize regional carriers, such as Northwest,

Continental, and USAir, offer point-to-point service in the Midwest, West, and East, respectively.

Another new development, especially prevalent among new carriers, is the contracting out of functions that do not involve direct contact with customers, such as maintenance, food service, and computer operations. Contracting out services reduces labor costs, vulnerability to union strikes, and capital expenses. These savings, in turn, make the airlines more attractive to capital investors. In recent years, some airlines have also contracted out personnel services at smaller airports, but this trend is not likely to spread because most airlines want direct control over their customer-contact employees, such as reservation and ticketing agents, gate personnel, pilots, and flight attendants, because those employees strongly influence customers' willingness to continue flying on that airline. Finally, some airlines, especially new start-ups, now lease a portion of their aircraft fleet. This reduces airline's capital expenses, making them more attractive to investors, who are often reluctant to invest money in an industry that is cyclical in nature, subject to labor stoppages, and no longer protected by national fare restrictions.[44]

It was argued during congressional hearings that deregulation might compromise air safety because airlines would be tempted to defer maintenance to reduce expenses. In 1990, Eastern Airlines was issued a 60-count indictment charging it with improper maintenance practices, but there was little other evidence to suggest that airlines cut back on maintenance. Statistically, flying became progressively safer during the 1980s and 1990s, with the death rate falling to one in every 2 million flights.[45]

Improvements in aircraft design and the natural recycling of older, less-safe aircraft with newer, safer ones played a role in improving the civilian air transportation industry's air safety record during the 1980s and 1990s.[46] Another important factor was the Federal Aviation Administration's continued issuance and enforcement of strict, mandatory maintenance rules. It also continued its long-term effort to automate portions of its air traffic control system. As announced in its National Airspace System Plan of 1982, the Federal Aviation Administration wanted to take advantage of improvements in computer technology to automate routine tasks surrounding takeoffs and landings, enabling air traffic controllers to concentrate on the separation of aircraft while en route between destinations. Under the plan (revised by the Capital Improvement Plan of 1991, which included even higher levels of automation and an added emphasis on radar, communications, and weather forecasting systems), the Federal Aviation Administration acquired new surveillance, data-processing, navigation, and communications equipment and constructed new air traffic control facilities. Between 1982 and 2000, 126 separate air traffic control projects were either completed or under way, at an estimated cost of $26.5 billion. Included in this cost estimate was $13 billion for 59 information technology projects. These projects were software-intensive information and communications systems that support the air traffic control system.[47]

The Federal Aviation Administration currently employs three types of facilities to manage and control air traffic. Airport towers direct aircraft on the ground, before landing, and after takeoff for up to five nautical miles and up to about 3,000 feet above the airport. Terminal radar approach control facilities sequence and separate aircraft as they approach and leave airports, beginning about five nautical miles and ending about 50 nautical miles from the airport. These facilities generally deal with aircraft flying below 10,000 feet. Air route traffic control centers control aircraft in transit and during approaches to airports. Most en route control centers deal with aircraft flying above 18,000 feet, although they sometimes assist airplanes flying at lower altitudes.

The Federal Aviation Administration embraced new, emerging technologies as a means to reduce human error and aircraft accidents. However, the still ongoing modernization program has not been without its critics. Employees have worried about job security and changes in work patterns and assignments. Also, the U.S. General Accounting Office noted numerous cost overruns, lengthy delays, and significant performance shortfalls in many of the newly installed systems. In a series of reports, it sharply criticized the Federal Aviation Administration's management of the modernization program, especially during the 1980s and early 1990s. It noted that until 1999, the Federal Aviation Administration lacked a centralized, standardized management information system and historical database for capturing and maintaining project information. This prevented it from tracking the progress of projects on a systemwide basis. The General Accounting Office also noted that several modernization projects started during the 1980s were never completed, largely because they were ill conceived from the start. It was especially critical of the management of the modernization program's centerpiece, the Advanced Automation System. Its cost has tripled (from an original estimate of $2.5 billion to $7.6 billion), and software development problems have delayed many of the system's promised capabilities for more than eight years.[48]

The Federal Aviation Administration responded to these criticisms by taking a more incremental approach to upgrade its air control facilities and operating systems. As Jane F. Garvey, federal aviation administrator, testified before Congress on February 3, 2000, "Our management approach can be summed up as . . . evolution, not revolution. Instead of taking a 'big bang' approach to modernization, we are moving incrementally, building upon each step that we have taken, reducing the potential for cost overruns and schedule delays."[49]

During the mid-1990s, the Federal Aviation Administration purposively lessened its reliance on the development of new, untested computer software. Instead, it increasingly relied on tested, on-the-shelf software. Although on-the-shelf software systems often did not provide all of the desired capabilities, they proved to be more reliable than custom-made software systems. In 1996, the Federal Aviation Administration also introduced a series of management reforms (called the Acquisition Management System) to provide a better assessment of a given project's potential costs and greater oversight of the project's progress during implementation. It also created a senior management investment review group to provide a central mechanism for determining if proposed projects meet the Federal Aviation Administration's needs. Although the formation of this new group has enabled the

Federal Aviation Administration to compare new projects in a more systematic manner, the General Accounting Office noted that projects already in operation are not part of this review process, making it difficult to fully assess and make trade-offs about the relative merits of spending funds to develop new systems, enhance current systems, or continue operating and maintaining existing systems.[50]

2000 AND BEYOND: *THE WENDELL FORD AVIATION INVESTMENT AND REFORM ACT FOR THE 21st CENTURY*

Throughout the 1980s and 1990s, Congress often diverted funds from the Airport and Airway Trust Fund to reduce the budget deficit. For example, in 1999, the Federal Aviation Administration received $9.8 billion, even though the Airport and Airway Trust Fund generated more than $11.1 billion.[51] The aviation industry's interest groups, particularly the Aircraft Owners and Pilots Association, complained that the diversion of Airport and Airway Trust Fund revenue seriously impeded the Federal Aviation Administration's ability to upgrade its air traffic control system to keep pace with the expansion of civilian air traffic, expected to exceed 1 billion passengers by 2010. During congressional hearings in 2001, they pointed out that the air traffic control system experienced 101 significant system failures (more than 10 minutes in duration) in 1998, with 43 of those failures lasting more than an hour and one lasting five days. They also noted that in March 1999 the air traffic control system at Dulles International Airport, outside Washington, D.C., was once down for over 10 hours. They argued that these problems could be resolved if Congress stopped diverting Airport and Airway Trust Fund revenue to other purposes. They also pointed to a General Accounting Office report released in 1999 that concurred with their conclusions. The General Accounting Office concluded that the Federal Aviation Administration needed at least another $700 million annually to address its air traffic control problems and an additional $2.3 billion annually for general operating expenses and airport aid just to keep pace with increasing air traffic. The aviation industry's interest groups noted that most of this revenue was available in the Airport and Airway Trust Fund but was being diverted to other uses.

Congress responded to the criticisms of the Federal Aviation Administration's management of the air traffic control system's modernization program by creating a series of blue-ribbon panels to study the issue. In 1997, the National Civil Aviation Review Commission recommended that the Federal Aviation Administration be operated in a more businesslike fashion. Specifically, it recommended that the air traffic control system be headed by a chief operating officer whose salary and tenure were linked to performance measures. Moreover, the system would be financed on a cost-basis, with airlines and other aircraft using the system contributing to its upkeep instead of passengers. The commission argued that switching to a cost-based financing system would increase pressure on the Federal Aviation Administration to reform its management practices because the aviation industry's various organized interest groups, who would be billed for using the system, had more political clout than passengers. If the aviation industry was displeased with the Federal Aviation Administration's management decisions, they were in a much stronger position than nonorganized passengers to force the Federal Aviation Administration to change its policies and procedures. Finally, in exchange for pricing reform, all revenue generated from the imposition of the cost-based financing system would be spent exclusively on air traffic control.

Although President Bill Clinton (D, 1993–2001) was aware of the National Civil Aviation Review Commission's recommendations, he was not convinced that the benefits that might accrue from switching to a cost-based financing system were worth the political fallout that was certain to be generated by the aviation industry if he endorsed the recommendation. However, by 1999, a number of studies from reputable sources, such as the General Accounting Office, had all concluded that the aviation industry's request for additional funding for the air traffic control system and airport development was appropriate. Therefore, he recommended that the Federal Aviation Administration's budget be increased to $11.2 billion annually, approximately the same amount generated by the Airport and Airway Trust Fund. Most of the money ($6.6 billion) was for general operating expenses, $1.95 billion for the Airport Improvement Program, $2.5 billion for facilities and equipment, and $184 million for research, engineering, and development. President Clinton also recommended that the passenger facility charge be increased from $3 to $4.50. This change was expected to increase Airport and Airway Trust Fund revenue by approximately $700 million annually.[52]

As noted in the previous chapter, Representative Bud Shuster (R-PA), chair of the House Transportation and Infrastructure Committee, led an effort in 1998 to ensure the nondiversion of Highway Trust Fund revenue. He announced in 1999 that he would fight to ensure the nondiversion of Airport and Airway Trust Fund revenue, primarily because he was convinced that the air traffic control system needed to be upgraded and improved to meet the continued expansion of civilian air traffic. He noted that although the civilian aviation industry's death rate was relatively low compared to other transportation modes, it had not improved in more than a decade. He cited the National Civil Aviation Review Commission's 1997 prediction that the safety of the aviation system would slowly erode over the next 10 to 15 years unless significant steps were taken to further improve aviation safety. In response to those who wanted to privatize the air traffic control system, he recommended the creation of an Air Traffic Management Oversight Board to oversee the Federal Aviation Administration's modernization efforts.[53]

Representative Shuster incorporated his ideas into the House-passed version of the *Wendell Ford Aviation Investment and Reform Act for the 21st Century*, known as AIR-21. The House initially passed its version of AIR-21 in June 1999, 316–110. It increased the Federal Aviation Administration's budget to $12.6 billion in FY 2001, 25 percent more than in FY 2000, with $2.1 billion from general revenue and the remainder from the Airport and Airway Trust Fund. It did not include the Clinton administration's proposal to increase passenger facility charges. The Senate, on the other hand, was more interested in enacting a general tax cut than increasing the Federal Aviation Administration's budget. It had targeted $14 billion in unspent Airport and Airway Trust Fund revenue to help fund the tax cut. The Senate's initial version of the act, passed in July 1999, retained the status quo by extending the Federal Aviation Administration's funding for two months.

Over the next 10 months, Congress enacted three short-term funding extensions to enable the Federal Aviation Administration to continue functioning as House and Senate conferees tried to hammer out a compromise. President Clinton supported the Senate's position. He opposed using general revenue for the Federal Aviation Administration because it would jeopardize funding for other programs. He singled out Amtrak and the Coast Guard as programs most likely to be affected.

During negotiations, Senator Pete Domenici (R-NM), chair of the Senate Budget Committee, and Senator Slade Gordon (R-WA), chair of the Senate Commerce Committee's Science and Transportation Aviation Subcommittee, offered to increase the Federal Aviation Administration's budget to the amount generated by Airport and Airway Trust Fund, plus interest collected on the trust fund's unspent funds. This amount, estimated at $10 billion to $11 billion annually, was similar to the Clinton administration's request. Representative Shuster rejected the offer because he was not convinced that the Senate would appropriate the promised funds. He insisted that the only way to ensure the nondiversion of Airport and Airway Trust Fund revenue was to take the trust fund off-budget.

As negotiations dragged on, an air traffic control computer malfunctioned on January 4, 2000, in Nashua, New Hampshire, delaying flights in Massachusetts, New York, and New Jersey. Then, on January 6, 2000, a major air traffic control failure knocked out most traffic control systems across the eastern seaboard. Hundreds of flights were grounded or canceled. Representative Shuster pointed to the failures as proof that the Federal Aviation Administration's funding was inadequate. Others viewed the failures as further proof of the Federal Aviation Administration's incompetence and the need to privatize the air traffic control system. They cited Canada's privatization of its civilian air traffic control system to NAV CANADA in 1996 as an example of how privatization can save money without compromising service.

A final agreement was reached following a series of private meetings in late February and early March 2000 between Representative Shuster and Senate Majority Leader Trent Lott (R-MS). Representative Shuster withdrew his proposal to move the Airport and Airway Trust Fund off-budget in exchange for increasing the Federal Aviation Administration's authorization level to nearly $40 billion over three years. That was a $10 billion increase over then-current funding levels. Most of the $40 billion ($33 billion) was guaranteed because it came from the Airport and Airway Trust Fund. The remainder ($6.7 billion) was subject to the annual congressional appropriations process. Representative Shuster initially insisted on a series of parliamentary points of order to guarantee that the $6.7 billion in discretionary funding was actually appropriated. However, Senate Appropriations Committee Chair Ted Stevens (R-AK) objected to the points of order because they infringed on his committee's power. Representative Shuster agreed to drop the provision after receiving letters from House Speaker Dennis Hastert (R-IL) and House Rules Committee Chairman David Drier (R-CA) indicating that the House would insist during the congressional appropriations process that the $6.7 billion in discretionary funding be appropriated. The Senate agreed to the compromise on March 8, 2000 (82–17), the House passed it on March 15, 2000 (318–102), and President Clinton signed it into law on April 5, 2000.

AIR-21 increased the Federal Aviation Administration's funding from $9.9 billion in FY 2000 to $12.6 billion in FY 2001, $13.3 billion in FY 2002, and $14 billion in FY 2003. The Federal Aviation Administration's general operating budget increased from $5.8 billion in FY 2000 to $6.5 billion in FY 2001, $6.9 billion in FY 2002, and $7.3 billion in FY 2003. The Airport Improvement Program received the largest funding increase, nearly doubling from $1.9 billion in FY 2000 to $3.2 billion in FY 2001, $3.3 billion in FY 2002, and $3.4 billion in FY 2003. During the AIR-21's signing ceremony, President Clinton reiterated his concern that AIR-21's funding increases and emphasis on airport construction and capital improvements could make it more difficult to find revenue for the Federal Aviation Administration's general operating budget and other discretionary programs in the future, particularly for Amtrak and the Coast Guard.[54]

During the reauthorization process, media attention focused on funding issues and Representative Shuster's effort to place the Airport and Airway Trust Fund off-budget. However, a number of less visible, but equally important, decisions concerning eligibility and distribution of Airport and Airway Trust Fund revenue were also reached. For example, general aviation airports were provided funding for the first time ($274 million annually). Also, funding for terminals, gates, taxiways, and other infrastructure to stimulate competition at airports was increased. In addition, airline access and competition were increased at Chicago's O'Hare Airport by abolishing slots in 2002, at New York's LaGuardia and Kennedy Airports by abolishing slots in 2007, and at Reagan National Airport by creating 24 new slots. Funding was also increased for noise abatement projects and safety improvements at small airports; minimum funding levels for nonhub airports was increased from $500,000 to $1 million annually; minimum funding for primary airports (10,000 or more passengers annually) was doubled (from $519 million to $1.06 billion annually); an incentive program to assist small airports secure air traffic control tower services was created; the cap on the passenger facility charge was raised by $1.50 (to $4.50) to enable airports to generate revenues for safety or noise abatement projects not funded through the Airport Improvement Program; and a 10-member Aviation Management Advisory Council, comprising representatives from the aviation industry, was created to oversee the Federal Aviation Administration's air traffic control modernization effort.[55]

CONCLUSION

AIR-21 provided significant funding increases for airports that had received funding in the past. By funding general aviation airports and increasing funding for small airports, AIR-21 also expanded the number of airports that receive national government assistance. This was politically popular within Congress because it provided congressional members additional opportunities to claim credit for securing funds for their respective districts and states. Credit-claiming is generally viewed as one of the primary goals of all congressional members because it enhances their reelection prospects. President Clinton's lack of enthusiasm when signing AIR-21 was, at least in part, explained by his and his predecessors' belief that funding should be concentrated on larger airports because they serve a national, as opposed to a state or local, purpose by carrying significant amounts of interstate and international passengers and cargo. Elected on a national ballot, presidents are less inclined than members of Congress to sympathize with efforts to disburse funds to as many congressional districts as possible.

AIR-21's funding increases will prevent the Federal Aviation Administration from blaming future program performance shortfalls on the lack of funding. Its management difficulties, documented by the General Accounting Office and others, highlight the importance of program implementation. The Federal Aviation Administration's introduction of automated, technologically advanced air traffic control systems during the last two decades has reduced human error as a contributing cause of air accidents. However, the software and hardware that constitute these new, automated systems are subject to their own operational difficulties. The trick is to get these systems to work and keep working, without experiencing cost overruns and program delays. Although adding an additional layer of bureaucracy to police the actions of an existing bureaucracy is always problematic, especially when that oversight body comprises members of the industry being served, the new Aviation Management Advisory Council will, at the very least, enhance the aviation industry's influence within the Federal Aviation Administration. If the Federal Aviation Administration continues to experience management difficulties under the new reorganization, the idea of privatizing the air traffic control system will be taken more seriously on Capitol Hill.

As in the past, the national government's civilian air transportation policies, embodied in AIR-21, were developed in relative isolation from its highway and mass transit policies and intercity passenger rail policies. As mentioned previously, there are several explanations for this behavior, including Congress's decentralized decision-making structure, the bureaucracy's interest in maintaining hegemony over its respective portion of transportation policy, and the desire of elected officials at all levels of government to avoid upsetting the various transportation modes' organized interest groups. Although ISTEA and its successor, TEA-21, promoted the use of intermodal solutions in surface transportation, the national government has avoided policies that mandate an integrated and comprehensive intermodal solution, involving all major transportation modes (air, highway, mass transit, and passenger rail), to improve the nation's mobility. This contrasts sharply with the actions under way in many European countries. For example, relatively few airports in the United States are served directly by passenger rail service. Baltimore/Washington International Airport, located just outside Baltimore, and airports in Atlanta, Chicago, Cleveland, Philadelphia, St. Louis, and Washington D.C., are among the exceptions. Part of the explanation for the absence of rail services at the nation's airports is the disjointed nature of the way that the national government deals with transportation policy in the United States. In Europe, where intermodal solutions to traffic mobility are a higher priority, intercity passenger trains serve nearly all major airports, enabling passengers to move relatively seamlessly from one transportation mode to the other. For example, several European nations allow airline passengers to buy a single ticket or an electronic ticketless record for both their airline flight and a trip by rail at one or both ends of their air travel. The Europeans call this latest innovation in travel intermodal interlining.[56] Given Europe's increased attention to intermodal transportation solutions, it is not surprising that this latest innovation in air travel ticketing originated there and not in the United States.

ADDENDUM: TERRORISM IN THE SKIES

On July 17, 1996, Trans World Airline's Flight 800 exploded off the coast of Long Island, New York, killing all 230 passengers and crew onboard. Media speculation focused on the possibility of the explosion's being caused by a bomb placed in the airplane's cargo bay by terrorists. Under intense media pressure to do something to ensure the public's safety, President Clinton announced on July 25, 1996, the creation of the White House Commission on Aviation Safety and Security to review the airline industry's safety procedures. To assure the American public that he was giving this issue a high priority, he asked Vice President Al Gore to chair the commission. After holding several hearings, the commission issued a preliminary report on September 9, 1996. It recommended that additional funding be provided to purchase new explosives detection systems for the nation's airports. The next month, Congress authorized $400 million for the systems. The commission continued its deliberations and issued its final report on February 12, 1997. Most of its recommendations focused on accelerating the Federal Aviation Administration's effort to modernize its air transportation control facilities and improve its cargo screening capacity. In response, the Federal Aviation Administration announced that it was already deploying new, high-tech explosives detection systems in the nation's airports and was training additional teams of bomb-sniffing dogs, hiring new security and hazardous materials agents, and preparing new rules to verify the background of airport employees and certify those working at airport checkpoints.

As media attention focused elsewhere, most analysts believed that the Federal Aviation Administration was doing what was necessary to protect the public from terrorists. Little thought was given to the possibility of terrorists hijacking airplanes and using them as bombs. The U.S. Commission on National Security in the 21st Century, a congressionally sanctioned independent commission headed by former U.S. Senators Warren Rudman and Gary Hart, did issue a series of reports in 2000 indicating that it was likely that terrorists would attack the United States with nuclear, chemical, or biological weapons at some point within the next

25 years. It recommended that the United States form a new Anti-Terrorism Cabinet Agency to deal with the increased likelihood of terrorist attacks in the United States. They also warned that unconventional terrorist attacks, such as the planting of viruses in the Federal Aviation Administration's air traffic control system, were also threats to national security.[57] But no one foresaw the tragic events that led to the attacks on the World Trade Center and Pentagon.

As mentioned earlier, the additional security measures imposed at the nation's airports in the wake of the events of September 11, 2001, coupled with the introduction of armed air marshals aboard commercial airliners and other measures, such as the fortification of cockpit doors to deny access from the cabin and the nationalization of airport security personnel, will reassure the American traveling public that flying is relatively safe. As they return to the skies, air traffic congestion is likely to reemerge as the number one issue facing the civilian air transportation system in the United States. However, although congressional and presidential debate will likely refocus on the modernization of the Federal Aviation Administration's air traffic control system and how to cope with air traffic congestion, the events of September 11, 2001, will have a lasting effect on those deliberations. Air safety is now firmly planted on the political agenda and will remain a very high priority for many years to come.

NOTES

1. Associated Press, "Airlines Hope to Avoid Summer of Travel Troubles," *CNN.com/Travel*, May 7, 2001. Available on-line at http://www.cnn.com/2001/Travel/News/05/07/airtime.asp/index.html; Jonathan D. Salant, "FAA Presents Plan to Reduce Delays," Associated Press News Release, June 5, 2001. Available on-line at http://dailynews.yahoo.com/h/ap/20010604/pl/airline_delays_3.html; and Sylvia Adcock, "FAA Plans Air Traffic Modernization Project," *Newsday.com*, June 4, 2001. Available on-line at: http://www.newsday.com/news/daily/faa605.htm.

2. Steven A. Morrison and Clifford Winston, *The Evolution of the Airline Industry* (Washington, DC: The Brookings Institution, 1995), p. 3.

3. Donald R. Whitnah, *Safer Skyways: Federal Control of Aviation, 1926–1966* (Ames, IA: The Iowa State University Press, 1966), pp. 9–14.

4. Barbara Sturken Peterson and James Glab, *Rapid Descent: Deregulation and the Shakeout in the Airlines* (New York: Simon & Schuster, 1994), p. 24.

5. Donald R. Whitnah, *Safer Skyways*, pp. 15–23; and Robert Burkhardt, *The Federal Aviation Administration* (New York: Frederick A. Praeger Publishers, 1967), pp. 11–14.

6. U.S. Federal Aviation Administration, "A Brief History of the Federal Aviation Administration and Its Predecessor Agencies," (Washington, DC: U.S. Department of Transportation, November 11, 1999). Available on-line at: http://www.faa.gov/historyinfo.htm.

7. Barbara Sturken Peterson and James Glab, *Rapid Descent*, p. 27.

8. Ibid., pp. 26, 27.

9. U.S. Federal Aviation Administration, "A Brief History of the Federal Aviation Administration and Its Predecessor Agencies."

10. Donald R. Whitnah, *Safer Skyways*, pp. 106, 107, 166, 167; and Robert Burkhardt, *The Federal Aviation Administration*, p. 17.

11. Donald R. Whitnah, *Safer Skyways*, pp. 137–191, 196–201.

12. Robert Burkhardt, *The Federal Aviation Administration*, p. 17.

13. John A. Volpe, Secretary of Transportation, "Letter to the Hon. Warren G. Magnuson, Chairman of the Committee on Commerce of the U.S. Senate, dated September 17, 1969," in *Airport/Airways Development*. Hearings before the Subcommittee on Aviation, U.S. Senate Committee on Commerce, 91st Congress, First Session (Washington, DC: U.S. Government Printing Office, July 23, 1969), p. 593; and Jeremy J. Warford, *Public Policy toward General Aviation* (Washington, DC: The Brookings Institution, 1971), pp. 112–115.

14. Dwight D. Eisenhower, President of the United States, "Letter to the Congress of the United States, dated June 13, 1958," in *Federal Aviation Agency Act*. Hearings before the Subcommittee on Aviation, U.S. Senate Committee on Interstate and Foreign Commerce, 85th Congress, Second Session (Washington, DC: U.S. Government Printing Office, June 16, 1958); and General E. R. Quesada, Chairman, Airways Modernization Board, "Statement before the Subcommittee on Aviation, U.S. Senate Committee on Interstate and Foreign Commerce," in *Federal Aviation Agency Act*. Hearings before the Subcommittee on Aviation, U.S. Senate Committee on Interstate and Foreign Commerce, 85th Congress, Second Session (Washington, DC: U.S. Government Printing Office, May 23, 1958).

15. E. Thomas Burnard, Executive Director, Airport Operators Council, "Statement before the Subcommittee on Aviation, U.S. Senate Committee on Interstate and Foreign Commerce," in *Federal Aviation Agency Act*. Hearings before the Subcommittee on Aviation, U.S. Senate Committee on Interstate and Foreign Commerce, 85th Congress, Second Session (Washington, DC: U.S. Government Printing Office, June 4, 1958).

16. James R. Durfee, Chairman, Civil Aeronautics Board, "Statement before the Subcommittee on Aviation, U.S. Senate Committee on Interstate and Foreign Commerce," in *Federal Aviation Agency Act*. Hearings before the Subcommittee on Aviation, U.S. Senate Committee on Interstate and Foreign Commerce, 85th Congress, Second Session (Washington, DC: U.S. Government Printing Office, June 16, 1958).

17. Donald R. Whitnah, *Safer Skyways*, pp. 279–296; and Robert Burkhardt, *The Federal Aviation Administration*, pp. 41–61, 87.

18. David R. Mayhew, *Congress: The Electoral Connection* (New Haven, CT: Yale University Press, 1974), pp. 52–61.

19. Robert Burkhardt, *The Federal Aviation Administration*, pp. 41–61.

20. Ibid., p. 90; and Donald R. Whitnah, *Safer Skyways*, p. 326.

21. Robert Burkhardt, *The Federal Aviation Administration*, pp. 92, 93.

22. Alan S. Boyd, Secretary, Department of Transportation, "Statement before the Subcommittee on Aviation, U.S. Senate Committee on Commerce," in *Airport Development Act of 1968*. Hearings before the Subcommittee on Aviation, U.S. Senate Committee on Commerce, 90th Congress, Second Session (Washington, DC: U.S. Government Printing Office, June 18, 1968), pp. 40, 41.

23. Joseph B. Hartranft, Jr., President, Aircraft Owners and Pilots Association, "Statement before the Subcommittee on Aviation, U.S. Senate Committee on Commerce," in *Airport Development Act of 1968*. Hearings before the Subcommittee on Aviation, U.S. Senate Committee on Commerce, 90th Congress, Second Session (Washington, DC: U.S. Government Printing Office, June 19 1968), pp. 181–183.

24. Stuart G. Tipton, President, Air Transport Association of America, "Statement before the Subcommittee on Aviation, U.S. Senate Committee on Commerce," in *Airport Development Act of 1968*. Hearings before the Subcommittee on Aviation, U.S. Senate Committee on Commerce, 90th Congress, Second Session (Washington, DC: U.S. Government Printing Office, June 18, 1968), pp. 107–113.

25. Lyndon Baines Johnson, President of the United States, "Letter to Alan S. Boyd, Secretary, Department of Transportation, dated September 20, 1967." Cited by Alan S. Boyd,

Secretary, Department of Transportation, "Letter to the Honorable Hubert H. Humphrey, President of the U.S. Senate, dated May 20, 1968," in *Airport Development Act of 1968*. Hearings before the Subcommittee on Aviation, U.S. Senate Committee on Commerce, 90th Congress, Second Session (Washington, DC: U.S. Government Printing Office, June 18, 1968), pp. 30, 31.

26. Alan S. Boyd, "Statement before the Subcommittee on Aviation, U.S. Senate Committee on Commerce," p. 42.

27. Clifton F. von Kann, Senior Vice President, Air Transport Association of America, "Statement before the Subcommittee on Aviation, U.S. Senate Committee on Commerce," in *Oversight Hearings on Noise Control Act*. Hearings before the Subcommittee on Aviation, U.S. Senate Committee on Commerce, 93rd Congress, First Session (Washington, DC: U.S. Government Printing Office, March 30, 1973), p. 125.

28. Jeremy J. Warford, *Public Policy toward General Aviation* (Washington, DC: The Brookings Institution, 1971), pp. 58–67; and U.S. Federal Aviation Administration, *Administrator's Fact Book, April 2000* (Washington, DC: U.S. Department of Transportation, April 2000), p. 37.

29. Jeremy J. Warford, *Public Policy toward General Aviation*, pp. 115–134.

30. Frederick A. Meister, Acting Association Administrator for Policy Development and Review, Federal Aviation Administration, "Statement before the Subcommittee on Aviation, U.S. Senate Committee on Commerce," in *Aircraft Noise Control Programs*. Hearings before the Subcommittee on Aviation, U.S. Senate Committee on Commerce, 93rd Congress, Second Session (Washington, DC: U.S. Government Printing Office, May 16, 1974), pp. 126–130.

31. Barbara Sturken Peterson and James Glab, *Rapid Descent*, pp. 33–43.

32. Edward M. Kennedy, U.S. Senator from Massachusetts, "Statement before the Subcommittee on Aviation, U.S. Senate Committee on Commerce," in *Regulatory Reform in Air Transportation*. Hearings before the Subcommittee on Aviation, U.S. Senate Committee on Commerce, 94th Congress, Second Session (Washington, DC: U.S. Government Printing Office, April 6, 1976), p. 163.

33. Barbara Sturken Peterson and James Glab, *Rapid Descent,* p. 30.

34. Edward M. Kennedy, "Statement before the Subcommittee on Aviation, U.S. Senate Committee on Commerce," p. 163.

35. William T. Coleman, Jr., Secretary of Transportation, "Statement before the Subcommittee on Aviation, U.S. Senate Committee on Commerce," in *Regulatory Reform in Air Transportation*. Hearings before the Subcommittee on Aviation, U.S. Senate Committee on Commerce, 94th Congress, Second Session (Washington, DC: U.S. Government Printing Office, April 7, 1976), p. 233.

36. Robert Six, Chairman of the Board and Chief Executive Officer of Continental Airlines, Inc., "Statement before the Subcommittee on Aviation, U.S. Senate Committee on Commerce," in *Regulatory Reform in Air Transportation*. Hearings before the Subcommittee on Aviation, U.S. Senate Committee on Commerce, 94th Congress, Second Session (Washington, DC: U.S. Government Printing Office, April 12, 1976), p. 425.

37. Edward E. Carlson, Chairman and Chief Executive Officer of United Airlines, Inc., "Statement before the Subcommittee on Aviation, U.S. Senate Committee on Commerce," in *Regulatory Reform in Air Transportation*. Hearings before the Subcommittee on Aviation, U.S. Senate Committee on Commerce, 94th Congress, Second Session (Washington, DC: U.S. Government Printing Office, April 13, 1976), p. 535.

38. Melvin A. Brenner, James O. Leet, and Elihu Schott, *Airline Deregulation* (Westport, CT: Eno Foundation for Transportation, Inc., 1985), pp. 8–10.

39. Ibid., pp. 10–12; and Barbara Sturken Peterson and James Glab, *Rapid Descent*, pp. 74–76.

40. Barbara Sturken Peterson and James Glab, *Rapid Descent*, pp. 106–108, 112–116.

41. Ibid., pp. 112–116.

42. Ibid., pp. 120, 121; Melvin A. Brenner, James O. Leet, and Elihu Schott, *Airline Deregulation*, pp. 75–96; and Steven A. Morrison and Clifford Winston, *The Evolution of the Airline Industry*, pp. 6–35.

43. Barbara Sturken Peterson and James Glab, *Rapid Descent*, p. 11.

44. James Ott and Raymond E. Neidl, *Airline Odyssey: The Airline Industry's Turbulent Flight into the Future* (New York: McGraw-Hill, Inc., 1995), pp. 42–44, 194–197.

45. Steven A. Morrison and Clifford Winston, *The Evolution of the Airline Industry*, pp. 31–35.

46. National Civil Aviation Review Commission, *NCARC Final Report: Avoiding Aviation Gridlock and Reducing the Accident Rate, A Consensus for Change* (Washington, DC: U.S. Department of Transportation, December 1997), executive summary. Complete report on-line at: http://www.library.unt.edu/gpo/ncarc/reports/pepele.htm.

47. U.S. General Accounting Office, *Air Traffic Control: FAA's Modernization Investment Management Approach Could Be Strengthened* (Washington, DC: U.S. General Accounting Office, April 1999), p. 15.

48. Ibid., pp. 14–52. Also see U.S. General Accounting Office, *Air Traffic Control: Observations on FAA's Air Traffic Control Modernization Program* (Washington, DC: U.S. General Accounting Office, March 1999); and U.S. General Accounting Office, *Air Traffic Control: Status of FAA's Modernization Program* (Washington, DC: U.S. General Accounting Office, December 1998).

49. Jane F. Garvey, Federal Aviation Administrator, "Statement before the Joint Hearing of the Senate Committee on Budget, U.S. Senate Appropriations Subcommittee on Transportation," in *FAA Modernization: Challenges and Solutions*. Hearings before the U.S. Senate Committee on the Budget and the U.S. Senate Appropriations Subcommittee on Transportation, 106th Congress, Second Session (Washington, DC: U.S. Government Printing Office, February 3, 2000).

50. U.S. General Accounting Office, *Air Traffic Control: FAA's Modernization Investment Management Approach Could Be Strengthened*, p. 5.

51. U.S. Federal Aviation Administration, *Administrator's Fact Book, April 2000* (Washington, DC: U.S. Department of Transportation, April 2000), p. 37.

52. Jane F. Garvey, Federal Aviation Administrator, "Statement before the House Subcommittee on Transportation and Related Agencies, House Committee on Appropriations," in *Federal Aviation Administration's Budget for Fiscal Year 2001*. Hearings before the U.S. House Committee on Appropriations, 106th Congress, Second Session (Washington, DC: U.S. Government Printing Office, March 22, 2000).

53. National Civil Aviation Review Commission, *NCARC Final Report*.

54. Bud Shuster and James L. Oberstar, Chair and Ranking Democratic Member of the House Committee on Transportation and Infrastructure, "Letter to Honorable Trent Lott, Majority Leader, U.S. Senate and Honorable Tom Daschle, Democratic Leader, U.S. Senate, dated September 9, 1999." Available on-line at http://www.house.gov/transportation/press/press114.html; and Airport Owners and Pilots Association, "AOPA Online—On Capitol Hill—106th Congress, Second Session." Available on-line at: http://www.aopa.org/whatsnew/caphill.html.

55. *The Wendell Ford Aviation Investment and Reform Act for the 21st Century*, Conference Report. U.S. House Committee on Transportation and Infrastructure, 106th Con-

gress, Second Session (Washington, DC: U.S. Government Printing Office, March 2000). Available on-line at: http://www.house.gov/transportation/air21conf/report.html.

56. Tom Belden, "Europe to Ease Moving from Plane to Train," *The Dominion Post*, October 8, 2000, p. 10-G.

57. U.S. Commission on National Security in the 21st Century, "Seeking a National Strategy: A Concert for Preserving Security and Promoting Freedom" (Washington, DC: U.S. Commission on National Security in the 21st Century, April 15, 2000). Available on-line at: http://www.nssg.gov/PhaseII.pdf.

6

THE FUTURE OF AMERICAN TRANSPORTATION POLICY

The Federal Highway Act of 1956 was a defining moment for American transportation policy during the twentieth century. It made the interstate highway system's completion the focal point of American transportation policy. For over 40 years, all other transportation issues, whether on land or in the air, were secondary to the interstate highway system's completion. When the interstate highway system was, for all practical purposes, completed in the early 1990s, consensus in American transportation policy disappeared, and the policy-making process entered into an era of relative instability, with policymakers and stakeholders searching for a new, still elusive consensus on how to proceed. Some, led by the highway lobby, argued for only minor deviations from the status quo. They wanted the emphasis on highway and bridge construction to continue, with additional funding for highway and bridge repair as well. Others, led by city planners, academics, and environmentally conscious organizations, such as the Surface Transportation Policy Project, advocated a more "balanced" transportation system, featuring a greater emphasis on highway and bridge maintenance, mass transit, and intermodal solutions to surface transportation congestion and additional funding for commuter and intercity passenger rail service. Some pointed to the European experience with congestion pricing and its stronger emphasis on intercity passenger rail transportation and more comprehensive intermodal transportation planning as a model for solving America's traffic congestion. Still others, primarily economists, viewed national transportation policy differently. Instead of debating the appropriate nature of governmental policies and institutional arrangements, they questioned the unchallenged assumption that government should determine the scope and nature of America's transportation infrastructure.

Theoretical arguments concerning government's role in providing and regulating use of transportation infrastructure have never had a significant effect on the policy-making process in the United States. Most national policymakers are not aware of the differences between toll goods, common-pool goods, private goods, and public goods. They do not know that transportation is a toll good and, theoretically, should be left to the private sector. Political considerations, especially the opportunities that transportation projects provide for congressional credit-claiming and the political activities of the various transportation industries' organized interest groups, led to the national government's now preeminent role in determining the scope and nature of America's transportation system. Of course, state and local governments are also influential. They spend more than the national government on transportation infrastructure, and ISTEA and TEA-21 increased their influence in planning and selecting surface transportation projects. Moreover, the private sector is also influential. It spends billions of dollars each year on transportation infrastructure, some transportation functions have been privatized, and other functions, such as the air traffic control system and Amtrak, have been recommended for privatization. However, overall, the national government has attained a hegemony over American transportation policy that is not likely to end anytime soon.

Policymakers now accept, without question, the national government's leading role in transportation policy making. However, there is little consensus concerning which policies are best. Those advocating a more balanced transportation system and smart growth strategies argue that the national government should place a greater emphasis on mass transit and intercity passenger rail service. They challenge the prevailing notion that highway and bridge construction enhances economic growth and national productivity. They point to a 1998 Congressional Budget Office report that found that most nationally financed infrastructure projects yielded net economic benefits that were small or negative, and only a select few yielded high economic returns. The report also found that many of the infrastructure projects financed by the national government absorbed resources that could have been used more productively by private firms. The Congressional Budget Office concluded that national government regulations and spending often distort infrastructure decisions made by state and local governments and the private sector.[1]

Advocates for a more balanced transportation system and the use of smart growth strategies note that the nation's transportation system continues to experience severe traffic congestion despite governmental expenditures exceeding $180 billion annually on transportation projects. In their view, this proves that resolving the nation's traffic congestion problem requires more than just spending money; it requires fundamental change. They note that deteriorating highway conditions and escalating traffic jams cost the nation well over $80 billion annually in lost wages and wasted fuel.[2] In addition, until the September 11, 2001, terrorist attacks on the World Trade Center and Pentagon, air traffic congestion was the most pressing issue facing the civilian air transportation system, especially at the nation's largest airports. Air traffic delays and flight cancellations were so common during the summer of 2000 that United Airlines ran nationwide television commercials apologizing to the public for the delays and cancellations. Although the air traffic congestion problem disappeared temporarily following the tragic events of September 11, 2001, it is expected to re-emerge as a major issue in the near future.

Advocates for change argue that America's transportation policies contain numerous provisions that result more from the congressional desire to enhance their reelection prospects than their desire to create a transportation system that moves goods and people in an efficient, cost-effective manner that also takes into account quality-of-life issues, such as the effect that transportation decisions have on noise and air pollution levels, the poor, and cities. They cite mandatory funding for special highway demonstration projects, lengthy and intense congressional debates over highway funding formulas, emphasis on highway and bridge construction over other transportation modes, congressional reluctance to support Amtrak funding unless it services their congressional district or state, and relatively wide dispersal of airport subsidies as examples of Congress's tendency to let political considerations influence the outcome of national transportation policy. They also argue that government bureaucrats, throughout American history, often become captives of the industries that they are supposed to be regulating. During the 1800s, the Interstate Commerce Commission promoted the railroad's economic interests, often to the detriment of passengers and small business. More recently, consumer prices fell after airlines were deregulated in 1978 and after the trucking and railroad industries were deregulated in 1980. Moreover, the Federal Aviation Administration took aggressive action to minimize aircraft noise only after legislation was adopted forcing them to do so. In their view, these examples prove that government regulatory powers are often used to promote the interests of the various transportation industries, not the interests of consumers and the public.

INFRASTRUCTURE FINANCING

Although there is little consensus concerning how government transportation funds should be spent and if the privatization of specific transportation services is warranted, most stakeholders agree that government should spend more than it does on transportation infrastructure. National, state, and local governments currently spend over $180 billion annually on transportation infrastructure, with states spending about half of that amount, the national government about a third, and local governments about one-fifth. The national government provides about 45 percent of government funding for highways and bridges, 54 percent of government funding for mass transit, and 20 percent of government funding for airport development. Nearly two-thirds of national government transportation funding is used to purchase or construct physical assets, while nearly two-thirds of state and local government transportation funding is used for improvements, maintenance, and repair of physical assets.[3]

Although transportation lobbies insist that government needs to spend more on transportation, government has, in fact, increased funding for transportation infrastructure, in both absolute dollars and as a percentage of gross domestic product, since 1980. This is in sharp contrast to funding reductions for other types of infrastructure, such as water supply and treatment, housing, schools, and military installations. The national government's transportation expenditures have increased continuously since 1980, rising from $21 billion in FY 1980, to $62 billion in 2002.[4] Moreover, TEA-21 and AIR-21's funding authorizations and spending agreements will continue that upward trend well into the future. These funding increases resulted from a combination of factors, including continued public pressure to resolve the nation's traffic congestion problem, the opportunity that transportation projects present for congressional credit-claiming, the political activities of transportation-related industries, the influence of reports issued by various think tanks and other organizations legitimating the transportation lobbies' demand for additional funding, the existence of the Highway Trust Fund and Airport and Airway Trust Fund, and Representative Bud Shuster's (R-PA) determined effort to prevent the diversion of transportation trust fund revenue to other purposes.

State and local government spending on transportation also increased significantly since 1980, both in absolute dollars and as a percentage of gross state product. In absolute dollars, state and local government spending on transportation increased from $21 billion in 1980 to over $120 billion in 2002. Most of the 2002 funding (84.8 percent) was spent on highways, bridges, and mass transit, 11.5 percent on air transportation, 2.7 percent on sea and inland port facilities, and 1 percent on parking facilities.[5]

IS MORE MONEY THE SOLUTION?

Most of the stakeholders involved in the transportation policy-making process argue that money is at least part of the solution to improving the nation's mobility. However, those advocating smart growth strategies and a more balanced transportation system note that government funding for transportation infrastructure has increased dramatically in recent years, yet traffic congestion remains a serious problem. They claim that this lack of progress proves that merely spending more money for transportation infrastructure is not enough. They argue that government should devise strategies that integrate the various transportation modes into a coherent, unified system instead of taking the more politically expedient route by increasing capacity in all transportation modes indiscriminately. They also argue that government should increase funding for mass transit and intercity passenger rail service significantly; impose higher fuel taxes and actively pursue other congestion pricing strategies to encourage people to prioritize their travel and use mass transit and other alternatives to the automobile; and adopt zoning ordinances and other measures to encourage people to locate closer to their places of employment. Government should also take into consideration the consequences of its transportation policy on both people and places. Sprawl, they argue, can, and should, be avoided and mitigated, and the destruction of viable urban neighborhoods should be avoided whenever possible.

Others dismiss balanced transportation system and smart growth strategies as unwanted and inappropriate "social engineering." In their view, the nation's traffic congestion "problem" does not suggest policy failure. On the contrary, traffic congestion results from policy success. Air traffic congestion, for example, would not be an issue if the government's air traffic control system and other safety measures had not convinced Americans that it was relatively safe to fly. Automobile traffic congestion also results from governmental policies that have created a transportation system that fosters economic growth. This growth, in turn, has enabled Americans to purchase record numbers of cars and trucks. Highways also provide millions of Americans an opportunity to improve their quality of life by locating in the suburbs. In their view, the suburbanization of American society is a sign of progress that should be hailed, not lamented. Instead of enacting policies that go against what most people want, their solution to traffic congestion is to continue increasing government funding for transportation infrastructure; continue emphasizing highway construction and repair over mass transit and intercity passenger rail service; avoid congestion pricing strategies and zoning ordinances that impinge on property rights; and require government bureaucracies to follow the best practices of leading government and private organizations when allocating resources.

Advocates of what can be called the free market approach to solving the nation's traffic congestion note that several U.S. General Accounting Office reports singled out the U.S. Department of Transportation, the Federal Aviation Administration, and Amtrak for having serious management deficiencies. In a summary report released in 2000, the General Accounting Office concluded that current management practices within these three agencies make it difficult to distinguish between genuine transportation needs and "wish lists." This makes it difficult for policymakers to determine if funding levels are too high, too low, or appropriate. Specifically, the General Accounting Office found that the national government agencies responsible for managing the national government's infrastructure programs (1) do not conduct needs assessments based on results-oriented goals, (2) do not have in place a consistent approach to analyze costs and benefits of potential infrastructure projects, and (3) until recently were not required to relate planned infrastructure spending to their missions and goals.

The General Accounting Office singled out the U.S. Department of Transportation for failing to conduct results-oriented needs assessments. It noted that the Department of Transportation inventories highway and bridge conditions every two years. That inventory is used to make surface transportation policy recommendations. As a result, the Department of Transportation regularly and predictably recommends policies emphasizing improvements to highways and bridges. The General Accounting Office concluded that because the Department of Transportation did not conduct a results-oriented needs assessment, it failed to consider alternative strategies for improving traffic mobility, such as congestion pricing, ridesharing programs, enhanced emphasis on mass transit and intercity passenger trains, and community planning.[6]

The General Accounting Office singled out the Federal Aviation Administration for not having in place a consistent approach to analyze the costs and benefits of potential infrastructure projects. This failure was evidenced by cost overruns, lengthy programmatic delays, and significant performance shortfalls experienced during the Federal Aviation Administration's long-term, multibillion-dollar effort to modernize its air traffic control system.[7] It also used the Federal Aviation Administration as an example of how the absence of a consistent approach to analyzing costs and benefits of potential infrastructure projects makes it difficult for policymakers to make informed infrastructure decisions. The General Accounting Office noted that in 1966 the Federal Aviation Administration reported that it would cost $6.5 annually to meet the nation's airport construction needs. That same year, representatives of the nation's airports claimed that it would cost $10 billion annually to meet those needs, and airline representatives said that it would cost $4 billion annually. The airport representatives' figure was based on the cost of all projects planned at more than 3,500 airports nationwide, regardless of their eligibility for national government funding. The airline industry's figure was based on the cost of projects planned at the nation's 421 largest airports. The airline industry included only those airports because they were eligible for national government funding and had, historically, been awarded funding for such projects in the past. The Federal Aviation Administration's figure was based on the cost of all projects eligible for national government funding at 3,300 airports.[8]

The General Accounting Office also pointed out that infrastructure expenditures are made by a variety of agencies and levels of government that have different goals and missions. This makes it difficult for policymakers to develop consistent rationales and decision-making processes to improve the nation's infrastructure investments. Its proposed solution was to require national government agencies to conduct goal-oriented needs assessments; inventory infrastructure assets to identify excess infrastructure capacity and current capabilities; use inventories to identify unmet maintenance and repair needs; identify alternative, noncapital approaches to investing in new infrastructure; use investment approaches to evaluate and select new infrastructure; consider innovative approaches to fund infrastructure; and better manage infrastructure improvements by regularly monitoring and validating information concerning costs, benefits, and risks.[9]

The U.S. Office of Management and Budget also issued a series of reports during the late 1990s concurring with the General Accounting Office's conclusion that the national government's management of transportation-related infrastructure programs is flawed. The Office of Management and Budget was especially critical of these agencies for lacking clear mission statements and guiding principles, an insufficient consideration of program life-cycle costs, and a general failure to analyze and manage risks inherent in the acquisition of infrastructure and other capital assets. Based on its findings, Congress passed the *Federal Acquisition Streamlining Act of 1994* to improve the national government's acquisition process; the *Clinger–Cohen Act of 1996*, requiring national government agencies to engage in capital planning and performance and results-based management for investments in information technology; and the *Government Performance and Results Act of 1993*, requiring agencies to develop mission statements, long-range strategic goals and objectives, and annual performance plans. In addition, in July 1997, the Office of Management and Budget added a section to its annual budget preparation guidance (Circular A-11) requiring agencies to provide it with information on major capital acquisitions and submit a capital asset plan and justification. The annual budget preparation guide was also supplemented by a Capital Programming Guide providing detailed steps on how to plan, budget, acquire, and manage infrastructure and other capital assets.[10]

The General Accounting Office also noted that the congressional budgetary process does not "prompt explicit debate about infrastructure spending that is intended to have long-term benefits."[11] Instead, Congress treats both short-term expenditures, such as supplies for government agencies, and long-term expenditures for infrastructure the same. This can favor consumption over investment because the initial cost of infrastructure projects seems high when compared to other expenditures. Its proposed solution was to include an investment component within the national government's budget that included specific funding targets to ensure that investment in infrastructure was considered formally in the congressional budget process.[12]

RECOMMENDATIONS

The administrative and budgetary reforms just mentioned are both necessary and appropriate measures to address management deficiencies and improve the implementation of American transportation policy. However, resolving the nation's continuing struggle with traffic congestion on land and in the air requires more than just improving the management and implementation of existing policies. It requires policies that transcend Congress's decentralized and disjointed nature. With two bodies and 535 voting members, both houses of Congress have historically relied on a decentralized committee system to enable it to function more efficiently. However, decentralized policy-making systems compartmentalize decisions into manageable pieces, making it difficult to develop broad-based policies. As a result, Congress addresses highway and bridge programs separately from mass transit programs, separately from Amtrak, and separately from air transportation programs. Although ISTEA and TEA-21 address this shortcoming, at least to some extent, by encouraging the consideration of intermodal transportation solutions to highway traffic congestion, there is no overarching national transportation policy in the United States. The national government has a highway and bridge policy, a mass transit policy, an intercity passenger rail policy, and a civilian aviation policy. It does not have a cohesive, comprehensive national transportation policy that identifies how the various transportation modes are to be integrated into a single national transportation system. The implementation of the 1961 Doyle Report's recommendation to form a House and Senate Joint Committee on Transportation to serve as a focal point for coordinating transportation legislation in Congress would be helpful in this regard. However, the prospects of this occurring remain slim. Just as in the 1960s, congressional members have little incentive to centralize the congressional committee system. Centralization upsets existing power relationships and has, historically, been opposed by those who would be deprived of power and by those who have been waiting, often impatiently, to obtain power through the seniority system. Moreover, as a practical matter, while this institutional reform would be a step forward, it is unlikely to result in a radical departure from the status quo because the path of least political resistance continues to be the indiscriminate enhancement of capacity for all transportation modes. Whenever possible, elected officials avoid making enemies. It is more expedient, both politically and intellectually, to provide additional resources to enhance the capacity of all transportation modes than it is to devise comprehensive intermodal solutions to improve traffic mobility.

As a federal system, it is important to distinguish between the desire to have the national government meld its disparate transportation policies into a cohesive national transportation policy and the creation of a nationally centered transportation policy. Although the national government plays a major role in transportation policy today, both ISTEA and TEA-21 have purposively granted more authority to state and local government officials in the implementation of surface transportation policy. Involving state and local governments in meaningful ways in the development and implementation of American transportation policy increases the number of decision makers. This has both positive and negative effects. On the positive side, it increases the likelihood that decisions will take into consideration all sides of the argument, are responsive to local needs, and are viewed as legitimate by all affected parties. This creates an atmosphere of mutual trust and respect that is helpful in overcoming program implementation problems that often arise. However, increasing the number of decision makers slows the policy-making process and increases the likelihood that one or more stakeholders will take an extreme position as a tactic to force other stakeholders to accept compromise simply to keep the process moving. Moreover, like their national government counterparts, state and local government transportation bureaucracies do not always follow the best practices of leading government and private organizations when managing resources. Allowing state and local government transportation bureaucracies to play a major role in transportation decision making can result in the same implementation problems that the General Accounting Office and Office of Management and Budget found in national bureaucracies.

CONCLUSION

American transportation policy has been in a state of disequilibrium since the interstate highway system's completion in the early 1990s. The transportation policy-making community is now more diverse and fluid, the highway lobby has lost its hegemony over the policy-making process, the congressional transportation committees have lost their hegemony over transportation financing, and there is no consensus on how to proceed. The majoritarian, client-based politics of the interstate highway era has been replaced by increasingly hostile and partisan interest group politics. As a result, American transportation policy making has become less predictable than in the past, and the national government has moved in several seemingly contradictory directions. For example, ISTEA and TEA-21 elevated the importance of metropolitan planning organizations in project selection, encouraged the development of intermodal solutions to surface transportation traffic congestion, and provided additional funding for mass transit. All of these actions were in accordance with the desires of smart growth advocates and those wanting the national government to follow the more balanced transportation system approach to solving traffic congestion. At the same time, the national government increased funding for highway and bridge construction significantly, continuing the historical bias favoring highways and bridges. In fact, mass transit's share of funding fell from 21 percent under ISTEA to 17 percent under TEA-21. These actions were in accordance with the desires of the highway lobby and other advocates of the free market approach to solving traffic congestion. Moreover, although Amtrak was made eligible for funding under the Congestion Mitigation and Air Quality Improvement program, the national government continued to address each transportation mode separately, instead of devising a strategy to meld the transportation modes into a single, unified system.

Congress's decentralized and disjointed policy-making process helps to explain why the national government has not devised a comprehensive intermodal strategy to address the nation's transportation traffic congestion problems. However, institutional factors are just part of the explanation. Politics also plays an important role. Devising comprehensive intermodal strategies to address the nation's transportation traffic congestion problems threatens the status quo. Congressional members who have worked hard to secure for themselves an influential position in the transportation policy-making process, the various transportation lobbies, and the various transportation-related national government bureaucracies are, naturally, risk- and change-averse. Devising intermodal strategies might hinder Congress's credit-claiming capacity, reduce the various transportation lobbies' respective share of available resources, and upset established management responsibilities and practices held by the various national transportation bureaucracies. The safer and far easier route, the one with the least political resistance, is to continue examining each transportation mode separately and to fight for additional resources to augment capacity in all transportation modes.

Most states have also moved in seemingly contradictory directions. For example, most states did not exercise their authority under ISTEA and TEA-21 to shift spending on surface transportation projects from highways and bridges to mass transit. However, nine states, Alaska, California, Connecticut, Illinois, New Jersey, New York, Rhode Island, Vermont, and Washington, were more likely than others to flex ISTEA and TEA-21 funds from highways to mass transit. These states spent a larger proportion of their funds than others on the maintenance and repair of highways and bridges than on new construction. They also spent more than one-third of their Congestion Mitigation and Air Quality Improvement funds on projects with long-term air quality benefits, were more likely than others to flex funds from traditional highway and bridge programs to alternative transportation modes, and spent a relatively high proportion of their funds on mass transit and safety programs. Delaware and Hawaii also increased their spending on alternative transportation modes and repairing highways and bridges.[13] Nevertheless, like the national government, most states addressed their traffic congestion problems by enhancing capacity in all transportation modes, rather than devising a comprehensive strategy to meld the various transportation modes into a single, unified system.

Although the trend is slow and best described as evolutionary as opposed to revolutionary, American transportation policy is incorporating some of the features desired by those who advocate smart growth strategies, a more balanced transportation system, and the European transportation model to improve the nation's mobility. For example, ISTEA and TEA-21 place a greater emphasis than in the past on automobile diversion strategies, intermodal planning, and additional funding for mass transit and intercity passenger rail. TEA-21 even included funding for congestion pricing demonstration projects. However, as has been documented earlier, most states did not exercise their authority to divert significant amounts to mass transit, primarily because their behavior is shaped by the same conditions existing at the national level. For example, credit-claiming is not limited to Congress. It applies to state legislators as well. Moreover, many state legislatures have modeled their institutional arrangements after Congress. As a result, many state legislatures have decentralized committee systems that, like Congress's decentralized committee system, break legislation into manageable pieces. Decentralization expedites the policy-making process but makes it difficult to consider broad-based, comprehensive transportation policies, such as those pursued in Europe and advocated by those desiring a more balanced transportation and the implementation of smart growth strategies.

There are at least three more, often overlooked explanations for why American transportation policy has not followed the European transportation model, which stresses automotive diversion strategies and intermodal solutions to traffic congestion. First, many European nations have population densities along established transportation corridors that make intercity passenger rail a more economically viable alternative than in most places in the United States. Second, many European countries have unitary political systems that place a great deal of authority in the central government. America's more decentralized federal system precludes, or at least makes more difficult, the imposition of intermodal solutions and automotive diversion strategies. The national government can exert great influence over state and local government transportation policy, particularly by threatening the withdrawal of financial support. But if state and local government officials determine that political support for intermodal solutions and automotive diversion strategies is absent, they are in a position to resist, obstruct, and delay the implementation of those policies. Their reluctance to exercise their authority granted by ISTEA and TEA-21 to flex funds from highways and bridges to mass transit is just one example of their important role in determining the outcome of American transportation policy.

The third, often overlooked reason that American transportation policy has not moved more quickly toward the European transportation model is that American political culture is decidedly different from that in most European nations. For example, gasoline prices spiked three times in 2000, once early in the year, once during the summer months, and a third time in September, reaching nearly $2 a gallon for unleaded gasoline each time. This was less than half and, in some cases, less than one-third the price paid in Europe. Europeans were not happy about the escalating price of gasoline. There were calls for tax relief in Great Britain, France, and Spain, especially from truckers. The price of gasoline topped out at nearly $7 a gallon in Great Britain, but the European reaction was mild compared to America's reaction. The American public demanded action, ranging from immediate tax relief to the use of force against the 11-member Organization of Petroleum Exporting Countries to encourage them to export more oil to reduce gasoline prices. In February 2000, a Gallup poll found that 40 percent of American households surveyed said that the spike in gasoline costs had created a "financial hardship" for them.[14] Reacting to the political tempest, Democratic presidential candidate Al Gore suggested that American oil companies were at least partially to blame, accusing them of price gouging and collusion. Republican presidential candidate George W. Bush, who had ties to the oil industry, countered that the Clinton–Gore administration had not done enough to pressure Saudi Arabia and other oil-producing nations to increase the supply of oil and had supported policies preventing the opening of oil fields in the United States. The oil companies and various other oil-related industries argued that much of the price increase resulted from environmental safeguards requiring refiners to manufacture and oil companies to sell reformulated gasoline containing relatively high levels of oxygenate in areas where air quality failed to meet national standards. They wanted those environmental standards suspended so motorists in those areas could purchase "normal," less expensive gasoline. Elected officials at all levels of government ducked for political cover. Congressional members took turns on their respective house floors denouncing the price increases and offering their proposed solutions, ranging from a temporary suspension of part of the national government's gasoline tax, to releasing oil from the nation's Strategic Petroleum Reserve to ease oil prices. Several governors announced plans to suspend a portion of their state fuel tax. Indiana's Governor Frank O'Bannon (D, 1996–), for example, suspended that state's 5 percent sales tax on gasoline. The first two gasoline price spikes were short-lived as market forces, in the form of higher exports from Saudi Arabia and other members of the Organization of Petroleum Exporting Countries, caused prices to moderate. The third price spike moderated following President Clinton's announcement on September 22, 2000, that he was ordering the release of 30 million gallons of oil from the nation's 590-million-barrel Strategic Petroleum Reserve.

This was just the second release from the Strategic Petroleum Reserve since its inception in 1973. The first occurred following Iraq's invasion of Kuwait in 1990. Republicans claimed that the move was a political ploy to bolster Democratic candidate Al Gore's presidential campaign, especially in the Northeast, where consumers were worried about the price of home heating oil. President Clinton countered that he was tapping into the reserve to assure that no American would have to choose between food and heat during the upcoming winter heating months.

The American reaction to the gasoline price spikes in 2000 brought into sharp focus America's relationship with the automobile. As noted earlier, automobile ownership is a powerful social symbol in the United States and an emotional outlet for millions of Americans. Obtaining a driver's license is a major life-altering event, signifying for millions of American teenagers the transition from childhood to adulthood. Although the highway lobby has lost its dominance over transportation policy making in the United States, and those seeking a more balanced transportation system and smart growth strategies have won some legislative concessions, the bond between the American public and the automobile/truck remains strong. Because that bond is so strong, American transportation policy may take on some of the characteristics seen in Europe, and it may incorporate some of the automobile diversion and congestion pricing strategies favored by those opposed to the free market approach to transportation policy making, but it will never embrace those policies completely. Americans love to drive and continue to demand that their political leaders put the automobile user's needs above all others.

NOTES

1. U.S. Congressional Budget Office, *The Economic Effects of Federal Spending on Infrastructure and Other Investments* (Washington, DC: U.S. Government Printing Office, June 1998), pp. 1–10.

2. U.S. Department of Transportation, Federal Highway Administration, *FY 2002 Performance Plan and FY 2000 Performance Report* (Washington, DC: U.S. Government Printing Office, 2002). Available on-line at: http://www.fhwa.dot.gov/reports/2002plan/index.htm.

3. U.S. General Accounting Office, *U.S. Infrastructure: Funding Trends and Opportunities to Improve Investment Decisions* (Washington, DC: U.S. Government Printing Office, February 2000), pp. 1–10.

4. Ibid., pp. 5, 6, 13–18; and U.S. Office of Management and Budget, *The Budget of the United States Government for FY 2003: Historical Tables* (Washington, DC: U.S. Government Printing Office, 2002), pp. 44–51.

5. U.S. Bureau of the Census, *Government Finances, 1998–99* (Washington, DC: U.S. Government Printing Office, 2001), p. 1.

6. U.S. General Accounting Office, *U.S. Infrastructure*, pp. 22, 23.

7. Ibid., p. 41.

8. Ibid., p. 26.

9. Ibid., p. 7.

10. Ibid., pp. 10, 11.

11. Ibid., p. 7.

12. Ibid., pp. 47, 48.

13. Barbara McCann, Roy Kienitz, and Bianca DeLille, *Changing Direction: Federal Transportation Spending in the 1990s* (Washington, DC: Surface Transportation Policy Project, 2000), p. 33.

14. Ellen Sung, "Cheap Gas, at Any Cost," *Policy.com*, June 27, 2000. Available on-line at: http://www.policy.com/news/dbrief/dbriefarc721.asp.

BIBLIOGRAPHY

ACIR (U.S. Advisory Commission on Intergovernmental Relations). 1978. *Categorical Grants: Their Role and Design*. Washington, DC: ACIR.

———. 1987. *Devolving Selected Federal-Aid Highway Programs and Revenue Bases: A Critical Appraisal*. Washington, DC: ACIR.

———. 1987. *Local Perspectives on State-Local Highway Consultation and Cooperation: Survey Responses from State Associations of Local Officials*. Washington, DC: ACIR.

———. 1988. *Devolution of Federal Aid Highway Programs: Cases in State-Local Relations and Issues in State Law*. Washington, DC: ACIR.

———. 1988. *State-Local Highway Consultation and Cooperation: The Perspective of State Legislators*. Washington, DC: ACIR.

Adcock, Sylvia. 2001. "FAA Plans Air Traffic Modernization Project," *Newsday.com*, June 4. Available on-line at: http://www.newsday.com/news/daily/faa605.htm.

Ailes, Stephen, President, Association of American Railroads. 1973. "Statement before the Subcommittee on Surface Transportation, U.S. Senate Committee on Commerce." In *Amtrak Oversight and Authorization*. Hearings before the Subcommittee on Surface Transportation, U.S. Senate Committee on Commerce, 93rd Congress, First Session. Washington, DC: U.S. Government Printing Office, May 16.

———. 1975. "Statement before the Subcommittee on Transportation and Commerce, U.S. House Committee on Interstate and Foreign Commerce." In *Railroad Revitalization*. Hearings before the Subcommittee on Transportation and Commerce, U.S. House Committee on Interstate and Foreign Commerce, 94th Congress, First Session. Washington, DC: U.S. Government Printing Office, July 23.

Airport Owners and Pilots Association, "AOPA Online—On Capitol Hill—106th Congress, Second Session." Available on-line at: http://www.aopa.org/whatsnew/caphill.html.

American Society of Civil Engineers. 2001. *Renewing America's Infrastructure: A Citizen's Guide*. Washington, DC: American Society of Civil Engineers.

American Public Transit Association. 1997. Testimony before the Senate Environment and Public Works Committee, Subcommittee on Transportation and Infrastructure. Washington, DC, March 13. Available on-line at: http://www.apta.com/govt/apatest/ epwtea.htm.

"Amtrak Authorization." 1983. *Congressional Quarterly Almanac, 1983.* Washington, DC: Congressional Quarterly, Inc.

Amtrak Reform Council. 2002. *An Action Plan for the Restructuring and Rationalization of the National Intercity Rail Passenger System.* Washington, DC: Amtrak Reform Council, February 7. Available on-line at: http://www.amtrakreformcouncil.gov/finalreport.html.

Arnold, Laurence. 2002. "House Railroad Panel Debates Proposal to Break Up Amtrak." *The Charleston Gazette*, February 15, p. 12A.

Associated Press. 2000. "Congress Approves National DUI Law." *The Charleston Gazette*, October 4, p. 3A.

———. 2001. "Airlines Hope to Avoid Summer of Travel Troubles." *CNN.com/Travel*, May 7. Available on-line at: http://www.cnn.com/2001/Travel/News/05/07/airtime. ap/index.html.

———. 2002. "Bill Would Abolish Amtrak." *The Charleston Gazette*, February 16, p. 6A.

Barlas, Stephen. 1997. "States, Locals Battle for ISTEA." *The American City & County* 112 (March): 12.

Baron, David P. 1990. "Distributive Politics and the Persistence of Amtrak." *Journal of Politics* 52 (August): 883–913.

Baumgartner, Frank R. and Bryan D. Jones. 1993. *Agendas and Instability in American Politics.* Chicago: The University of Chicago Press.

Beam, David R. 1981. "Washington's Regulation of States and Localities: Origins and Issues." *Intergovernmental Perspective* 7:3 (Summer): 8–18.

Belden, Tom. 2000. "Europe to Ease Moving from Plane to Train." *The Dominion Post*, October 8, p. 10-G.

Bowman, Ann O'M. and Michael A. Pagano. 1990. "The State of American Federalism 1989–1990." *Publius: The Journal of Federalism* 20 (Summer): 1–25.

Boyd, Alan S., Secretary, Department of Transportation. 1968. "Statement before the Subcommittee on Aviation, U.S. Senate Committee on Commerce." In *Airport Development Act of 1968.* Hearings before the Subcommittee on Aviation, U.S. Senate Committee on Commerce, 90th Congress, Second Session. Washington, DC: U.S. Government Printing Office, June 18.

Brenner, Melvin A., James O. Leet, and Elihu Schott. 1985. *Airline Deregulation.* Westport, CT: Eno Foundation for Transportation, Inc.

Burkhardt, Robert. 1967. *The Federal Aviation Administration.* New York: Frederick A. Praeger Publishers.

Burnard, E. Thomas, Executive Director, Airport Operators Council. 1958. "Statement before the Subcommittee on Aviation, U.S. Senate Committee on Interstate and Foreign Commerce." In *Federal Aviation Agency Act.* Hearings before the Subcommittee on Aviation, U.S. Senate Committee on Interstate and Foreign Commerce, 85th Congress, Second Session. Washington, DC: U.S. Government Printing Office, June 4.

Burwell, David G., Keith Bartholomew, and Deborah Gordon. 1990. "Energy and Environmental Research Needs." In *Transportation, Urban Form, and the Environment.* Transportation Research Board, pp. 81–99. Washington, DC: Transportation Research Board.

Camp, Donald H. 1996. "Transportation, the ISTEA, and American Cities." Washington, DC: Surface Transportation Policy Project. Available on-line at: http://www.trans-act.org/mono/city.htm.

Carlson, Edward E., Chairman and Chief Executive Officer of United Airlines, Inc. 1976. "Statement before the Subcommittee on Aviation, U.S. Senate Committee on Commerce." In *Regulatory Reform in Air Transportation*. Hearings before the Subcommittee on Aviation, U.S. Senate Committee on Commerce, 94th Congress, Second Session. Washington, DC: U.S. Government Printing Office, April 13.

Carmichael, Gilbert E., Chairman, Amtrak Reform Council. 2000. "Statement before the Committee on Commerce, Science, and Transportation's Subcommittee on Surface Transportation and Merchant Marine." Washington, DC, February 23. Available on-line at: http://www.amtrakreformcouncil.gov/testimony.html.

Chen, Don. 1999. "It's the Regional Economy, Stupid!: Misinterpreting the Benefits of Highway Construction." Washington, DC: The Surface Transportation Policy Project. Available on-line at: http://www2.istea.org/progress/febr99/region.htm.

"Chronology of Action of Transportation and Communications." 1985. In *Congress and the Nation, 1981–1985*. Washington, DC: Congressional Quarterly Service.

Clay, Lucius D., Chairman of President Eisenhower's Committee on a National Highway Program. 1955. "Statement before the House Committee on Public Works." In *National Highway Program*. Hearings before the House Committee on Public Works, 84th Congress, First Session. Washington, DC: U.S. Government Printing Office, April 20.

"Claytor Insists Amtrak Will Not Need Operating Subsidies by 2000." 1990. *Traffic World* (July 9): 223.

Clinton, President William Jefferson. 1998. "1998 State of the Union Address." Washington, DC, January 27. Available on-line at: http://www.whitehouse.gov/WH/SOTU98/address.html.

Coleman, William T., Jr., Secretary of Transportation. 1976. "Statement before the Subcommittee on Aviation, U.S. Senate Committee on Commerce." In *Regulatory Reform in Air Transportation*. Hearings before the Subcommittee on Aviation, U.S. Senate Committee on Commerce, 94th Congress, Second Session. Washington, DC: U.S. Government Printing Office, April 7.

Commission of the European Communities. 1998. "White Paper on Fair Payment for Infrastructure Use: A Phased Approach to a Common Transport Infrastructure Charging Framework in the EU." Brussels, Belgium, July 22. Available on-line at: ftp://ftp.ttr-ltd.com/cupid/white_paper.pdf.

Conlan, Timothy J. 1991. "And the Beat Goes On: Intergovernmental Mandates and Preemption in an Era of Deregulation." *Publius: The Journal of Federalism* 21:3 (Summer): 43–57.

Conlan, Timothy J. and David B. Walker. 1983. "Reagan's New Federalism: Design, Debate, and Discord." *Intergovernmental Perspective* 8:4 (Winter): 6–23.

Curley, Ann. 1998. "Fiscally Conservative Republicans Take Aim at Highway Bill." *allpolitics*, March 27. Available on-line at: http://allpolitics.com/1998/03/27/highway.house/index.html.

Dentzer, Susan. 1985. "Amtrak's Struggle to Stay on Track." *Newsweek* 105 (June 3): 50.

Diamond, Etan. 1998. "Middle Class in Suburbs." In *Encyclopedia of Urban America: The Cities and Suburbs*. Vol. 2, edited by Neil Larry Shumsky, 463–465. Santa Barbara, CA: ABC-CLIO.

Dilger, Robert Jay. 1982. *The Sunbelt-Snowbelt Controversy: The War Over Federal Funds.* New York: New York University Press.

——. 1989. *National Intergovernmental Programs.* Englewood Cliffs, NJ: Prentice-Hall.

——. 1992. "ISTEA: A New Direction for Transportation Policy." *Publius: The Journal of Federalism* 22:3 (Summer): 67–78.

——. 1998. "TEA-21: Transportation Policy, Pork Barrel Politics, and American Federalism." *Publius: The Journal of Federalism* 28:1 (Winter): 49–69.

Dittmar, Hank. 1996. "Defining and Managing the Metropolitan Transportation System." In *ISTEA Planner's Workbook.* Washington, DC: Surface Transportation Policy Project.

——. 1999. "Highway Capital and Economic Productivity." Surface Transportation Policy Project, February. Available on-line at: http://www2.istea.org/progress/febr99/hcep.htm.

Dunn, James A., Jr. 1998. *Driving Forces: The Automobile, Its Enemies, and the Politics of Mobility.* Washington, DC: The Brookings Institution.

Durfee, James R., Chairman, Civil Aeronautic Board. 1958. "Statement before the Subcommittee on Aviation, U.S. Senate Committee on Interstate and Foreign Commerce." In *Federal Aviation Agency Act.* Hearings before the Subcommittee on Aviation, U.S. Senate Committee on Interstate and Foreign Commerce, 85th Congress, Second Session. Washington, DC: U.S. Government Printing Office, June 16.

Ebner, Michael. 1998. "Suburbanization." In *Encyclopedia of Urban America: The Cities and Suburbs.* Vol. 2, edited by Neil Larry Shumsky, 756–764. Santa Barbara, CA: ABC-CLIO.

Eisenhower, Dwight D., President of the United States. 1958. "Letter to the Congress of the United States, dated June 13, 1958." In *Federal Aviation Agency Act.* Hearings before the Subcommittee on Aviation, U.S. Senate Committee on Interstate and Foreign Commerce, 85th Congress, Second Session. Washington, DC: U.S. Government Printing Office, June 16.

Erickson, Stanford. 1983. "Rail Systems." In *Introduction to Transportation,* edited by Paul W. DeVore, 81–116. Worcester, MA: Davis Publications.

The European Local Transport Information Service. 2000. "Demand Management and Pricing." Brussels, Belgium. Available on-line at: http://www.eltis.org/en/index.htm.

Fehr, Stephen, C. 1991. "Policy Must Address Flight Delays, Crumbling Roads, Traffic Jams." *The Washington Post,* February 21, p. A12.

Fessler, Pamela. 1990. "This Year's Battle May Be Over, But the War Has Just Begun." *Congressional Quarterly Weekly Report* (November 3): 3714–3717.

Foster, Mark S. 1998. "Automobiles." In *Encyclopedia of Urban America: The Cities and Suburbs.* Vol. 2, edited by Neil Larry Shumsky, 52–58. Santa Barbara, CA: ABC-CLIO.

——. 1998. "Roads." In *Encyclopedia of Urban America: The Cities and Suburbs.* Vol. 2, edited by Neil Larry Shumsky, 671–675. Santa Barbara, CA: ABC-CLIO.

——. 1998. "Transportation." In *Encyclopedia of Urban America: The Cities and Suburbs.* Vol. 2, edited by Neil Larry Shumsky, 793–799. Santa Barbara, CA: ABC-CLIO.

Fowler, Wyche, Democratic Representative from Georgia. 1979. "Statement before the Subcommittee on Transportation and Commerce, U.S. House Committee on Interstate and Foreign Commerce." In *Amtrak Fiscal Year 1980 Authorization and Amtrak Route Restructuring.* Hearings before the Subcommittee on Transportation and Commerce, U.S. House Committee on Interstate and Foreign Commerce, 96th Congress, First Session. Washington, DC: U.S. Government Printing Office, April 3.

Friedman, Milton and Rose Friedman. 1979. *Free to Choose*. New York: Avon Books.

Gage, Robert W. and Bruce D. McDowell. 1995. "ISTEA and the Role of MPOs in the New Transportation Environment: A Midterm Assessment." *Publius: The Journal of Federalism* 25:3 (Summer): 133–154.

Garvey, Jane F., Federal Aviation Administrator. 2000. "Statement before the Joint Hearing of the Senate Committee on Budget, U.S. Senate Appropriations Subcommittee on Transportation." In *FAA Modernization: Challenges and Solutions*. Hearings before the U.S. Senate Committee on the Budget and the U.S. Senate Appropriations Subcommittee on Transportation, 106th Congress, Second Session. Washington, DC: U.S. Government Printing Office, February.

———. 2000. "Statement before the House Subcommittee on Transportation and Related Agencies, House Committee on Appropriations." In *Federal Aviation Administration's Budget for Fiscal Year 2001*. Hearings before the U.S. House Committee on Appropriations, 106th Congress, Second Session. Washington, DC: U.S. Government Printing Office, March 22.

Gleckman, Howard. 1987. "Reagan's Budget Won't Wash—But Can Congress Do Better?" *Business Week* (January 19): 32.

Gomez-Ibanz, Jose A. and John R. Meyer. 1993. *Going Private: The International Experience with Transport Privatization*. Washington, DC: The Brookings Institution.

Governors' Task Force on Transportation Infrastructure. 1991. *America in Transition*. Washington, DC: National Governors' Association.

Grodzins, Morton. 1966. *The American System*. Chicago: Rand McNally.

Hall, Kevin G. 1992. "Lawmaker Wants Amtrak Trust Fund to Be Paid for with Fuel-Tax Dollars." *Traffic World* (March 2): 13.

Hartke, Vance, Chair, Surface Transportation Subcommittee, U.S. Senate Committee on Commerce. 1976. "Statement before the Subcommittee on Surface Transportation, U.S. Senate Committee on Commerce." In *Criteria and Procedures for Making Route and Service Decisions by Amtrak*. Hearings before the Subcommittee on Surface Transportation, U.S. Senate Committee on Commerce, 94th Congress, Second Session. Washington, DC: U.S. Government Printing Office, March 3.

Hartranft, Joseph B., Jr., President, Aircraft Owners and Pilots Association. 1968. "Statement before the Subcommittee on Aviation, U.S. Senate Committee on Commerce." In *Airport Development Act of 1968*. Hearings before the Subcommittee on Aviation, U.S. Senate Committee on Commerce, 90th Congress, Second Session. Washington, DC: U.S. Government Printing Office, June 19.

Haswell, Anthony, Chairman of the National Association of Railroad Passengers. 1973. "Statement before the Subcommittee on Surface Transportation, U.S. Senate Committee on Commerce." In *Amtrak Oversight and Authorization*. Hearings before the Subcommittee on Surface Transportation, U.S. Senate Committee on Commerce, 93rd Congress, First Session. Washington, DC: U.S. Government Printing Office, May 16.

Hazard, John L. 1977. *Transportation: Management Economics Policy*. Cambridge, MD: Cornell Maritime Press, Inc.

Hilton, George W. 1980. *Amtrak: The National Railroad Passenger Corporation*. Washington, DC: American Enterprise Institute.

Hosansky, David. 1997. "Web of Alliances and Interests Set to Snare Highway Funds." *Congressional Quarterly Weekly Report* 55:10 (March 8): 583.

————. 1997. "Clinton Unveils Omnibus Bill to Mixed Reviews." *Congressional Quarterly Weekly Report* 55:11 (March 15): 623.

————. 1997. "ISTEA Reauthorization Stalls Over Highway Funding." *Congressional Quarterly Weekly Report* 55:19 (May 10): 1066–1068.

Hosansky, David and Alisa J. Rubin. 1997. "Shuster's Steamroller Stopped—For Now." *Congressional Quarterly Weekly Report* 55:21 (May 24): 1183.

"House Oks $218.3 Billion Highway Bill." 1998. *allpolitics*, April 1. Available on-line at: http://allpolitics.com/1998/04/01/highway.bill/.

"How Is Amtrak in 1990? Busy." 1990. *Sunset* (February): 68, 69.

Jackson, Brooks. 1998. "Proposed West Virginia Highway Under Fire." *allpolitics*, April 1. Available on-line at: http://allpolitics.com/1998/04/01/jackson.highway/.

Jesdanun, Anick. 1998. "Panel Approves Transportation Bill." *The Charleston Gazette*, March 25, p. 3A.

Johnson, Lyndon Baines, President of the United States. 1967. "Letter to Alan S. Boyd, Secretary, Department of Transportation, dated September 20, 1967." Cited by Alan S. Boyd, Secretary, Department of Transportation, "Letter to the Honorable Hubert H. Humphrey, President of the U.S. Senate, dated May 20, 1968." In *Airport Development Act of 1968*. Hearings before the Subcommittee on Aviation, U.S. Senate Committee on Commerce, 90th Congress, Second Session. Washington, DC: U.S. Government Printing Office, June 18.

Karmin, Monroe W. 1986. "Hanging a 'For Sale' Sign on Government." *U.S. News and World Report* 100 (January 13): 18, 19.

Kasarda, John D. 1985. "Urban Change and Minority Opportunities." In *The New Urban Reality*, edited by Paul E. Peterson, 33–68. Washington, DC: The Brookings Institution.

Kennedy, Edward M., U. S. Senator from Massachusetts. 1976. "Statement before the Subcommittee on Aviation, U.S. Senate Committee on Commerce." In *Regulatory Reform in Air Transportation*. Hearings before the Subcommittee on Aviation, U.S. Senate Committee on Commerce, 94th Congress, Second Session. Washington, DC: U.S. Government Printing Office, April 6.

Kohler, Walter J., Governor of Wisconsin and Chair, National Governors' Conference's Committee on Highways. 1955. "Statement before the House Committee on Public Works." In *National Highway Program*. Hearings before the House Committee on Public Works, 84th Congress, First Session. Washington, DC: U.S. Government Printing Office, May 4.

Leach, Richard H. and Timothy G. O'Rourke. 1988. *State and Local Government: The Third Century of Federalism*. Englewood Cliffs, NJ: Prentice-Hall, Inc.

Leis, Rodney and Thomas F. Murphy. 1983. "Marine Systems." In *Introduction to Transportation*, edited by Paul W. DeVore, 51–81. Worcester, MA: Davis Publications.

Lewis, Roger, President of Amtrak. 1971. "Letter to Honorable Vance Hartke, Chairman, Surface Transportation Subcommittee, U.S. Senate Committee on Commerce, dated November 23, 1971." In *Administration's Request for Additional Funding for Amtrak*. Hearing before the Subcommittee on Surface Transportation, U.S. Senate Committee on Commerce, 92nd Congress, First Session. Washington, DC: U.S. Government Printing Office, October 26.

————. 1971. "Statement before the Subcommittee on Surface Transportation, U.S. Senate Committee on Commerce." In *Administration's Request for Additional Funding for Amtrak*. Hearings before the Subcommittee on Surface Transportation, U.S. Senate

Committee on Commerce, 92nd Congress, First Session. Washington, DC: U.S. Government Printing Office, October 26.

Love, Jean, Wendell Cox, and Stephen Moore. 1996. "Amtrak at Twenty-Five: End of the Line for Taxpayer Subsidies." Cato Policy Analysis No. 266. Washington, DC: The Cato Institute, December 19.

Lyons, W. M. 1995. "The FTA-FHA MPO Reviews—Planning Practice Under the ISTEA and the CAA." Washington, DC: U.S. Department of Transportation.

Mayhew, David R. 1974. *Congress: The Electoral Connection.* New Haven, CT: Yale University Press.

McCann, Barbara, Roy Kienitz, and Bianca DeLille. 2000. *Changing Direction: Federal Transportation Spending in the 1990s.* Washington, DC: Surface Transportation Policy Project.

McDowell, Bruce D. 1983. "Transportation and Governmental Organizations." In *Introduction to Transportation,* edited by Paul W. DeVore, 325–348. Worcester, MA: Davis Publications.

———. 1984. "Governmental Actors and Factors in Mass Transit." *Intergovernmental Perspective* 10:3 (Summer): 6–13.

———. 1992. "Reinventing Surface Transportation: New Intergovernmental Challenges." *Intergovernmental Perspective* 18:1 (Winter): 6–8, 18.

Meister, Frederick A., Acting Association Administrator for Policy Development and Review, Federal Aviation Administration. 1974. "Statement before the Subcommittee on Aviation, U.S. Senate Committee on Commerce." In *Aircraft Noise Control Programs.* Hearings before the Subcommittee on Aviation, U.S. Senate Committee on Commerce, 93rd Congress, Second Session. Washington, DC: U.S. Government Printing Office, May 16.

Mertins, Herman, Jr. 1972. *National Transportation Policy in Transition.* Lexington, MA: Lexington Books.

Meyer, John R. and Jose A. Gomez-Ibanez. 1981. *Autos Transit and Cities.* Cambridge, MA: Harvard University Press.

Miller, James C., III. 1975. "An Economic Policy Analysis of the Amtrak Program." In *Perspectives on Federal Transportation Policy,* edited by James C. Miller, III, 158. Washington, DC: American Enterprise Institute. Reprinted in *Criteria and Procedures for Making Route and Service Decisions by Amtrak.* Hearings before the Subcommittee on Surface Transportation, U.S. Senate Committee on Commerce, 94th Congress, Second Session. Washington, DC: U.S. Government Printing Office, March 3, 1976.

Miller, William, President, American Public Transportation Association. 2000. "Statement before the Committee on Commerce, Science, and Transportation's Subcommittee on Surface Transportation and Merchant Marine." Washington, DC, February 23. Available on-line at: http://www.amtrakreformcouncil.gov/testimony.html.

Mills, Mike. 1991. "Administration Asks States to Carry the Transit Load." *Congressional Quarterly Weekly Report* (March 9): 598–600.

———. 1991. "Senate Bill Would Alter Path of Nation's Road Policy." *Congressional Quarterly Weekly Report* (April 27): 1054.

———. 1991. "Senate Panel Passes Overhaul of Federal Highway Policy." *Congressional Quarterly Weekly Report* (May 25): 1366–1368.

———. 1991. "Senate Endorsement Paves Way for a New Highway System." *Congressional Quarterly Weekly Report* (June 15): 1575–1577.

————. 1991. "House Travels Favorite Road to Funding Local Highways." *Congressional Quarterly Weekly Report* (July 13): 1884–1888.

————. 1991. "House Bill's Gas Tax Increase May Stall Highway Overhaul." *Congressional Quarterly Weekly Report* (July 20): 1973–1974.

————. 1991. "Lawmakers Lard Highway Bill with $6.8 Billion in Projects." *Congressional Quarterly Weekly Report* (July 27): 2063–2066.

————. 1991. "House Leaders Withdraw on Nickel for America." *Congressional Quarterly Weekly Report* (September 21): 2683.

————. 1991. "Surface Transportation." *Congressional Quarterly Weekly Report* (November 2): 3227–3234.

————. 1991. "Highway and Transit Overhaul Is Cleared for President." *Congressional Quarterly Weekly Report* (November 30): 3518–3522.

Mills, Mike and David S. Cloud. 1991. "House Dispute Over Gas Tax Puts Highway Bill on Hold." *Congressional Quarterly Weekly Report* (August 3): 2153–2155.

Moore, Cassandra Chrones. 1994. "Intrastate Trucking: Stronghold of the Regulations." *Policy Analysis* 204 (February 16). Available on-line at: http://www.cato.org/pubs/pas/pa-204.html.

Morganthau, Tom. 1984. "A New War on Spending." *Newsweek* 104 (December 17): 45, 46.

Morrison, Steven A. and Clifford Winston. 1995. *The Evolution of the Airline Industry*. Washington, DC: The Brookings Institution.

Mudge, Richard. 1994. "ISTEA Legislation: The Promise versus the Reality." *Municipal Finance Journal* 64 (Winter): 35.

National Civil Aviation Review Commission. 1997. *NCARC Final Report: Avoiding Aviation Gridlock and Reducing the Accident Rate, A Consensus for Change*. Washington, DC: U.S. Department of Transportation, December. Executive summary. Complete report on-line at: http://www.library.unt.edu/gpo/ncarc/reports/pepele.htm.

National Railroad Passenger Corporation. 2002. "Amtrak Announces $285 Million in Cuts and Federal Appropriations Request of $1.2 Billion." Press Release. Washington, DC: National Railroad Passenger Corporation, February 1.

National Research Council. 1994. *Curbing Gridlock: Peak Period Fees to Relieve Traffic Congestion*. Vol. 1. Washington, DC: National Academy Press.

Nice, David C. 1991. "Financial Performance of the Amtrak System." *Public Administration Review* 51:2 (March/April): 138–144.

————. 1998. *Amtrak: The History and Politics of a National Railroad*. Boulder, CO: Lynne Rienner Publishers, Inc.

"Now the Railpax Row Will Begin." 1970. *Business Week* (November 28): 38.

Office of Program Administration, U.S. Department of Transportation. n.d. "The Dwight D. Eisenhower Interstate System." Available on-line: http://www.fhwa.dot.gov/infra-structure/progadmin/Interstate.html. Viewed on February 28, 2000.

Ott, James and Raymond E. Neidl. 1995. *Airline Odyssey: The Airline Industry's Turbulent Flight into the Future*. New York: McGraw-Hill, Inc.

Parker, Jeffrey A. 1990. "Does Transportation Finance Influence Urban Form?" In *Transportation, Urban Form, and the Environment*. Transportation Research Board, pp. 43–62. Washington, DC: Transportation Research Board.

Payne, Seth. 1989. "Why Amtrak Won't Stop to Let the Taxpayer Off." *Business Week* (January 30): 90.

Pena, Frederico. 1996. "Statement before the House Committee on Transportation and Infrastructure Subcommittee on Surface Transportation." Washington, DC, May 2. Available on-line at: http://www.dot.gov/affairs/1996/5296te.htm.

Percy, Stephen L. 1993. "ADA, Disability Rights, and Evolving Regulatory Federalism." *Publius: The Journal of Federalism* 23:4 (Fall): 87–105.

Peterson, April. 2000. "Sprawl: A Growing Political Concern." *Policy.com* (March 24). Available on-line at: http://www.policy.com/news/dbrief/dbriefarc534.asp.

Peterson, Barbara Sturken and James Glab. 1994. *Rapid Descent: Deregulation and the Shakeout in the Airlines.* New York: Simon & Schuster.

Phillips, Don. 1990. "Transportation Proposals Decried for Shifting Costs." *The Washington Post,* March 9, p. A10.

Pikarsky, Milton and Daphne Christensen. 1976. *Urban Transportation Policy and Management.* Lexington, MA: Lexington Books.

"Postwar Highway Program." 1965. In *Congress and the Nation, 1945–1964.* Washington, DC: Congressional Quarterly Service.

Pressler, Larry, Democratic Senator from South Dakota. 1983. "Statement before the Subcommittee on Surface Transportation, U.S. Senate Committee on Commerce, Science, and Transportation." In *Staggers Rail Act of 1980.* Hearings before the Subcommittee on Surface Transportation, U.S. Senate Committee on Commerce, Science, and Transportation, 98th Congress, First Session. Washington, DC: U.S. Government Printing Office, July 26.

"Public Strongly Supports Continuing Government Subsidies for Amtrak." 1997. *The Gallup Poll,* October 27. Available on-line at: http://trainweb.com/crocon/poll.html.

Putnam, Robert D. 2000. *Bowling Alone: The Collapse and Revival of American Community.* New York: Simon & Schuster.

Pytte, Alyson. 1990. "Bush Transportation Policy Is Non-Starter in Congress." *Congressional Quarterly Weekly Report* (March 10): 746, 747.

Quesada, E. R., Chairman, Airways Modernization Board. 1958. "Statement before the Subcommittee on Aviation, U.S. Senate Committee on Interstate and Foreign Commerce." In *Federal Aviation Agency Act.* Hearings before the Subcommittee on Aviation, U.S. Senate Committee on Interstate and Foreign Commerce, 85th Congress, Second Session. Washington, DC: U.S. Government Printing Office, May 23.

Rae, John B. 1971. *The Road and Car in American Life.* Cambridge, MA: MIT Press.

Rail Shippers Association. 1983. "Statement before the Subcommittee on Surface Transportation, U.S. Senate Committee on Commerce, Science, and Transportation." In *Staggers Rail Act of 1980.* Hearings before the Subcommittee on Surface Transportation, U.S. Senate Committee on Commerce, Science, and Transportation, 98th Congress, First Session. Washington, DC: U.S. Government Printing Office, July 26.

Rephann, Terance and Andrew Isserman. 1994. "New Highways as Economic Development Tools: An Evaluation Using Quasi-Experimental Matching Methods." *Regional Science and Urban Economics* 24:6: 723–751.

Reuters News Service. 2002. "Key Senator Opposed to Amtrak Breakup Plan." Press Release, February 11.

Roberts, Robert. 1991. "New Direction for Amtrak." *Railway Age* (June): 59, 60.

Robinson, Melissa B. 2001. "Lawmakers Debate Amtrak's Future." Associated Press Release, November 1. Available on-line at: http://biz.yahoo.com/apf/011101/amtrak_future_2.html.

Robyn, Dorothy. 1987. *Braking the Special Interests: Trucking Deregulation and the Politics of Policy Reform.* Chicago: The University of Chicago Press.

Rose, Mark H. 1990. *Interstate: Express Highway Politics, 1939–1989.* Rev. Ed. Knoxville, TN: The University of Tennessee Press.

Salant, Jonathan D. 2001. "U.S. Traffic Congestion Has Increased Greatly, Study Finds." *The Charleston Gazette,* May 8, p. 2A.

———. 2001. "FAA Presents Plan to Reduce Delays." Associated Press Release, June 5. Available on-line at http://dailynews.yahoo.com/h/ap/20010604/pl/ airline_delays_3.html.

Salholz, Eloise. 1989. "Bush Proposes to Eliminate Amtrak." *Newsweek* 113 (January 16): 26, 27.

Savas, E. S. 1987. *Privatization: The Key to Better Government.* Chatham: NJ: Chatham House.

———. 2000. *Privatization and Public-Private Partnerships.* New York: Chatham House.

Schultz, David F. 1990. "Keynote Address: Decision Makers Need Help." In *Transportation, Urban Form, and the Environment.* Transportation Research Board, pp. 11–22. Washington, DC: Transportation Research Board.

Shuster, Bud. 1997. "Chairman Shuster, Chairwoman Molinari Applaud Committee Approval of Amtrak Reform Bill." Press Release. Washington, DC: U.S. House Committee on Transportation and Infrastructure, July 30.

Shuster, Bud and James L. Oberstar, Chair and Ranking Democratic Member of the House Committee on Transportation and Infrastructure. 1999. "Letter to Honorable Trent Lott, Majority Leader, U.S. Senate and Honorable Tom Daschle, Democratic Leader, U.S. Senate, dated September 9." Available on-line at http://www.house.gov/transportation/press/press114.html.

Shuster, Bud, James L. Oberstar, Thomas Petri, and Nick J. Rahall, II. 2000. "The Impact of Reducing the Federal Fuel Tax on Transportation Programs." Dear Colleague Letter. Washington, DC: U.S. House Committee on Transportation and Infrastructure, March 4.

Six, Robert, Chairman of the Board and Chief Executive Officer of Continental Airlines, Inc. 1976. "Statement before the Subcommittee on Aviation, U.S. Senate Committee on Commerce." In *Regulatory Reform in Air Transportation.* Hearings before the Subcommittee on Aviation, U.S. Senate Committee on Commerce, 94th Congress, Second Session. Washington, DC: U.S. Government Printing Office, April 12.

Slater, Rodney E., U.S. Secretary of Transportation. 2000. "Remarks as Prepared for Delivery, U.S. Secretary of Transportation Rodney E. Slater Notice of Proposed Rule Making on Hours-of-Service." Press Release. Washington, DC: U.S. Department of Transportation, April 25. Available on-line at: http://www.dot.gov/affairs/2000/042500sp.htm.

———. 2000. "U.S. Transportation Secretary Slater Calls on Truck Safety Stakeholders to Discuss Driver Fatigue Safety Standard." Press Release. Washington, DC: U.S. Department of Transportation, August 9. Available on-line at: http://www.dot.gov/affairs/fmcsa1100.htm.

Small, Kenneth A. 1985. "Transportation and Urban Change." In *The New Urban Reality,* edited by Paul E. Peterson, 197–223. Washington, DC: The Brookings Institution.

Snelling, Richard, Governor of Vermont, and Rene Levesque, Premier, Province of Quebec, Canada. 1979. "Letter to James L. Florio, Chair, Subcommittee on Transportation and Commerce, U.S. House Committee on Interstate and Foreign Commerce." In *Amtrak Fiscal Year 1980 Authorization and Amtrak Route Restructuring.* Hearings before the

Subcommittee on Transportation and Commerce, U.S. House Committee on Interstate and Foreign Commerce, 96th Congress, First Session. Washington, DC: U.S. Government Printing Office, April 3.

Stafford, George N., Chairman, Interstate Commerce Commission. 1976. "Letter to Honorable Vance Hartke, Chairman, Surface Transportation Subcommittee, U.S. Senate Committee on Commerce, dated March 17, 1976." In *Criteria and Procedures for Making Route and Service Decisions by Amtrak: Additional Articles, Letters, and Statements.* Hearings before the Subcommittee on Surface Transportation, U.S. Senate Committee on Commerce, 94th Congress, Second Session. Washington, DC: U.S. Government Printing Office, March 3.

Stanfield, Rochelle L. 1982. "The New Federalism Is Reagan's Answer to Decaying Highways, Transit Systems." *National Journal.* June 12, pp. 1040–1044.

Sung, Ellen. 2000. "Cheap Gas, at Any Cost." *Policy.com*, June 27. Available on-line at: http://www.policy.com/news/dbrief/dbriefarc721.asp.

Surface Transportation Policy Project. 1995. "ISTEA Year Four." Washington, DC: Surface Transportation Policy Project. Available on-line at: http://www.transact.org/yf/over.htm.

―――. 2001. *Ten Years of Progress: Building Better Communities Through Transportation* Washington, DC: Surface Transportation Policy Project.

Thomas, June Manning. 1998. "Urban Renewal." In *Encyclopedia of Urban America: The Cities and Suburbs.* Vol. 2, edited by Neil Larry Shumsky, 826–829. Santa Barbara, CA: ABC-CLIO.

Tipton, Stuart G., President, Air Transport Association of America. 1968. "Statement before the Subcommittee on Aviation, U.S. Senate Committee on Commerce." In *Airport Development Act of 1968.* Hearings before the Subcommittee on Aviation, U.S. Senate Committee on Commerce, 90th Congress, Second Session. Washington, DC: U.S. Government Printing Office, June 18.

Transportation and the Early Nation. 1982. Papers presented at an Indiana American Revolution Bicentennial Symposium. Indianapolis: Indiana Historical Society.

"Transportation Policy." 1973. In *Congress and the Nation, 1969–1972.* Washington, DC: Congressional Quarterly Service.

Transportation Research Board, National Research Council. 1996. *Institutional Barriers to Intermodal Transportation Policies and Planning in Metropolitan Areas.* Washington, DC: National Academy Press.

―――. 1998. *The Costs of Sprawl-Revisited.* TCRP Report 39. Washington, DC: National Academy Press.

"Two-Year Reauthorization for Amtrak Clears." 1993. *Congressional Quarterly Almanac 1992.* Washington, DC: Congressional Quarterly, Inc.

"The Unloved Passenger." 1970. *TIME* (January 5): 48.

U.S. Bureau of the Census. 1999. *State and Local Government Finance Estimates, by State.* Washington, DC: U.S. Government Printing Office.

―――. 2001. *Government Finances, 1998–99.* Washington, DC: U.S. Government Printing Office.

U.S. Commission on National Security in the 21st Century. 2000. "Seeking a National Strategy: A Concert for Preserving Security and Promoting Freedom." Washington, DC: U.S. Commission on National Security in the 21st Century, April 15. Available on-line at: http://www.nssg.gov/PhaseII.pdf.

U.S. Congressional Budget Office. 1998. *The Economic Effects of Federal Spending on Infrastructure and Other Investments*. Washington, DC: U.S. Government Printing Office, June.

U.S. Department of Transportation. 1990. *Moving America: New Directions, New Opportunities*. Washington, DC: U.S. Department of Transportation.

———. 1996. "ISTEA Reauthorization Policy Statement and Principles." Washington, DC: U.S. Department of Transportation. Available on-line at: http://www.dot.gov/ost/govtaffairs/istea/isteap&p.html.

———. 1998. *Transportation Statistics Annual Report 1998*. Washington, DC: U.S. Department of Transportation.

———. 2000. *Transportation Statistics Annual Report 1999*. Washington, DC: U.S. Department of Transportation. Available on-line at: http://www.bts.gov/programs/transtu/tsar/tsar99pt.html.

———. 2002. *Transportation Indicators: January 2002*. Washington, DC: U.S. Government Printing Office.

U.S. Department of Transportation, Federal Highway Administration. 1976. *America's Highways, 1776/1976*. Washington, DC: U.S. Government Printing Office.

———. 2000. *Highway Statistics 1998*. Washington, DC: U.S. Government Printing Office. Available on-line at: http://fhinter.fhwa.dot.gov/ohim/hs98/roads.htm.

———. 2002. *FY 2002 Performance Plan and FY 2000 Performance Report*. Washington, DC: U.S. Government Printing Office. Available on-line at: http://www.fhwa.dot.gov/reports/2002plan/index.htm.

U.S. Federal Aviation Administration. 1999. "A Brief History of the Federal Aviation Administration and Its Predecessor Agencies." Washington, DC: U.S. Department of Transportation, November 11. Available on-line at: http://www.faa.gov/historyinfo.htm.

———. 2000. *Administrator's Fact Book, April 2000*. Washington, DC: U.S. Department of Transportation.

U.S. General Accounting Office. 1993. *Transportation Infrastructure: Better Tools Needed for Making Decisions on Using ISTEA Funds Flexibly*. RCED-94-25. Washington, DC: U.S. General Accounting Office, October.

———. 1995. *Intercity Passenger Rail: Financial and Operating Conditions Threaten Amtrak's Long-Term Viability*. Washington, DC: U.S. General Accounting Office, February.

———. 1995. *Amtrak's Northeast Corridor: Information on the Status and Cost of Needed Improvements*. Washington, DC: U.S. General Accounting Office, April.

———. 1997. *Intercity Passenger Rail: Amtrak's Financial Crisis Threatens Continued Viability*. Washington, DC: U.S. General Accounting Office, April.

———. 1998. *Air Traffic Control: Status of FAA's Modernization Program*. Washington, DC: U.S. General Accounting Office, December.

———. 1999. *Air Traffic Control: Observations on FAA's Air Traffic Control Modernization Program*. Washington, DC: U.S. General Accounting Office, March.

———. 1999. *Air Traffic Control: FAA's Modernization Investment Management Approach Could Be Strengthened*. Washington, DC: U.S. General Accounting Office, April.

———. 1999. *Intercity Passenger Rail: Amtrak Faces Challenges in Improving Its Financial Condition*. Washington, DC: U.S. General Accounting Office, October 28.

———. 2000. *U.S. Infrastructure: Funding Trends and Opportunities to Improve Investment Decisions*. Washington, DC: U.S. General Accounting Office, February.

————. 2000. *Intercity Passenger Rail: Amtrak Needs to Improve Its Accountability for Tax-payer Relief Act Funds.* Washington, DC: U.S. General Accounting Office, February 29.

U.S. Office of Management and Budget (OMB). 2002. *The Budget of the United States Government for FY 2003: Historical Tables.* Washington, DC: U.S. Government Printing Office.

Victor, Kirk. 1991. "Skinner's Final Act." *National Journal,* December 14, pp. 3016–3019.

Vivier, Jean. 1999. "Urban Transport Pricing." *Public Transport International* (May): 28–35.

Volpe, John A., Secretary of Transportation. 1969. "Letter to the Hon. Warren G. Magnuson, Chairman of the Committee on Commerce of the U.S. Senate, dated September 17, 1969." In *Airport/Airways Development.* Hearings before the Subcommittee on Aviation, U.S. Senate Committee on Commerce, 91st Congress, First Session. Washington, DC: U.S. Government Printing Office, July 23.

von Kann, Clifton F., Senior Vice-President, Air Transport Association of America. 1973. "Statement before the Subcommittee on Aviation, U.S. Senate Committee on Commerce." In *Oversight Hearings on Noise Control Act.* Hearings before the Subcommittee on Aviation, U.S. Senate Committee on Commerce, 93rd Congress, First Session. Washington, DC: U.S. Government Printing Office, March 30.

Walters, Jonathan. 1995. "The Highway Revolution That Wasn't." *Governing* 8:8 (May): 30–33, 35–37.

Ward, Richard E. 1983. "Transportation and Society." In *Introduction to Transportation,* edited by Paul W. DeVore, 1–22. Worcester, MA: Davis Publications.

Warford, Jeremy J. 1971. *Public Policy toward General Aviation.* Washington, DC: The Brookings Institution.

Weingroff, Richard F. 1996. "Federal-Aid Highway Act of 1956: Creating the Interstate System." *Public Roads* 60:1 (Summer). Available on-line at: http://www.tfhrc.gov/pubrds/summer96/p96su10.htm.

————. 1996. "From 1916 to 1939: The Federal-State Partnership at Work." *Public Roads* 60:1 (Summer). Available on-line at: http://www.tfhrc.gov/pubrds/summer96/p96su7.htm.

Weissert, Carol S. and Sanford F. Schram. 1996. "The State of American Federalism, 1995–1996." *Publius: The Journal of Federalism* 26:3 (Summer): 1–26.

Welch, William H. 1998. "Extra $31B Paved the Way for Passage of Road Bill." *USA Today,* March 15, p. 11A.

————. 1998. "Senate OKs $214 Billion Transport Bill." *USA Today,* March 15, p. 1A.

The Wendell Ford Aviation Investment and Reform Act for the 21st Century (Conference Report). 2000. U.S. House Committee on Transportation and Infrastructure, 106th Congress, Second Session. Washington, DC: U.S. Government Printing Office, March. Available on-line at: http://www.house.gov/transportation/air21conf/report.html.

Whitnah, Donald R. 1966. *Safer Skyways: Federal Control of Aviation, 1926–1966.* Ames, IA: The Iowa State University Press.

Will, George, F. 1991. ". . . Congealed in Traffic." *The Washington Post,* March 11, p. B7.

Williams, Larry. 1997. "Road Bill Faces Potholes." *Charleston Gazette,* March 13, p. 9A.

Wilner, Frank N. 1994. *The Amtrak Story.* Omaha, NE: Simmons-Boardman Books, Inc.

Wilson, James Q. 1980. "The Politics of Regulation." In *The Politics of Regulation,* edited by James Q. Wilson. New York: Basic Books.

Index

About the Author

ROBERT JAY DILGER is the Director of the Institute for Public Affairs, West Virginia University, Morgantown.